O.P. LANE

D1134642

DNA Repair
and Recombination

DNA Repair
and Recombination

Edited by

T. Lindahl
Deputy Director of Research
Imperial Cancer Research Fund
Hertfordshire, UK

and

S.C. West
Principal Scientist
Imperial Cancer Research Fund
Hertfordshire, UK

CHAPMAN & HALL
London · Glasgow · Weinheim · New York · Tokyo · Melbourne · Madras

Published by Chapman & Hall, 2–6 Boundary Row, London SE1 8HN, UK

Chapman & Hall, 2–6 Boundary Row, London SE1 8HN, UK

Blackie Academic & Professional, Wester Cleddens Road, Bishopbriggs, Glasgow G64 2NZ, UK

Chapman & Hall GmbH, Pappelallee 3, 69469 Weinheim, Germany

Chapman & Hall USA, 115 Fifth Avenue, New York, NY 10003, USA

Chapman & Hall Japan, ITP-Japan, Kyowa Building, 3F, 2-2-1 Hirakawacho, Chiyoda-ku, Tokyo 102, Japan

Chapman & Hall Australia, 102 Dodds Street, South Melbourne, Victoria 3205, Australia

Chapman & Hall India, R. Seshadri, 32 Second Main Road, CIT East, Madras 600 035, India

Printed in Great Britain by The Alden Press, Osney Mead, Oxford

ISBN 0 412 64040 6

A catalogue record for this book is available from the British Library

∞ Printed on permanent acid-free text paper, manufactured in accordance with ANSI/NISO Z39.48-1992 (Permanence of Paper).

Contents

Contributors

Munna L Agarwal

Department of Molecular Biology, Research Institute, The Cleveland Clinic Foundation, 9500 Euclid Avenue, Cleveland, Ohio 44195, USA

Susan K Amundsen

Fred Hutchinson Cancer Research Center, 1124 Columbia Street, Seattle, WA 98104, USA

Lidia K Arciszewska

Microbiology Unit, Department of Biochemistry, University of Oxford, South Parks Road, Oxford, OX1 3QU

A Jane Bardwell

Laboratory of Molecular Pathology, Department of Pathology, The University of Texas Southwestern Medical Center, Dallas, Texas 75235, USA
Current address: Genelabs Technologies Inc, Redwood City, California 94063, USA

Lee Bardwell

Laboratory of Molecular Pathology, Department of Pathology, The University of Texas Southwestern Medical Center, Dallas, Texas 75235, USA
Current address: Department of Molecular and Cell Biology, University of California at Berkeley, Berkeley, California 94720, USA

Garry Blakely

Microbiology Unit, Department of Biochemistry, University of Oxford, South Parks Road, Oxford, OX1 3QU

Dirk Bootsma

Medical Genetics Centre, Department of Cell Biology and Genetics, Erasmus University Rotterdam, PO Box 1738, 3000 DR Rotterdam, The Netherlands

Michail V Chernov

Department of Molecular Biology, Research Institute, The Cleveland Clinic Foundation, 9500 Euclid Avenue, Cleveland, Ohio 44195, USA

Olga B Chernova

Department of Molecular Biology, Research Institute, The Cleveland Clinic Foundation, 9500 Euclid Avenue, Cleveland, Ohio 44195, USA

Sean Colloms

Microbiology Unit, Department of Biochemistry, University of Oxford, South Parks Road, Oxford, OX1 3QU

Patrick Dabert

Fred Hutchinson Cancer Research Center, 1124 Columbia Street, Seattle, WA 98104, USA

Yutaka Deguchi

Department of Molecular Biology, Research Institute, The Cleveland Clinic Foundation, 9500 Euclid Avenue, Cleveland, Ohio 44195, USA

Grigory Dianov

Imperial Cancer Research Fund, Clare Hall Laboratories, South Mimms, Hertfordshire EN6 3LD

Derek R Duckett

CRC Nucleic Acid Structure Research Group, Department of Biochemistry, University of Dundee, Dundee DDl 4HN

William J Feaver

Department of Cell Biology, Stanford University School of Medicine, Stanford, California 94305, USA

Errol C Friedberg

Laboratory of Molecular Pathology, Department of Pathology, The University of Texas Southwestern Medical Center, Dallas, Texas 75235, USA

Martin Gellert

Laboratory of Molecular Biology, National Institute of Diabetes and Digestive and Kidney Diseases, Building 5, Room 241, National Institute of Health, Bethesda, Maryland 20892, USA

Marie-Josèphe E Giraud-Panis

CRC Nucleic Acid Structure Research Group, Department of Biochemistry, University of Dundee, Dundee DD1 4HN

Karen Grant

Microbiology Unit, Department of Biochemistry, University of Oxford, South Parks Road, Oxford, OXl 3QU

Current address: Wellcome Molecular Parasitology Unit, Anderson College, Church Street, Glasgow G11 5JS

J A Halliday

Laboratoire de Mutagénèse, Institut J Monod, 2 Place Jussieu, 75251 Paris, France

Jan Hoeijmakers

Medical Genetics Centre, Department of Cell Biology and Genetics, Erasmus University Rotterdam, PO Box 1738, 3000 DR Rotterdam, The Netherlands

Ted R Hupp

CRC Cell Transformation Group, Department of Biochemistry, University of Dundee, Dundee DDl 4HN

Yukihito Ishizaka

Department of Molecular Biology, Research Institute, The Cleveland Clinic Foundation, 9500 Euclid Avenue, Cleveland, Ohio 44195, USA

Roger D Kornberg

Department of Cell Biology, Stanford University School of Medicine, Stanford, California 94305, USA

David P Lane

CRC Cell Transformation Group, Department of Biochemistry, University of Dundee, Dundee DDl 4HN

Nick Leslie   Microbiology Unit, Department of Biochemistry,
                               University of Oxford, South Parks Road,
                               Oxford, OXl 3QU

David M J Lilley   CRC Nucleic Acid Structure Research Group,
                               Department of Biochemistry, University of Dundee,
                               Dundee DDl 4HN

Tomas Lindahl   Imperial Cancer Research Fund, Clare Hall
                               Laboratories, South Mimms, Hertfordshire EN6 3LD

Xin Lu   Ludwig Institute for Cancer Research, St Mary's
                               Hospital Medical School, Norfolk Place, London W2 lPG

I Matic   Laboratoire de Mutagénèse, Institut J Monod,
                               2 Place Jussieu, 75251 Paris, France
                               Laboratory of Biology and Microbial Genetics, Faculty of
                               Food Technology and Biotechnology, University of
                               Zagreb, 41000 Zagreb, Croatia

J Fraser McBlane   Laboratory of Molecular Biology, National Institute of
                               Diabetes and Digestive and Kidney Diseases, Building 5,
                               Room 241, National Institute of Health, Bethesda,
                               Maryland 20892, USA

Richard McCulloch   Microbiology Unit, Department of Biochemistry,
                               University of Oxford, South Parks Road,
                               Oxford, OXl 3QU
                               Current address: Netherlands Cancer Institute, Antoni
                               Van Leeuwenhoek Huis, Plesmanlaan 121, 1066 CX
                               Amsterdam, The Netherlands

Carol A Midgley   CRC Cell Transformation Group, Department of
                               Biochemistry, University of Dundee, Dundee DDl 4HN

Paul Modrich   Department of Biochemistry and Howard Hughes
                               Medical Institute, Duke University Medical School,
                               Durham, North Carolina, USA

Alistair I H Murchie   CRC Nucleic Acid Structure Research Group,
                               Department of Biochemistry, University of Dundee,
                               Dundee DDl 4HN

Thomas E Patterson   Department of Molecular Biology, Research Institute,
                               The Cleveland Clinic Foundation, 9500 Euclid Avenue,
                               Cleveland, Ohio 44195, USA

Steven M Picksley   CRC Cell Transformation Group, Department of
                               Biochemistry, University of Dundee, Dundee DDl 4HN

J Richard Pöhler   CRC Nucleic Acid Structure Research Group,
                               Department of Biochemistry, University of Dundee,
                               Dundee DDl 4HN

Marie-France Poupon CNRS URA 620, Institut Curie Section de Biologie, 26 rue d'Ulm, F-75231 Paris, Cedex 05, France

C M Radding Departments of Genetics, and Molecular Biophysics and Biochemistry, Yale University School of Medicine, New Haven, Connecticut 06510, USA

M Radman Laboratoire de Mutagénèse, Institut J Monod, 2 Place Jussieu, 75251 Paris, France

B J Rao Departments of Genetics, and Molecular Biophysics and Biochemistry, Yale University School of Medicine, New Haven, Connecticut 06510, USA

Masahiko K Satoh Imperial Cancer Research Fund, Clare Hall Laboratories, South Mimms, Hertfordshire EN6 3LD

David J Sherratt Microbiology Unit, Department of Biochemistry, University of Oxford, South Parks Road, Oxford, OXl 3QU

Gerald R Smith Fred Hutchinson Cancer Research Center, 1124 Columbia Street, Seattle, WA 98104, USA

Kathleen A Smith Imperial Cancer Research Fund, 44 Lincoln's Inn Fields, London WC2A 3PX

George R Stark Department of Molecular Biology, Research Institute, The Cleveland Clinic Foundation, 9500 Euclid Avenue, Cleveland, Ohio 44195, USA

Jesper Q Svejstrup Department of Cell Biology, Stanford University School of Medicine, Stanford, California 94305, USA

F Taddei Laboratoire de Mutagénèse, Institut J Monod, 2 Place Jussieu, 75251 Paris, France
Ecole Nationale du Génie Rural des Eaux et des Forêts, 19 Avenue du Maine, 75015 Paris, France

Andrew F Taylor Fred Hutchinson Cancer Research Center, 1124 Columbia Street, Seattle, WA 98104, USA

Alan E Tomkinson Institute of Biotechnology, The University of Texas Health Science Center at San Antonio, San Antonio, Texas 78245, USA

Christine Troelstra Medical Genetics Centre, Department of Cell Biology and Genetics, Erasmus University Rotterdam, PO Box 1738, 3000 DR Rotterdam, The Netherlands

Peter van der Spek Medical Genetics Centre, Department of Cell Biology and Genetics, Erasmus University Rotterdam, PO Box 1738, 3000 DR Rotterdam, The Netherlands

Hanneke van Vuuren Medical Genetics Centre, Department of Cell Biology and Genetics, Erasmus University Rotterdam, PO Box 1738, 3000 DR Rotterdam, The Netherlands

Wim Vermeulen Medical Genetics Centre, Department of Cell Biology and Genetics, Erasmus University Rotterdam, PO Box 1738, 3000 DR Rotterdam, The Netherlands

Borivoj Vojtesek Masaryk Memorial Cancer Institute, Zluty Kopex, 656 53 Brno, Czech Republic

Zhigang Wang Laboratory of Molecular Pathology, Department of Pathology, The University of Texas Southwestern Medical Center, Dallas, Texas 75235, USA

Geert Weeda Medical Genetics Centre, Department of Cell Biology and Genetics, Erasmus University Rotterdam, PO Box 1738, 3000 DR Rotterdam, The Netherlands

Stephen C West Imperial Cancer Research Fund, Clare Hall Laboratories, South Mimms, Herts EN6 3LD

Richard D Wood Imperial Cancer Research Fund, Clare Hall Laboratories, South Mimms, Herts EN6 3LD

Preface

Genomic instability is a major threat to living organisms. To counteract the damaging effects posed by endogenous and environmental agents, such as chemicals or radiation, micro-organisms devote several percent of their genome to encode proteins that function in the repair and recombination of DNA. For many years, a relatively small group of scientists have carefully delineated the molecular mechanisms of these repair processes, using the simplest model systems available, namely *Escherichia coli* and *Saccharomyces cerevisiae*. These studies, which until recently had only moderate impact outside of the field, now provide the cornerstone for exciting new research into analogous processes in human cells. The reason for this is the revelation that the biochemical pathways for the accurate replication, repair and recombination of DNA have been conserved through evolution.

New research shows that human cells use DNA repair mechanisms that are analogous to those found in bacteria to overcome the damaging effects of environmental mutagens and carcinogens. Of particular significance is the observation that certain cancers are caused by defects in DNA repair enzymes. For example, the human inherited non-polyposis colon cancer is now known to be caused by defects in the enzymes that repair DNA mismatches. Because much detailed information has been accumulated in studies of analogous mismatch repair proteins from bacteria, rapid progress can now be made. Without these model systems, progress would be dependent upon the usual time-consuming and laborious attempts to carry out positional cloning of human disease genes, followed by often painstaking efforts to identify the function of each gene product. The structural and functional homologies between the *E. coli* MutS and MutL proteins, and the *S. cerevisiae* and human MSH2 and MLH1 proteins, now guide research into understanding the basis of this form of colon cancer.

In the realm of model systems, few have been studied in more detail than the mechanism of recombination catalysed by the *E. coli* RecA protein. This protein, which is responsible for the pairing of homologous chromosomes during recombination and the post-replicational repair of DNA damages, has a counterpart in yeast and man (Rad51), again emphasizing the evolutionary conservation of important biological processes. The same can be said of the primary mechanism by which human cells are resistant towards the mutagenic effects of ultraviolet light since the mechanism of nucleotide excision repair, carried out in bacteria by the UvrABC proteins, has been conserved in yeast and human cells. Again, defects in this DNA repair system exhibit themselves in man as a predisposition to cancer, i.e. the human inherited disease xeroderma pigmentosum.

Most likely, there are additional lessons to be learnt by extending model systems to man. For example, when exposed to a hostile environment, bacteria attempt to defend themselves by induction of an error-prone DNA repair system; over twenty years ago, Brenner and Milstein proposed that a similar mechanism of local error-prone DNA repair synthesis might be employed by higher cells as a hypermutation mechanism to generate antibody diversity. This intriguing hypothesis is now open to experimental test. However, it is obvious that higher eukaryotes also have unique organizational problems that do not occur in bacteria. The presence of a large amount of repeated DNA sequences in higher cells poses problems in avoiding the loss or gain of DNA sequences, resulting from slippage of the template during replication and recombination. It is difficult to imagine the consequences of the high level of spontaneous recombination characteristic of *S. cerevisiae* if it occurred in human cells (actually, it is not difficult to imagine, but the thought of it sends a shiver down our DNA backbones!).

The aim of this Discussion meeting was to provide a current authoritative account of a rapidly developing field. We thank our distinguished colleagues who contributed to this volume for making this possible.

November 1994

Thomas Lindahl
Stephen C. West

1

RecA protein mediates homologous recognition via non-Watson–Crick bonds in base triplets

B. J. RAO AND C. M. RADDING

Departments of Genetics, and Molecular Biophysics & Biochemistry, Yale University School of Medicine, New Haven, Connecticut 06510, U.S.A.

SUMMARY

E. coli RecA protein, the prototype of a class, forms a helical nucleoprotein filament on single-stranded DNA that recognizes homology in duplex DNA, and initiates the exchange of strands in homologous recombination. The discovery of this reaction some years ago posed a quandary on how a third strand recognizes homology in duplex DNA, whose Watson–Crick bonds face inward in a hydrophobic core of stacked bases. Recent studies have shown that RecA protein promotes homologous recognition via non-Watson–Crick bonds in base triplets. The intermediates in the RecA reaction differ distinctly from triplex DNA that forms non-enzymically. The biological significance of the novel set of DNA interactions by which RecA protein effects homologous recognition is indicated by the importance of this protein in recombination, and the widespread distribution of homologous proteins in prokaryotes and eukaryotes.

1. AN OVERVIEW OF THE RecA REACTION

E. coli RecA protein, the prototype of a class that is widespread in both prokaryotes and eukaryotes, plays essential roles in recombination and repair (Ogawa *et al.* 1993; Shinohara *et al.* 1993; Story *et al.* 1993; for reviews, see Kowalczykowski *et al.* 1994; Radding 1991; West 1992). *In vitro*, RecA protein forms a right-handed helical nucleoprotein filament by head-to-tail polymerization on single-stranded DNA. This nucleoprotein filament recognizes homology in duplex DNA, which it quickly assimilates to form a three-stranded nucleoprotein filament that can be kilobases long (Stasiak *et al.* 1984; G. Reddy, B. Burnett & C. M. Radding, unpublished observations). The filament effects a switch of base pairs, creating heteroduplex DNA and a third strand which it displaces by a process that is fuelled by ATP hydrolysis (figure 1) (Menetski *et al.* 1990; Roca & Cox 1990; Rosselli & Stasiak 1990; Radding 1991; Burnett *et al.* 1994; Cox 1994).

2. RECOGNITION OF HOMOLOGY

Biologists have long known that in homologous genetic recombination, DNA molecules of different parentage are ultimately joined by Watson–Crick pairing of complementary strands in a molecular splice, called a heteroduplex joint; but the way in which homologous molecules initially recognize one another has remained mysterious.

The actions of RecA protein, as discovered fifteen years ago, brought to light a reaction in which a single strand recognizes homology in duplex DNA (figure 2) (McEntee *et al.* 1979; Shibata *et al.* 1979). Although three strands are involved, rather than two, recognition might nonetheless entail the Watson–Crick pairing of complementary strands, provided that RecA protein were to cause at least a local unpairing of strands in the duplex partner (figure 3). A non-enzymic precedent exists for such a mechanism, namely the thermally induced formation of D-loops by single strands and homologous superhelical DNA (Holloman *et al.* 1975). Characterization of the non-enzymic reaction, in which superhelicity plays an essential role, showed that it is based on the Watson–Crick pairing of an incoming single strand with its complement in a locally unwound region of duplex DNA (Beattie *et al.* 1977; Wiegand *et al.* 1977).

According to an alternative model, base triplets might mediate the recognition of homology in duplex DNA: an additional set of bonds would form between a third strand and duplex DNA while the latter temporarily maintains its Watson–Crick connections (figure 3) (Hsieh *et al.* 1990; Rao *et al.* 1993). A non-enzymic precedent also exists for this *base triplet* model, namely the spontaneous formation in solution of triplex DNA involving Hoogsteen and other non-Watson–Crick bonds which bind a third strand in the wide groove of duplex DNA. The formation of such triplex DNA, however, requires special sequences, runs of purines and pyrimidines, and produces a structure in which the third strand is antiparallel rather than parallel to its homologue (see figure 3) (Felsenfeld *et al.* 1957; Moser & Dervan 1987; Cooney *et al.* 1988;

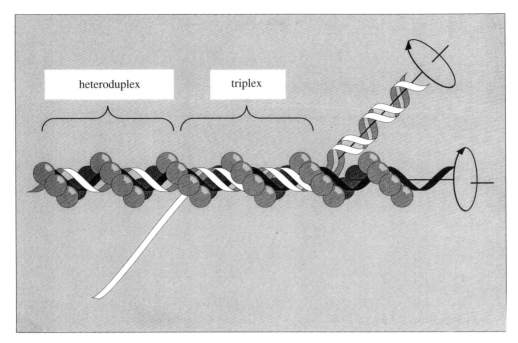

Figure 1. A model of strand exchange promoted by RecA protein (Howard-Flanders *et al.* 1984; Radding 1991). *In vitro*, the RecA nucleoprotein filament and duplex DNA meld to form a triplex intermediate, leading to exchange of base pairs and the separation of one strand from the original duplex.

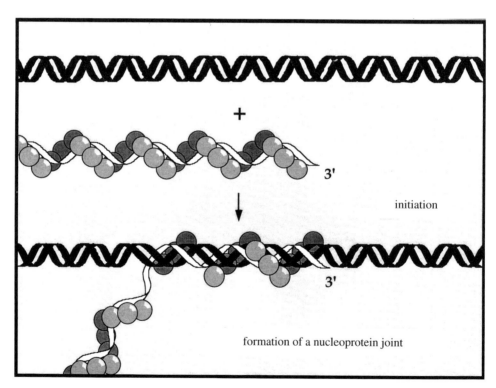

Figure 2. Recognition of homology in duplex DNA by the RecA nucleoprotein filament.

Rajagopal & Feigon 1989; Radhakrishnan *et al.* 1991). Neither the special sequences nor the antiparallel orientation pertains to the RecA reaction, which requires homologous rather than specific sequences, and which requires parallel homologues that undergo stepwise directional exchange that extends over kilobase lengths (cf. figures 1 and 3).

3. HOMOLOGOUS RECOGNITION BY NON-WATSON–CRICK INTERACTIONS OF TWO STRANDS

Evidence of a triplet interaction that precedes switching of base pairs has come from observations on the interactions of single-stranded oligonucleotides

base-pair model   base-triplet model

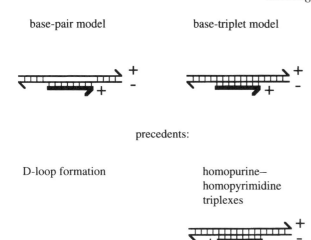

precedents:

D-loop formation   homopurine–
           homopyrimidine
           triplexes

Figure 3. Alternative models for the recognition of homology in duplex DNA.

with DNA, either single-stranded or double-stranded, in the RecA filament (Rao & Radding 1993, 1994).

With a single strand in the RecA filament, homologous complexes were formed when a complementary oligonucleotide was added, as had been observed previously. Surprisingly, however, a single strand in the RecA filament recognized not only its complement, but also recognized an oligonucleotide of identical sequence (figure 4).

The pairing of identical strands, called *self-recognition*, required RecA protein, Mg^{2+}, and ATP or ATPγS. Pairing was observed with several homologous sequences, but not with heterologous sequences. A computer search at various levels of partial matches revealed no fortuitous complementary sequences that could account for the different behaviour of homologous versus heterologous oligonucleotides (Rao & Radding 1993).

Self-recognition promoted by RecA protein is not to be confused with the non-enzymic formation of parallel strand DNA (Van de Sande *et al.* 1988; Rippe *et al.* 1992; Rippe & Jovin 1992), which, like the non-enzymic formation of triplex DNA, requires specific sequences, and in some cases, acidic pH (Robinson *et al.* 1992; Robinson & Wang 1993). Moreover, unlike parallel strand DNA, which is a stable DNA structure in solution, the self-recognition complexes formed by RecA protein do not survive deproteinization; they are not stable DNA structures, but rather are transient intermediates in homologous pairing and strand exchange.

4. HOMOLOGOUS RECOGNITION INVOLVING THREE STRANDS OF DNA IN RecA FILAMENTS

The experiments described above revealed that the RecA filament is capable of using non-Watson–Crick bonds to recognize homology. Are these the bonds that mediate recognition of homology in duplex DNA, and what does the pairing of two identical strands have to do with the prototypic RecA reaction in which three strands are involved? When the pairing reaction was further explored, not with a single strand in the RecA

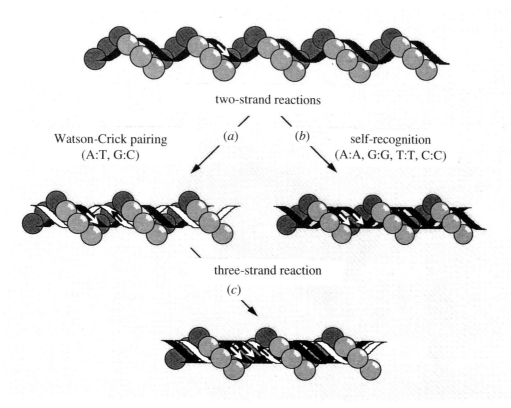

two-strand reactions

Watson-Crick pairing (*a*) (*b*) self-recognition
(A:T, G:C)   (A:A, G:G, T:T, C:C)

three-strand reaction

(*c*)

Figure 4. Experimental models of homologous recognition in the RecA filament. (*a*) Watson–Crick pairing of a complementary oligonucleotide with a single strand in the RecA filament; (*b*) Self-recognition of an oligonucleotide of identical sequence; (*c*) Recognition of a third strand by a RecA filament that contains a pair of complementary strands.

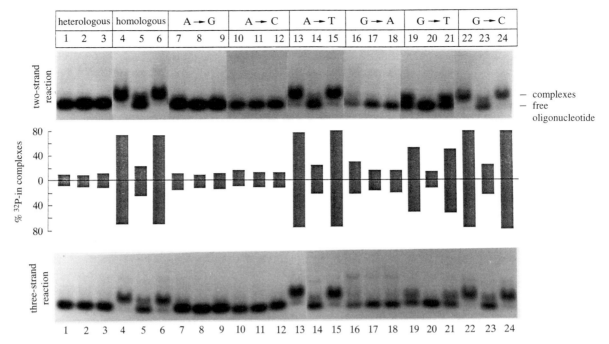

Figure 5. Comparison of the effects of base substitutions in an oligonucleotide on self-recognition (figure 4*b*) versus the recognition of that same oligonucleotide by duplex DNA in the RecA filament (figure 4*c*) (Rao & Radding 1994). The top of each panel shows the effects of base substitutions on the two-strand reaction, the bottom on the three-strand reaction. For the two-strand reaction, a RecA filament was formed on an 83 mer oligonucleotide in the presence of ATPγS; for the three-strand reaction, the filament was formed on the same 83 mer to which a complementary 43 mer had been annealed. Pairing was initiated by adding 5′ labelled 33 mer homologous oligonucleotide, a homologous oligonucleotide carrying base substitutions, or a heterologous 33 mer oligonucleotide, in the presence of a 24-fold excess of heterologous unlabelled carrier oligonucleotide. Each pairing reaction was done in three ways: without any additional competitor (first lane in each set of three, e.g. lane 4), with a tenfold excess of unlabelled competitor of the same sequence as the labelled 33 mer (second lane in each set of three, e.g. lane 5), or with another heterologous competitor (third lane in each set of three, e.g. lane 6). Pairing was done for 6 min at 37 °C, the samples were analysed by a gel retardation assay and quantitated by scanning the gel (PhosphorImager, Molecular Dynamics) (Rao & Radding 1993). The quantitative data from the three-strand reactions are plotted as inverted bars for ease of comparison with the two-strand reactions. Additional controls included: omission of RecA protein, omission of ATPγS, and deproteinization of wild-type reactions with SDS and proteinase K as described (Rao & Radding 1993), all of which resulted in no detectable pairing. (Copyright permission from *Proc. natn. Acad. Sci. U.S.A.*, 1994.)

filament, but rather with a segment of homologous duplex DNA in the filament, observations were made that closely paralleled those made on self-recognition. The nucleoprotein filament containing duplex DNA recognized a single-stranded oligonucleotide that had the sequence of either the Watson or the Crick strand, and all the requirements and stereochemical properties of two-strand and three-strand reactions were the same (figure 4, and see (§7) below).

5. IDENTICAL EFFECTS OF BASE SUBSTITUTIONS ON REACTIONS INVOLVING TWO VERSUS THREE STRANDS OF DNA

A comparison of the effects of base substitutions on self-recognition versus the recognition of homology in duplex DNA revealed that these two reactions are either the same or nearly so: Base substitutions that affected the two-strand reaction had the same quantitative effect on the three-strand reaction, and, likewise, those substitutions that did not affect one reaction did not affect the other (figure 5) (for

information on other substitutions, see Rao & Radding 1994). As the mutual recognition of two identical sequences occurs by non-Watson–Crick bonds, it follows that recognition of homology involving three strands must occur via the same or similar bonds, and hence that base triplets rather than Watson–Crick base pairs mediate the initial recognition in the three-strand reaction. Controls showed that similar base substitutions had no detectable effect on the pairing of complementary strands.

As illustrated in figure 6, the reaction of the RecA nucleoprotein filament with oligonucleotides can be written as a reversible reaction whose equilibrium lies to the right. In the experiments on the three-strand reaction cited here, we have studied the reverse reaction. To the extent that the reaction is freely reversible, the mechanisms of the reverse reaction should be the same as those of the forward reaction. Our interpretation that recognition in the reverse reaction reflects recognition in the forward reaction rests on the assumption of reversibility, which has been justified by preliminary experiments and is being studied in more detail (R. L. Bazemore and C. M. Radding, unpublished observations).

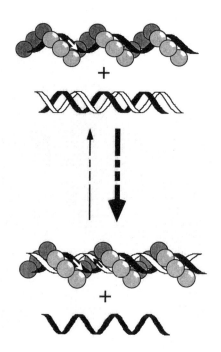

Figure 6. The reversibility of strand exchange when a duplex oligonucleotide is one of the substrates.

6. RECOGNITION VIA NOVEL TRIPLETS

On the basis of studies of deproteinized products of the RecA reaction, Rao & Radding proposed a model for homologous recognition via base triplets that was similar to several earlier proposals (figure 7) (Lacks 1966; Umlauf *et al.* 1990; Chiu *et al.* 1993; Rao *et al.* 1993). Such models, however, fail to account satisfactorily for self-recognition if the third complementary strand (C(−) in figure 7) is simply removed from the triplet. Recently, Zhurkin and colleagues pointed out that in such triplet schemes, there is a complementary pattern of partial charges, including the well-known charges that produce hydrogen bonds, and weaker charges as well (Zhurkin *et al.* 1994) (see figure 7); they specifically suggested that this pattern of complementary charges might constitute an electrostatic code for recognition. That complementary pattern is precisely the same for a two-strand versus a three-strand reaction, although major rotations are required to bring pairs of complementary charges into proximity (see figure 7). Thus in principle, the electrostatic code rationalizes the observed identity of the two- and three-strand reactions: but further chemical and physical studies are required to identify the bonds that mediate the formation of these base triplets and to determine the structure of the intermediate.

Three sets of observations now support the view that base triplets and non-Watson–Crick bonds mediate homologous recognition: These are the similar requirements and similar stereochemistry of the two-strand versus three-strand reactions (Rao & Radding 1993), the indistinguishable effects of base substitutions on both reactions (Rao & Radding 1994), and studies of a RecA mutant that promotes Watson–Crick pairing normally, but is partly defective both in self-recognition

and recognition of homology in duplex DNA (Ogawa *et al.* 1992; Kurumizaka *et al.* 1994*a,b*).

7. THE PERMISSIVE NATURE OF RECOGNITION

Two properties that are common to both non-Watson–Crick self-recognition and the recognition of homology in duplex DNA reveal that the initial stage of recognition is not fastidious. The stereochemical specificity of these reactions was explored by pairing the usual RecA filaments with oligonucleotides in which the linear array of bases was the same, but the 5 to 3 orientation of the phosphodiester backbone was reversed. Surprisingly, this major stereochemical alteration had virtually no effect on homologous recognition, although it did completely eliminate any strand exchange (Rao & Radding 1993).

When, as described above, the specificity of the pairing reactions was examined by base substitutions, homologous sequences were distinguished from heterologous sequences, but the number of base substitutions required to eliminate the recognition of an otherwise homologous sequence was surprisingly large. In a 33 mer oligonucleotide, out of nine G residues, more than six had to be changed to A before homologous recognition was abolished (Rao & Radding 1994). At present, we can only speculate about the significance of the lack of stringency of homologous recognition. Perhaps reduced stringency permits a more rapid search, facilitating the location of the right sequence out of many. Previous observations have shown that strand exchange promoted by RecA protein is also very permissive (DasGupta & Radding 1982*a, b*, Livneh & Lehman 1982; Bianchi & Radding 1983; Hahn *et al.* 1988). Further studies with oligonucleotides are in progress to determine if strand exchange plays a separate role in discriminating homologous from heterologous sequences.

8. IMPLICATIONS FOR INTERCHROMOSOMAL COMMUNICATION

Several groups demonstrated that a segment of the RecA nucleoprotein filament containing duplex DNA can recognize homology in a completely duplex molecule (Conley & West 1990; Lindsley & Cox 1990; Chiu *et al.* 1990). In light of the experiments described above, it seems likely that non-Watson–Crick interactions also mediate such four-strand reactions.

In certain lower eukaryotes, there are striking instances of interchromosomal communication. In *S. cereviseae*, homologous genes that are located at non-allelic positions on the same or non-homologous chromosomes undergo gene conversion at rates that are similar to conversion between genes at allelic sites (Petes & Hill 1988; Haber *et al.* 1991). In *Neurospora crassa* and *Ascobolus immersus* repeated sequences, which may also be at ectopic sites, are inactivated prior to meiosis by extensive methylation or mutation (Faugeron *et al.* 1990; Selker 1990). In each of these cases, the data indicate that recognition occurs by

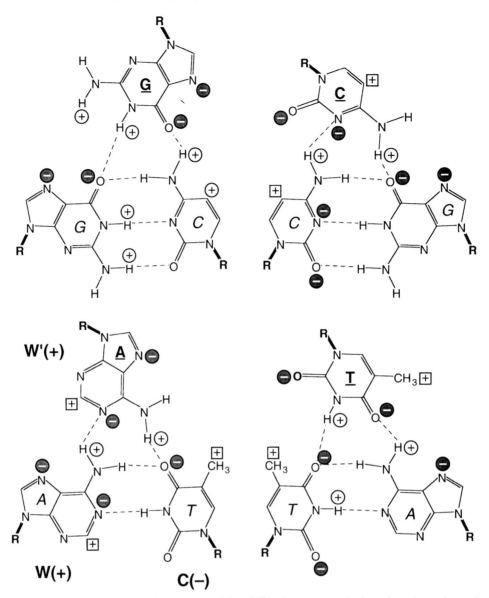

Figure 7. A base-triplet model for homologous recognition. W′(+) represents the base from incoming naked 33 mer oligonucleotide which is recognized by strands in the filament, either a single strand, W(+) (self-recognition in a two-strand reaction), or a pair of complementary strands, W(+):C(−) (triplet-recognition in a three-strand reaction). Charges in circles are stronger than those in squares (Renugopalakrishnan *et al.* 1971; Saenger 1984). This scheme was originally proposed to explain the effects of methylation of N-4 Cytosine and N-6 Adenine and the lack of effect of methylation of N-7 Guanine (Rao *et al.* 1993). The complementarity of partial charges suggested by Zhurkin *et al.* (1994) as an electrostatic recognition code, rationalizes the identity of two-strand and three-strand pairings as reported here. When the strand labelled C(−) is removed, the identical pattern of charge complementarity of a two-strand reaction with that of a three-strand reaction may be realized by either clockwise or counter-clockwise rotation of bases in W′(+). (Copyright permission from *Proc. natn. Acad. Sci. U.S.A.*, 1994.)

pairing of the interacting sequences even though they are not located near one another nor on homologous chromosomes, implying the existence of a rapid search that can scan the entire genome prior to the alignment of homologues later in meiosis. Recognition in these cases may involve non-Watson–Crick interactions of the kind that are promoted by RecA protein.

We are grateful to Ning Ye for technical assistance, to Jan Zulkeski for secretarial assistance, and to SungKay Chiu, Rochelle Reves Bazemore, Guruchuran Reddy, Efim Golub, Hitoshi Kurumizaka, and Takehiko Shibata for collegial advice. We are especially grateful to Victor Zhurkin for discussion prior to publication of his ideas on base recognition by electrostatic interactions. This research was sponsored by Grant 2R01GM33504 from the National Institutes of Health.

REFERENCES

Adzuma, K. 1992 Stable synapsis of homologous DNA molecules mediated by the *Escherichia coli* RecA protein involves local exchange of DNA strands. *Genes Dev.* **6**, 1679–1694.

Beattie, K.L., Wiegand, R.C. & Radding, C.M. 1977 Uptake of homologous single-stranded fragments by superhelical DNA. II. Characterization of the reaction. *J. molec. Biol.* **116**, 783–803.

Bianchi, M.E. & Radding, C.M. 1983 Insertions, deletions,

and mismatches in heteroduplex DNA made by recA protein. *Cell* **35**, 511–520.

Burnett, B., Rao, B.J., Jwang, B., Reddy, G. & Radding, C.M. 1994 Resolution of the three-stranded recombination intermediate made by RecA protein: An essential role of ATP hydrolysis. *J. molec. Biol.* **238**, 540–554.

Chiu, S.K., Rao, B.J., Story, R.M. & Radding, C.M. 1993 Interactions of three strands in joints made by RecA protein. *Biochemistry* **32**, 13146–13155.

Chiu, S.K., Wong, B.C. & Chow, S.A. 1990 Homologous pairing in duplex DNA regions and the formation of four stranded paranemic joints promoted by RecA protein. Effect of gap length. *J. Biol. Chem.* **265**, 21262–21268.

Conley, E.C. & West, S.C. 1990 Underwinding of DNA associated with duplex–duplex pairing by RecA protein. *J. biol. Chem.* **265**, 10156–10163.

Cooney, M., Czernuszewicz, G., Postel, E.H., Flint, S.J. & Hogan, M.E. 1988 Site-specific oligonucleotide binding represses transcription of the human *c-myc* gene *in vitro*. *Science, Wash.* **241**, 456–459.

Cox, M.M. 1994 Why does RecA protein hydrolyze ATP? *Trends biochem. Sci.* (In the press.)

DasGupta, C. & Radding, C.M. 1982*a* Lower fidelity of RecA protein catalyzed homologous pairing with a superhelical substrate. *Nature, Lond.* **295**, 71–73.

DasGupta, C. & Radding, C.M. 1982*b* Polar branch migration promoted by recA protein: Effect of mismatched base pairs. *Proc. natn. Acad. Sci. U.S.A.* **79**, 762–766.

Faugeron, G., Rhounim, L. & Rossignol, J.L. 1990 How does the cell count the number of ectopic copies of a gene in the premeiotic inactivation process acting in *Ascobolus immersus*? *Genetics* **124**, 585–591.

Felsenfeld, G., Davies, D.R. & Rich, A. 1957 Formation of a three-stranded polynucleotide molecule. *J. Am. chem. Soc.* **79**, 2023–2024.

Haber, J.E., Leung, W.-Y., Borts, R. & Lichten, M. 1991 The frequency of meiotic recombination in yeast is independent of the number and position of homologous donor sequences: Implications for chromosome pairing. *Proc. natn. Acad. Sci. U.S.A.* **88**, 1120–1124.

Hahn, T.R., West, S.C. & Howard-Flanders, P. 1988 RecA-mediated strand exchange reactions between duplex DNA molecules containing damaged bases, deletions and insertions. *J. biol. Chem.* **263**, 7431–7436.

Holloman, W.K., Wiegand, R., Hoessli, C. & Radding, C.M. 1975 Uptake of homologous single stranded fragments by superhelical DNA: A possible mechanism for the initiation of genetic recombination. *Proc. natn. Acad. Sci. U.S.A.* **72**, 2394–2398.

Howard-Flanders, P., West, S.C. & Stasiak, A.J. 1984 Role of RecA spiral filaments in genetic recombination. *Nature, Lond.* **309**, 215–220.

Hsieh, P., Camerini-Otero, C.S. & Camerini-Otero, R.D. 1990 Pairing of homologous DNA sequences by proteins: Evidence for three-stranded DNA. *Genes Dev.* **4**, 1951–1963.

Kowalczykowski, S.C., Dixon, D.A., Eggleston, A.K., Lauder, S.D. & Rehrauer, W.M. 1994 Biochemistry of homologous recombination in *Escherichia coli*. *Microbiol. Rev.* **58**, 401–465.

Kurumizaka, H., Ikawa, S., Ikeya, T., Ogawa, T. & Shibata, T. 1994*a* A chimeric RecA protein exhibits altered double-stranded DNA binding. *J. biol. Chem.* **269**, 3068–3075.

Kurumizaka, H., Rao, B.J., Ogawa, T., Radding, C.M. & Shibata, T. 1994*b* A chimeric RecA protein that implicates non-Watson–Crick interactions in homologous pairing. *Nucl. Acids Res.* **22**, 3387–3391.

Lacks, S. 1966 Integration efficiency and genetic recom-

bination in pneumococcal transformation. *Genetics* **53**, 207–235.

Lindsley, J.E. & Cox, M.M. 1990 On RecA protein-mediated homologous alignment of two DNA molecules. *J. biol. Chem.* **265**, 10164–10171.

Livneh, Z. & Lehman, I.R. 1982 Recombinational bypass of pyrimidine dimers promoted by the RecA protein of *Escherichia coli*. *Proc. natn. Acad. Sci. U.S.A.* **79**, 3171–3175.

McEntee, K., Weinstock, G.M. & Lehman, I.R. 1979 Initiation of general recombination catalyzed *in vitro* by the RecA protein of Escherichia coli. *Proc. natn. Acad. Sci. U.S.A.* **76**, 2615–2619.

Menetski, J.P., Bear, D.G. & Kowalczykowski, S.C. 1990 Stable DNA heteroduplex formation catalyzed by the *Escherichia coli* RecA protein in the absence of ATP hydrolysis. *Proc. natn. Acad. Sci. U.S.A.* **87**, 21–25.

Moser, H.E. & Dervan, P.B. 1987 Sequence-specific cleavage of double helical DNA by triple helix formation. *Science, Wash.* **238**, 645–650.

Ogawa, T., Shinohara, A., Ogawa, H. & Tomizawa, J.-I. 1992 Functional structures of the RecA protein found by chimera analysis. *J. molec. Biol.* **226**, 651–660.

Ogawa, T., Yu, X., Shinohara, A. & Egelman, E.H. 1993 Similarity of the yeast RAD51 filament to the bacterial RecA filament. *Science, Wash.* **259**, 1896–1899.

Petes, T.D. & Hill, C.W. 1988 Recombination between repeated genes in microorganisms. *A. Rev. Genet.* **22**, 147–168.

Radding, C.M. 1991 Helical interactions in homologous pairing and strand exchange driven by RecA protein. *J. biol. Chem.* **266**, 5355–5358.

Radhakrishnan, I., de los Santos, C. & Patel, D.J. 1991 Nuclear magnetic resonance structural studies of intramolecular purine–purine–pyrimidine DNA triplexes in solution. *J. molec. Biol.* **221**, 1403–1418.

Rajagopal, P. & Feigon, J. 1989 NMR studies of triple-strand formation from the homopurine–homopyrimidine deoxyribonucleotides d(GA)4 and d(TC)4. *Biochemistry* **28**, 7859–7870.

Rao, B.J., Chiu, S.K. & Radding, C.M. 1993 Homologous recognition and triplex formation promoted by RecA protein between duplex oligonucleotides and single-stranded DNA. *J. molec. Biol.* **229**, 328–343.

Rao, B.J. & Radding, C.M. 1993 Homologous recognition promoted by RecA protein via non-Watson–Crick bonds between identical DNA strands. *Proc. natn. Acad. Sci. U.S.A.* **90**, 6646–6650.

Rao, B.J. & Radding, C.M. 1994 The formation of base triplets by non-Watson–Crick bonds mediates homologous recognition in genetic recombination. *Proc. natn. Acad. Sci. U.S.A.* **91**, 6161–6165.

Renugopalakrishnan, V., Lakshminarayanan, A.V. & Sasisekharan, V. 1971 Stereochemistry of nucleic acids and polynucleotides. 3. Electronic charge distribution. *Biopolymers* **10**, 1159–1167.

Rippe, K., Fritsch, V., Westhof, E. & Jovin, T.M. 1992 Alternating d(G–A) sequences form a parallel-stranded DNA homoduplex. *EMBO J.* **11**, 3777–3786.

Rippe, K. & Jovin, T.M. 1992 Parallel-stranded duplex DNA. *Methods Enzymol.* **211**, 199–220.

Robinson, H., van der Marel, G.A., van Boom, J.H. & Wang, A.H.-J. 1992 Unusual DNA conformation at low pH revealed by NMR: Parallel-stranded DNA duplex with homo base pairs. *Biochemistry* **31**, 10510–10517.

Robinson, H. & Wang, A.H.-J. 1993 5'-CGA sequence is a strong motif for homo base-paired parallel-stranded DNA duplex as revealed by NMR analysis. *Proc. natn. Acad. Sci. U.S.A.* **90**, 5224–5228.

Roca, A.I. & Cox, M.M. 1990 The RecA protein: Structure and function. *CRC Crit. Rev.* **25**, 415–456.

Rosselli, W. & Stasiak, A. 1990 Energetics of RecA-mediated recombination reactions. Without ATP hydrolysis RecA can mediate polar strand exchange but is unable to recycle. *J. molec. Biol.* **216**, 335–352.

Saenger, W. 1984 *Principles of nucleic acid structure.* New York, NY: Springer-Verlag.

Selker, E.U. 1990 Premeiotic instability of repeated sequences in *Neurospora crassa. A. Rev. Genet.* **24**, 579–613.

Shibata, T., DasGupta, C., Cunningham, R.P. & Radding, C.M. 1979 Purified *E. coli* recA protein catalyses homologous pairing of superhelical DNA and single-stranded fragments. *Proc. natn. Acad. Sci. U.S.A.* **76**. 1638–1642.

Shinohara, A., Ogawa, H., Matsuda, Y., Ushio, N., Ikeo, K. & Ogawa, T. 1993 Cloning of human, mouse and fission yeast recombination genes homologous to RAD51 and recA. *Nature Genet.* **4**, 239–243.

Stasiak, A., Stasiak, A.Z. & Koller, T. 1984 Visualization of RecA–DNA complexes involved in consecutive stages of an *in vitro* strand exchange reaction. *CSH Symp. Quant. Biol.* **49**, 561–570.

Story, R.M., Bishop, D.K., Kleckner, N. & Steitz, T.A. 1993 Structural relationship of bacterial RecA proteins to recombination proteins from bacteriophage T4 and yeast. *Science, Wash.* **259**, 1892–1896.

Umlauf, S.W., Cox, M.M. & Inman, R.B. 1990 Triple-helical pairing intermediates formed by RecA protein. *J. biol. Chem.* **265**, 16898–16912.

Van de Sande, J.H., Ramsing, N.B., Germann, M.W. *et al.* 1988 Parallel stranded DNA. *Science, Wash.* **241**, 551–557.

West, S.C. 1992 Enzymes and molecular mechanisms of genetic recombination. *A. Rev. Biochem.* **61**, 603–640.

Wiegand, R.C., Beattie, K.L., Holloman, W.K. & Radding, C.M. 1977 Uptake of homologous single-stranded fragments by superhelical DNA. III. The product and its enzymic conversion to a recombinant molecule. *J. molec. Biol.* **116**, 805–824.

Zhurkin, V.B., Raghunathan, G., Ulyanov, N.B., Camerini-Otero, R.D. & Jernigan, R.L. 1994 A parallel DNA triplex as a model for the intermediate in homologous recombination. *J. molec. Biol.* **239**, 181–200.

2

The initiation and control of homologous recombination in *Escherichia coli*

GERALD R. SMITH, SUSAN K. AMUNDSEN, PATRICK DABERT
AND ANDREW F. TAYLOR

Fred Hutchinson Cancer Research Center, 1124 Columbia Street, Seattle, WA 98104, U.S.A.

SUMMARY

The chromosome of *Escherichia coli* recombines at low frequency when it is an intact circle but recombines at high frequency when it is broken, for example by X-rays, or when a linear DNA fragment is introduced into the cell during conjugation or transduction. The high recombinogenicity of double-strand (ds) DNA ends is attributable to RecBCD enzyme, which acts on ds DNA ends and is essential for recombination and ds DNA break repair. RecBCD enzyme initiates DNA unwinding at ds DNA ends, and its nuclease activity is controlled by Chi sites (5′ G-C-T-G-G-T-G-G 3′) in such a way that the enzyme produces a potent single-stranded DNA substrate for homologous pairing by RecA and single-stranded DNA binding proteins. We discuss a unifying model for recombination and ds DNA break repair, based upon the enzymic activities of these and other proteins and upon the behaviour of *E. coli* mutants altered in these proteins.

1. INTRODUCTION

Homologous recombination plays a dual role for living organisms. First, in diploid or partly diploid organisms it produces new allelic combinations and thereby increases the variability required for evolution. Second, faithful repair of double-strand (ds) breaks in DNA provides the genomic stability required for continuity from one cell or one generation to the next. Recombination and ds DNA break repair appear to proceed by a common mechanism (Resnick 1976; Szostak *et al.* 1983) that is controlled, like many other cellular processes, at the initial stages. This article discusses the initiation and control of homologous recombination in *Escherichia coli*.

The genetic map of *E. coli* is circular, and its DNA is also circular at least some of the time. Recombination between repeated segments of the circular genome, for example the genes encoding ribosomal RNA, is rare, occurring at a rate of about 10^{-4} per cell division (Petes & Hill 1988). In contrast, broken (i.e. linear) DNA often recombines at a rate exceeding 1 per cell division (Krasin & Hutchinson 1977). The low frequency of recombination of an intact, circular genome provides stability and survival of *E. coli* as a species, whereas the high frequency of recombination of a broken genome provides rapid repair and survival of individual *E. coli* cells. Apparently, ds DNA breaks trigger recombination just when appropriate for the cell. We focus our discussion on the molecular mechanism of this control.

2. SOURCES OF DOUBLE-STRANDED DNA ENDS

Double-stranded (ds) DNA ends arise in several ways in *E. coli*. Direct DNA damage, such as that from X-irradiation, may make ds breaks. Single-strand (ss) DNA breaks (nicks or gaps) produced by other agents may be converted to ds breaks during attempted repair of a ss break or replication past it. Linear DNA is introduced into the cell during transduction, transformation (with linear DNA), or conjugation; in the last case ss DNA injected from the donor is converted into ds DNA in the recipient (Ippen-Ihler & Minkley 1986). In each case recombination (or repair) occurs at high frequency when ds DNA ends are present. The high reactivity of ds DNA ends is attributable to the strong preference for DNA ends by RecBCD enzyme, which is required for recombination and ds DNA break repair in *E. coli* (Emmerson 1968).

3. ACTIVITIES OF RecBCD ENZYME

RecBCD enzyme has multiple enzymic activities, which can be broadly separated into unwinding of linear ds DNA and DNA hydrolysis (see Taylor 1988, for review and references). Both activities require the concurrent hydrolysis of ATP, which in turn is dependent on DNA. The enzyme contains three large polypeptides, encoded by the *recB*, *recC*, and *recD* genes (M_r 134 kDa, 129 kDa, and 67 kDa, respectively). The isolated RecB polypeptide has strong DNA-dependent ATPase activity, but no other activity is present at high level with any combination except that of all three polypeptides (Masterson *et al.* 1992). Reconstitution with the three isolated polypeptides produces about 5 % of the native enzyme's specific activity (Masterson *et al.* 1992); whether reconstitution is inefficient or another factor is missing is unclear. The RecB and RecD polypeptides bind ATP (Julin & Lehman 1987) and may provide the 'motor' to move RecBCD enzyme along DNA.

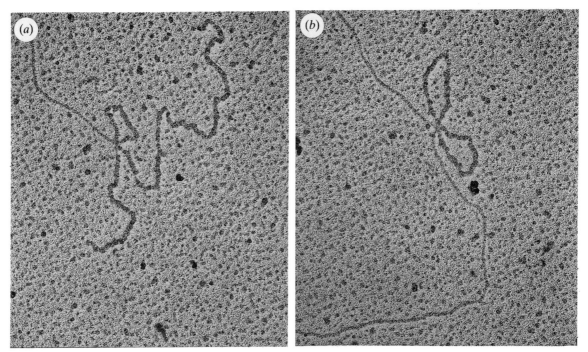

Figure 1. Loop-tail (*a*) and twin-loop (*b*) structures formed by RecBCD enzyme unwinding DNA. Thin lines are ds DNA, and thick lines are ss DNA coated with SSB. From Smith *et al.* 1984.

RecBCD enzyme has no detectable activity on circular ds DNA, but it has a high affinity for ds DNA ends: the dissociation constant is estimated to be 0.1 nM (A. F. Taylor & G. R. Smith, unpublished data). This concentration is about 1/10 that of a single ds DNA end per *E. coli* cell; consequently, the enzyme should act at its maximal rate whenever a ds DNA end occurs in the cell. This feature assures that linear ds DNA will be quickly repaired or recombined in *E. coli*.

In the absence of ATP RecBCD enzyme forms a well-defined complex with a ds DNA end (Ganesan & Smith 1992). The enzyme protects from DNase I digestion the terminal 16–17 nucleotides (nuc) of the strand with a 3′ end in the complex, and 20–21 nuc of the 5′ ended strand. uv-irradiation of the complex crosslinks the RecB polypeptide to the 3′ end and the RecC and RecD polypeptides to the 5′ end. These asymmetries are presumably responsible for the asymmetries of the unwinding and nuclease reactions, but the details remain unknown.

Upon addition of ATP to the complex, RecBCD enzyme rapidly moves along the DNA and unwinds it, with the production of a growing ss DNA loop and two ss DNA tails (figure 1*a*). These 'loop-tail' structures and the rates of their growth and movement were elucidated by electron microscopy (Taylor & Smith 1980; Telander-Muskavitch & Linn 1982). The strand with a 5′ end in the initiation complex forms the longer of the two tails, while the 3′ ended strand forms the loop and the shorter tail (Braedt & Smith 1989). Unwinding occurs at about 350 base pairs (b.p.) per second, and the loop grows at about 100 nuc per second, as measured by electron microscopy of molecules acted upon by RecBCD enzyme for 20–60 s (Taylor & Smith 1980); a similar estimate of the rate of unwinding was obtained by a continuous fluorescence-based spectroscopic assay (Roman &

Kowalczykowski 1989). The loop-tail structures are frequently preserved by single-stranded DNA binding (SSB) protein when it is present in the reaction mixture; alternatively, the two tails may anneal to form a twin-loop structure (figure 1*b*). The loops of this structure grow and move along the DNA at the same rate as the loop of the loop-tail structure. RecBCD enzyme's unwinding of DNA produces ss DNA, an essential substrate for RecA protein, which pairs homologous DNA (see Rao & Radding in this volume).

During its unwinding of DNA RecBCD enzyme cuts the DNA at a frequency that depends upon the Mg^{2+} and ATP concentrations (among other factors) (reviewed by Taylor 1988). With excess Mg^{2+} (relative to ATP) the nuclease is maximally active, and oligonucleotides are quickly produced from linear ds DNA. With excess ATP, which chelates the Mg^{2+}, the nuclease activity is markedly reduced, and long ss DNA is produced by the unwinding reaction. RecBCD enzyme also hydrolyses linear ss DNA to oligonucleotides. The degradation of DNA to oligonucleotides seems antithetical to the production of intact recombinant molecules, but the interaction of RecBCD enzyme with special nucleotide sequences, Chi sites, has helped resolve this paradox.

4. CHI SITES: HOTSPOTS OF HOMOLOGOUS RECOMBINATION

During their studies of phage λ recombination in *E. coli* Stahl and his collaborators found that certain λ mutations, which they called χ, enhance homologous recombination but only near themselves (see Thaler & Stahl (1988) and Smith (1988, 1994) for reviews and references); in other words the χ mutations create a site, called Chi, that locally stimulates recombination.

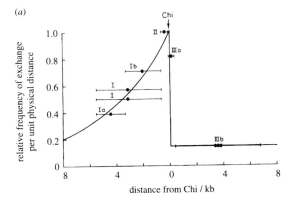

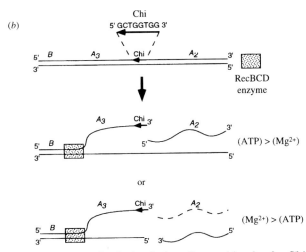

Figure 2. (*a*) Localized stimulation of recombination by Chi in phage λ crosses. I, Ia, etc. are genetic intervals bounded by markers located the indicated distance from a Chi site in λ. Solid circles indicate the midpoints of each interval and the frequency of recombinants per physical length of that interval, normalized to interval II = 1. From Cheng & Smith 1989. (*b*) Action of purified RecBCD enzyme at Chi. With (ATP) > (Mg^{2+}), RecBCD enzyme unwinds ds DNA, nicks the upper strand 4–6 nuc to the right of Chi, and continues unwinding (Taylor *et al.* 1985). With (Mg^{2+}) > (ATP), RecBCD enzyme degrades the upper strand up to, but not beyond, Chi (Dixon & Kowalczykowski 1993); the lower strand is cut near Chi and is unwound beyond Chi (A.F. Taylor & G.R. Smith, unpublished). Both conditions produce a ss DNA fragment with a 3′ end near Chi and extending to its left. A_2, A_3, and B are genetic markers discussed in the text.

Chi stimulates RecBCD enzyme-dependent recombination but not other types, such as that promoted by λ's own recombination functions. Chi stimulates recombination, including the formation of heteroduplex DNA (hDNA), to its left but not to its right (as defined by the conventional λ genetic map) (figure 2*a*). Inversion of a Chi site in λ greatly reduces its activity. These two asymmetries – leftward directionality and orientation dependence – are accounted for in the following way. RecBCD enzyme gains access to λ DNA primarily when the circular replicative form is cut by the λ terminase complex at the cohesive end site *cos* in preparation for packaging of the linear DNA into the virion; terminase remains bound to the left cohesive end, and RecBCD enzyme enters the right end. As it travels along the DNA, RecBCD enzyme recognizes

the asymmetric Chi sequence in one orientation but not the other.

Nucleotide sequence analyses of λ wild-type and χ mutants revealed Chi to be 5′ G-C-T-G-G-T-G-G 3′ (or its complement or the duplex). This sequence is recognized as Chi only when RecBCD enzyme approaches it from the right (as written here). Although wild-type λ lacks this sequence, the *E. coli* chromosome has about 1000 Chi sites, or about 1 per 5 kilobase pairs (kb). Chi is active in *E. coli* RecBCD enzyme-dependent recombination following conjugation and transduction; as far as tested, the properties of Chi in λ recombination apply to *E. coli* recombination. The *E. coli* Chi sites appear to be non-randomly oriented on the chromosome: about 80 % of those in the 136 kb sequenced region around the origin of replication *oriC* are oriented such that the 5′ end of the Chi sequence above is pointed toward *oriC* over the shorter arc of the chromosome (Burland *et al.* 1993). It is unclear whether this bias reflects a role of Chi in the repair of broken replication forks (Kuzminov *et al.* 1994; see below) or the occurrence of frequently used codons within Chi (Triman *et al.* 1982) plus a bias for transcription away from *oriC* (Brewer 1988). The abundance of Chi sites on the *E. coli* chromosome makes it likely that RecBCD enzyme entering a ds DNA break anywhere on the chromosome will find within a few tens of kb a Chi site properly oriented to interact with it and effectively repair or recombine the chromosome.

5. INTERACTION OF RecBCD ENZYME AND CHI SITES

The first evidence that RecBCD enzyme interacts with Chi was the hotspot activity of Chi in RecBCD enzyme-dependent recombination but not in other pathways of recombination, as noted above. Certain non-null alleles of *recB* and *recC* that reduce or abolish Chi activity but not recombination further implicated RecBCD enzyme as the factor that recognizes Chi. Direct evidence came from the finding of Chi-dependent DNA strand cleavage (Chi nicking) by purified RecBCD enzyme; mutations of Chi or of *recB* or *recC* coordinately reduce or abolish both Chi activity in cells and Chi nicking in cell-free extracts. This correlation indicates that Chi nicking or another activity not mutationally separated from it is required for Chi's stimulation of recombination.

Chi nicking was initially studied using a reaction condition with (ATP) > (Mg^{2+}), which minimizes the Chi-independent nuclease activity (Ponticelli *et al.* 1985). Under these conditions RecBCD enzyme cuts one DNA strand, that containing 5′ G-C-T-G-G-T-G-G 3′, 4–6 nuc to the right of this sequence (figure 2*b*) (Taylor *et al.* 1985). The complementary strand is not detectably cut. Up to 40 % of the substrate molecules are cut at Chi by a single passage of the enzyme (Taylor & Smith 1992), and high yields of the DNA fragments extending to the right and left of the nick are obtained. The nicked fragments are released as ss DNA, indicating that RecBCD enzyme unwinds the DNA before and after cutting at Chi. The ss DNA fragment extending from Chi to the left bears a 3′ OH end and is hypothesized to be a substrate for RecA and SSB protein-promoted pairing with a homologous duplex and to be a primer for repair DNA synthesis (see §7 for further discussion).

The pairing of this Chi-dependent fragment with a homologous supercoiled DNA has been demonstrated in a coupled system containing purified RecBCD enzyme, RecA protein and SSB protein (Dixon & Kowalczykowski 1991). Formation of the joint molecule product requires that all three proteins be present simultaneously, suggesting a coordinated action among the proteins. The joint molecule contains the supercoiled DNA and the ss DNA fragment extending from Chi to the left but apparently not the other parts of the linear Chi-containing substrate.

The reaction condition used by Dixon & Kowalczykowski (1991) to produce these joint molecules employs $(Mg^{2+}) > (ATP)$, which maximizes the activity of RecA protein. Under this condition RecBCD nuclease activity is strong, though it is inhibited by SSB protein (see Taylor 1988), and the enzyme degrades some of the DNA to oligonucleotides. Degradation is strongest on the strand with a 3′ end at which RecBCD enzyme initiated its action but is greatly diminished on that strand after encounter with a properly oriented Chi site (Dixon & Kowalczykowski 1993) (figure 2b). Thus, under these conditions Chi attenuates on one DNA strand the nuclease activity of RecBCD enzyme, rather than inducing the nicking activity of the enzyme, as under the conditions $((ATP) > (Mg^{2+}))$ discussed above. Under both conditions, however, RecBCD enzyme produces from the strand containing 5′ G-C-T-G-G-T-G-G 3′ a Chi-dependent fragment extending to the left of this site.

Under conditions with $(Mg^{2+}) > (ATP)$ the RecBCD enzyme reaction at Chi is complex (A. F. Taylor & G. R. Smith, unpublished results). In addition to degradation of the 3′ ended ('upper') strand up to Chi, we observe high frequency Chi-dependent cutting of the complementary ('lower') strand (figure 2b). Cuts on the 'upper' strand are distributed over a 10 nuc interval encompassing the Chi octamer, rather than being concentrated 4–6 nuc to the right of Chi as under conditions with $(ATP) > (Mg^{2+})$. Cuts on the 'lower' strand are distributed over a 15 nuc interval slightly offset to the left of the interval on the 'upper' strand. This reaction therefore produces three DNA fragments, one with a 5′ end near Chi ('lower' left, figure 2b) and two with 3′ ends near Chi ('upper' left and 'lower' right). The last two fragments are potential substrates for RecA protein-promoted homologous pairing.

A major question is which reaction condition, $(ATP) > (Mg^{2+})$ or $(Mg^{2+}) > (ATP)$, more nearly reflects the condition inside *E. coli* cells. Estimates of the free (ATP) and free (Mg^{2+}) are approximately 3 mM (Matthews 1972; Alatossava *et al.* 1985); thus, the entity in excess is uncertain. We have used mutant Chi sites, mutant *E. coli* RecBCD enzyme, and RecBCD enzymes from other bacterial species in both intracellular and extracellular reactions to address this question. There is an excellent correlation of Chi

hotspot activity inside cells and Chi nicking outside cells using conditions with $(ATP) > (Mg^{2+})$ (Ponticelli *et al.* 1985; Cheng & Smith 1987; McKittrick & Smith 1989); similar studies using conditions with $(Mg^{2+}) > (ATP)$ have not, to our knowledge, been done but may help resolve this question. Regardless of the reaction condition, a 3′ OH ss DNA fragment extending from Chi to its left is produced by RecBCD enzyme. In §7 we discuss how this fragment may produce recombinants and prime DNA synthesis for ds DNA break repair.

In addition to the DNA being changed (cut) at Chi, RecBCD enzyme is also changed when it cuts at Chi. With $(ATP) > (Mg^{2+})$ the enzyme loses the ability to cut at a subsequently encountered Chi site, even though the enzyme continues to travel past this site (Taylor & Smith 1992). With $(Mg^{2+}) > (ATP)$ the enzyme's nuclease activity, at least on the 'upper' strand discussed above, is attenuated (Dixon & Kowalczykowski 1993), so that a DNA end would not be expected to be produced at a subsequently encountered Chi site; this prediction has not, to our knowledge, been tested. The physical basis for the change of RecBCD enzyme upon cutting at Chi has not been established. Taking note of the phenotypes of *recD* mutants and Chi sites, Thaler *et al.* (1988) hypothesized that the RecD subunit is lost from RecBCD enzyme upon its encounter with Chi. The similar effect of (Mg^{2+}) on RecBCD enzyme after its encounter with Chi and on RecBC protein (i.e. lacking RecD polypeptide) has been interpreted as support for this hypothesis (Dixon, Churchill & Kowalczykowski 1994). Alternatively, the change may be the loss or alteration of a small RNA that is associated with purified RecBCD enzyme and which appears to be required for DNA unwinding and Chi cutting by RecBCD enzyme (S. K. Amundsen & G. R. Smith, unpublished data). Regardless of the physical basis for the change, cutting at only a single Chi site provides an enzymic basis for RecBCD enzyme promoting only a single recombinational or repair event near a ds DNA end (see §7).

6. FURTHER ENZYMIC STEPS FOR RECOMBINATION AND REPAIR

Production of ss DNA at and distal to a Chi site by RecBCD enzyme only initiates recombination or repair; further enzymic steps are required to convert this intermediate into completed recombinants or repaired molecules. These steps include homologous pairing, strand exchange, branch migration, and resolution, and can be promoted by the RecA, RuvAB, RecG, and RuvC proteins of *E. coli* (see below and articles by Rao & Radding and by West in this volume).

7. A UNIFYING MODEL FOR RECOMBINATION AND DS DNA BREAK REPAIR IN *E. COLI*

Based upon other people's work and ideas, as well as our own, we previously proposed a model (figure 3) for recombination by the RecBCD pathway of *E. coli*

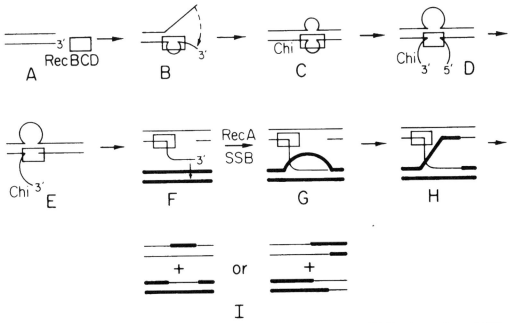

Figure 3. Model for recombination promoted by RecBCD enzyme (open box), Chi, RecA protein, and SSB protein. Thin and thick lines represent parental ds DNA. Resolving enzymes, such as RuvABC and RecG proteins, acting at the last two steps are not shown. For explanation see text. Modified from Smith *et al.* (1984).

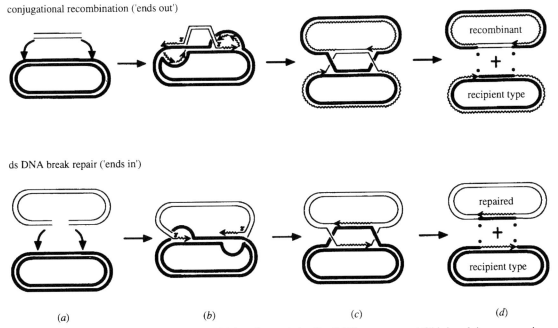

Figure 4. Model for recombination and ds DNA break repair by RecBCD enzyme and Chi, involving non-reciprocal resolution by DNA synthesis. Thin and thick lines are parental ds DNA, and wavy lines are newly synthesized DNA. Solid dots are probable sites of heteroduplex DNA. For explanation, see text and figure 3. From Smith (1991).

(Smith *et al.* 1984). In this model RecBCD enzyme binds to a ds DNA end, produced by any of several means (see §2). The enzyme unwinds DNA with the production of growing ss DNA loops (steps B and C) and cuts one strand at a properly oriented Chi site (D), to produce with continued unwinding a ss DNA 'tail' with Chi near the free 3′ OH end (E and F). RecA and SSB proteins pair this ss DNA with a homologous duplex to form a D-loop (G). Continued DNA unwinding by RecBCD enzyme and DNA strand transfer by RecA and SSB proteins extends the heteroduplex DNA in the D-loop.

At this point we envisage two alternatives for resolution of the joint molecule into recombinants. In the first alternative the D-loop is cut to allow RecA and SSB proteins to convert the D-loop into a Holliday junction (figure 3, step H). Branch migration and resolution of the Holliday junction by RuvAB and RuvC proteins or by RecG protein plus others produce reciprocal recombinants, either 'patches' (I, left) or 'splices' (I, right) depending upon which pair of strands is cleaved in the resolution.

In the second alternative (figure 4) the invading ss DNA with its 3′ OH in the D-loop primes DNA replication, which may be converted into a replication fork (Smith 1991). This process is especially attractive for recombination and repair of circular chromosomes, such as *E. coli*'s, in which a linear (broken or fragmented) DNA molecule interacts with an intact circular molecule. Action of RecBCD enzyme at properly oriented Chi sites near each end of the linear fragment (step *a*), followed by D-loop formation by RecA and SSB proteins (*b*), produces two replication primers pointed in opposite directions. Replication from these two points produces two intact circles joined by two Holliday junctions (*c*). Resolution of the Holliday junctions in the same directions (both 'horizontal' or both 'vertical') produces two intact monomeric circles (*d*); resolution in the opposite directions produces a dimeric circle (not shown), which can be resolved into monomeric circles by the XerCD site-specific recombination enzyme (see Sherratt *et al.* in this volume). In either case the occurrence of intact circles stops recombination, as circular DNA is refractory to RecBCD enzyme.

The model in figure 4 has several attractive features for *E. coli* recombination and ds DNA break repair. Note that repair of a broken chromosome (bottom panels) is topologically equivalent to recombination of a linear fragment introduced into *E. coli* during conjugation or transduction (top panels).

1. The same mechanism can account for both processes, as proposed by Resnick (Resnick 1976) and amplified by Szostak *et al.* (1983). In *E. coli* several enzymes are required for both processes: RecA protein, SSB protein, RecBCD enzyme, DNA polymerase I, and DNA ligase (see Smith 1988 for references). In addition a second genome is required for repair or recombination of a chromosome fragment (Krasin & Hutchinson 1977).

2. The loss of Chi nicking activity by RecBCD enzyme upon cutting at one Chi site (Taylor & Smith 1992) ensures that a RecBCD enzyme at each end will promote a single exchange (i.e., two exchanges on the linear fragment). As the donor DNA in conjugation or transduction is a linear chromosomal fragment, even numbers of exchanges are required to produce a circular (viable) chromosome. In conjugation and transduction the majority of the events (about 80% and > 95%, respectively) appear to involve exactly two exchanges (reviewed by Smith 1991). Breakage of the linear fragment into two, three, ...*n* pieces would result in four, six, ...2*n* exchanges, or always an even number, as required for viability. During DNA repair this feature of RecBCD enzyme would limit the process to the minimum number of exchanges needed for repair.

3. The generation of circular DNA molecules would limit recombination and repair to a single cycle of events. In contrast, reciprocal resolution without replication (figure 3) would generate a succession of linear fragments and cycles of recombination, perhaps until the linear fragment were destroyed by exonucleolytic degradation. The occurrence of recombinants with just two exchanges in the majority of the cases argues against repeated recombination being a principal outcome, but it may occur occasionally.

The model in figure 4 can account for both reciprocal and non-reciprocal exchange of markers during recombination, depending upon their location. Consider a set of markers A_1, A_2, A_3 and B, with B to the left of a leftward-directed Chi (figure 2*b*). If A_1 is outside the linear fragment, recombination between it and B will, of course, be non-reciprocal. If A_2 is on the linear fragment but to the right of Chi, recombination will be non-reciprocal if the linear fragment is degraded by RecBCD enzyme up to Chi but may be reciprocal if RecBCD enzyme nicks DNA at Chi (see §5). If A_3 is between Chi and B, recombination may be either reciprocal or non-reciprocal depending upon whether heteroduplex DNA covers both B and A_3 or just A_3 and depending upon the correction of mismatches in the heteroduplex DNA. The available evidence from Chi-stimulated recombination of phage λ in *E. coli* suggests that both types of recombination may occur (see Smith 1994 for references); this evidence is inconclusive, however, primarily because of the inability to monitor all of the substrate and product molecules. Further studies are needed to resolve this issue.

8. TEST OF THE TWO CHI MODEL: TRANSFORMATION WITH LINEAR DNA

The model in figure 4 predicts that recombination of a linear DNA fragment with the *E. coli* chromosome requires two Chi sites on the fragment, each oriented to activate RecBCD enzyme approaching it from the nearer end. We have begun such a test with a linear fragment bearing about 3.0 kb of a Chi-free part of the *E. coli his* operon flanked by about 1.5 and 0.8 kb of Chi-free pBR322 vector (P. Dabert & G. R. Smith, unpublished). The test χ^+ DNA has a properly oriented Chi site at each *his*–pBR322 junction, whereas the control χ^0 DNA has no Chi sites. Addition of these DNA's to CaCl$_2$-treated *E. coli* produced, in 15 independent transformations, a total of 155 *his* integrated transformants with χ^+ DNA but 0 with an equal amount of χ^0 DNA. (Neither DNA transformed a *recA* mutant, but both transformed a *recD* *E. coli* mutant with equal efficiencies. *recD* mutants are recombination-proficient but have no detectable ATP-dependent nuclease, Chi-cutting or Chi-hotspot activity; these mutants may recombine by a pathway different from that of wild-type *E. coli* (Smith 1988).) The strong Chi-dependence of transformation of wild-type *E. coli* with linear DNA supports the model in figure 4, but additional tests, such as transformation using DNA's with one Chi site or with inverted Chi sites, are needed.

9. PERSPECTIVES

The mechanism of homologous recombination and ds DNA break repair discussed here may apply, with modifications, to other organisms. RecBCD-like enzymes and RecA-like proteins are widely distributed in bacteria (Telander-Muskavitch & Linn 1981; Miller & Kokjohn 1990), and they may use a mechanism very similar to that of *E. coli*. Although Chi sites are, as expected, frequently found in genomes from diverse organisms, they appear to be active as recombinational hotspots only in the enteric bacteria (McKittrick & Smith 1989 and references therein). Chi is active in phage λ crosses in *Salmonella typhimurium*. Diverse enteric bacteria, both terrestrial and marine, contain RecBCD-like enzymes with Chi cutting activity, and cloned *recBCD* genes from several of these bacteria confer Chi hotspot activity to *E. coli recBCD* deletion mutants. Non-enteric bacteria contain RecBCD-like enzymes that do not detectably recognize Chi, even when, in the case of two *Pseudomonas* spp, their genes are in *E. coli*. These bacteria may use another nucleotide sequence as a recombinational hotspot, but with this modification they may repair and recombine their DNA by the same mechanism as *E. coli*.

In eukaryotes ds DNA breaks also trigger repair and recombination (Thaler & Stahl 1988). Furthermore, genes encoding proteins with amino acid sequences homologous to that of *E. coli* RecA protein have been described, and, in the case of *Saccharomyces cerevisiae*, mutants lacking these proteins are deficient in recombination and repair (Bishop *et al.* 1992; Shinohara *et al.* 1992). It is likely, therefore, that enzymes enter ds DNA ends and form ss DNA substrates for homologous pairing with intact duplexes by the RecA-like proteins. Alternative mechanisms, such as initiation by ss nicks and gaps, have not been excluded, however. To our knowledge, there are no substantiated reports of RecBCD-like enzymes (i.e. ATP-dependent nucleases) from eukaryotes. Thus, the putative ss DNA substrates for pairing may be produced by exonucleases that digest one DNA strand (perhaps in conjunction with helicases); such a mechanism has been inferred for the λ Red and *E. coli* RecE and RecF pathways (reviewed by Smith 1988; Thaler & Stahl 1988). Fungi and perhaps other eukaryotes contain hotspots of meiotic recombination with genetic properties similar to those of Chi (Smith 1994). In *S. cerevisiae* these appear, however, to be sites of ds DNA break formation controlled by chromatin structure (Wu & Lichten 1994), rather than sites acting, as Chi does, spatially and temporally downstream of the ds DNA break. Such secondary control sites in eukaryotes have not been excluded, however. The overall mechanism of homologous recombination and repair in eukaryotes may be similar to that in *E. coli*, but the details of the mechanism may be different. The control of the initiation of recombination in eukaryotes also remains to be elucidated; knowledge of that control in *E. coli* may aid its elucidation.

We are grateful to our past and present colleagues for their contributions to our work. We thank Wayne Wahls for figure 2*b*. Research in our laboratory is supported by grants from the United States Public Health Service (NIH grants GM31693 and GM32194). P.D. is a scientist of the Institut National de la Recherche Agronomique (France) and the recipient of an EMBO fellowship (ALTF 622–1992).

REFERENCES

Alatossava, T., Jütte, H., Kuhn, A. & Kellenberger, E. 1985 Manipulation of intracellular magnesium content by polymyxin B nonapeptide-sensitized *Escherichia coli* by ionophore A23187. *J. Bacteriol.* **162**, 413–419.

Bishop, D.K., Park, D., Xu, L. & Kleckner, N. 1992 *DMC1*: A meiosis-specific homolog of *E. coli recA* required for recombination, synaptonemal complex formation, and cell cycle progression. *Cell* **69**, 439–456.

Braedt, G. & Smith, G.R. 1989 Strand specificity of DNA unwinding by RecBCD enzyme. *Proc. natn. Acad. Sci. U.S.A.* **86**, 871–875.

Brewer, B.J. 1988 When polymerases collide: replication and the transcriptional organization of the *Escherichia coli* chromosome. *Cell* **53**, 679–686.

Burland, V., Plunkett III, G., Daniels, D.L. & Blattner, F.R. 1993 DNA sequence and analysis of 136 kilobases of the *Escherichia coli* genome: Organizational symmetry around the origin of replication. *Genomics* **16**, 551–561.

Cheng, K.C. & Smith, G.R. 1987 Cutting of Chi-like sequences by the RecBCD enzyme of *Escherichia coli*. *J. molec. Biol.* **194**, 747–750.

Cheng, K.C. & Smith, G.R. 1989 Distribution of Chi-stimulated recombinational exchanges and heteroduplex endpoints in phage lambda. *Genetics* **123**, 5–17.

Dixon, D.A., Churchill, J.J. & Kowalczykowski, S.C. 1994 Reversible inactivation of the *Escherichia coli* RecBCD enzyme by the recombination hotspot χ *in vitro*: Evidence for functional inactivation or loss of the RecD subunit. *Proc. natn. Acad. Sci. U.S.A.* **91**, 2980–2984.

Dixon, D.A. & Kowalczykowski, S.C. 1991 Homologous pairing *in vitro* stimulated by the recombination hotspot, Chi. *Cell* **66**, 361–371.

Dixon, D.A. & Kowalczykowski, S.C. 1993 The recombination hotspot χ is a regulatory sequence that acts by attenuating the nuclease activity of the *E. coli* RecBCD enzyme. *Cell* **73**, 87–96.

Emmerson, P.T. 1968 Recombination deficient mutants of *Escherichia coli* K12 that map between *thyA* and *argA*. *Genetics* **60**, 19–30.

Ganesan, S. & Smith, G.R. 1992 Strand-specific binding to duplex DNA ends by the subunits of *Escherichia coli* RecBCD enzyme. *J. molec. Biol.* **229**, 67–78.

Ippen-Ihler, K.A. & Minkley, E.G. Jr 1986 The conjugation system of F, the fertility factor of *Escherichia coli*. *A. Rev. Genet.* **20**, 593–624.

Julin, D.A. & Lehman, I.R. 1987 Photoaffinity labeling of the recBCD enzyme of *Escherichia coli* with 8-azidoadenosine 5-triphosphate. *J. biol. Chem.* **262**, 9044–9051.

Krasin, F. & Hutchinson, F. 1977 Repair of DNA double-strand breaks in *Escherichia coli*, which requires *recA* function and the presence of a duplicate genome. *J. molec. Biol.* **116**, 81–98.

Kuzminov, A., Schabtach, E. & Stahl, F.W. 1994 Chi sites in combination with RecA protein increase the survival of linear DNA in *Escherichia coli* by inactivating exoV activity of RecBCD nuclease. *EMBO J.* **13**, 2764–2776.

Masterson, C., Boehmer, P.E., McDonald, F., Chaudhuri, S., Hickson, I.D. & Emmerson, P.T. 1992 Reconstitution of the activities of the RecBCD holoenzyme of *Escherichia coli* from the purified subunits. *J. biol. Chem.* **267**, 13564–13572.

Matthews, C.K. 1972 Biochemistry of deoxyribonucleic acid-defective amber mutants of bacteriophage T4. III. *J. biol. Chem.* **247**, 7430–7438.

McKittrick, N.H. & Smith, G.R. 1989 Activation of Chi recombinational hotspots by RecBCD-like enzymes from enteric bacteria. *J. molec. Biol.* **210**, 485–495.

Miller, R.V. & Kokjohn, T.A. 1990 General microbiology of *recA*: Environmental and evolutionary significance. *A. Rev. Microbiol.* **44**, 365–394.

Petes, T.D. & Hill, C.W. 1988 Recombination between

repeated genes in microorganisms. *A. Rev. Genet.* **22**, 147–168.

Ponticelli, A.S., Schultz, D.W., Taylor, A.F. & Smith, G.R. 1985 Chi-dependent DNA strand cleavage by RecBC enzyme. *Cell* **41**, 145–151.

Resnick, M.A. 1976 The repair of double-strand breaks in DNA: a model involving recombination. *J. theor. Biol.* **59**, 97–106.

Roman, L.J. & Kowalczykowski, S.C. 1989 Characterization of the helicase activity of *Escherichia coli* RecBCD enzyme using a novel helicase assay. *Biochemistry* **28**, 2863–2873.

Shinohara, A., Ogawa, A.H. & Ogawa, T. 1992 Rad51 protein involved in repair and recombination in *S. cerevisiae* is a RecA-like protein. *Cell* **69**, 457–470.

Smith, G.R. 1988 Homologous recombination in procaryotes. *Microbiol. Rev.* **52**, 1–28.

Smith, G.R. 1991 Conjugational recombination in *E. coli*: Myths and mechanisms. *Cell* **64**, 19–27.

Smith, G.R. 1994 Hotspots of homologous recombination. *Experientia* **50**, 234–241.

Smith, G.R., Amundsen, S.K., Chaudhury, A.M., Cheng, K.C., Ponticelli, A.S., Roberts, C.M., Schultz, D.W. & Taylor, A.F. 1984 Roles of RecBC enzyme and Chi sites in homologous recombination. *Cold Spring Harbor Symp. quant. Biol.* **49**, 485–495.

Smith, G.R., Schultz, D.W., Taylor, A.F. & Triman, K. 1981 Chi sites, RecBC enzyme, and generalized recombination. *Stadler Genet. Symp.* **13**, 25–37.

Szostak, J.W., Orr-Weaver, T.L., Rothstein, R.J. & Stahl, F.W. 1983 The double-strand-break repair model for recombination. *Cell* **33**, 25–35.

Taylor, A.F. 1988 RecBCD enzyme of *Escherichia coli*. In *Genetic recombination* (ed. R. Kucherlapati & G.R. Smith), pp. 231–263. Washington, DC: American Society for Microbiology.

Taylor, A.F. & Smith, G.R. 1980 Unwinding and rewinding of DNA by the RecBC enzyme. *Cell* **22**, 447–457.

Taylor, A.F. & Smith, G.R. 1992 RecBCD enzyme is altered upon cutting DNA at a Chi recombination hotspot. *Proc. natn. Acad. Sci. U.S.A.* **89**, 5226–5230.

Taylor, A.F., Schultz, D.W., Ponticelli, A.S. & Smith, G.R. 1985 RecBC enzyme nicking at Chi sites during DNA unwinding: Location and orientation dependence of the cutting. *Cell* **41**, 153–163.

Telander-Muskavitch, K.M. & Linn, S. 1981 RecBC-like enzymes: the exonuclease V deoxyribonucleases. In *The enzymes* (ed. P.D. Boyer), pp. 233–250. New York: Academic Press.

Telander-Muskavitch, K.M. & Linn, S. 1982 A unified mechanism for the nuclease and unwinding activities of the *recBC* enzyme of *Escherichia coli*. *J. biol. Chem.* **257**, 2641–2648.

Thaler, D.S. & Stahl, F.W. 1988 DNA double-chain breaks in recombination of phage lambda and of yeast. *A. Rev. Genet.* **22**, 169–197.

Thaler, D.S., Sampson, E., Siddiqi, I., Rosenberg, S.M., Stahl, F.W. & Stahl, M., 1988 A hypothesis: Chi-activation of RecBCD enzyme involves removal of the RecD subunit. In *Mechanisms and consequences of DNA damage processing* (ed. E. Friedberg & P. Hanawalt), pp. 413–422. New York: Alan R. Liss.

Triman, K.L., Chattoraj, D.K. & Smith, G.R. 1982 Identity of a Chi site of *Escherichia coli* and Chi recombinational hotspots of bacteriophage lambda. *J. molec. Biol.* **154**, 393–399.

Wu, T.-C. & Lichten, M. 1994 Meiosis-induced double-strand break sites determined by yeast chromatin structure. *Science, Wash.* **263**, 515–518.

3

Formation, translocation and resolution of Holliday junctions during homologous genetic recombination

STEPHEN C. WEST

Imperial Cancer Research Fund, Clare Hall Laboratories, South Mimms, Herts. EN6 3LD, U.K.

SUMMARY

Over the past three or four years, great strides have been made in our understanding of the proteins involved in recombination and the mechanisms by which recombinant molecules are formed. This review summarizes our current understanding of the process by focusing on recent studies of proteins involved in the later steps of recombination in bacteria. In particular, biochemical investigation of the *in vitro* properties of the *E. coli* RuvA, RuvB and RuvC proteins have provided our first insight into the novel molecular mechanisms by which Holliday junctions are moved along DNA and then resolved by endonucleolytic cleavage.

1. INITIATION OF RECOMBINATION

A simple scheme which attempts to coordinate the properties of the enzymic activities involved in recombination in *E. coli* is shown in figure 1. Recombination in bacteria, and probably also in eukaryotic organisms, requires the formation of single-stranded DNA (West 1993). Single strands are generated by the combined helicase/nuclease activities of RecBCD enzyme (see accompanying article by G. R. Smith), following cleavage at specific sites known as Chi (Smith 1990; Taylor 1988). Mutations in *recB*, or *recC*, reduce the frequency of recombination but do not block it completely, because in the absence of functional RecBCD, other proteins can provide the single-stranded DNA required for initiation. For example, a DNA helicase such as RecQ (Umezu *et al.* 1990) or a single-strand specific exonuclease such as RecJ, or their combined action, would suffice (Lovett & Kolodner 1989). A similar function could be played by DNA helicase II (*uvrD* gene product) or helicase IV (*helD* gene product) (Matson & George 1987; Mendonca *et al.* 1993; Wood & Matson 1987).

2. PAIRING AND STRAND EXCHANGE

The presence of single-stranded DNA triggers recombination reactions catalysed by the RecA protein. This 38 kDa protein is quite remarkable in that it plays a dual role in recombination by providing: (i) the catalytic activity for homologous pairing and strand exchange; and (ii) the structural framework within which recombination reactions take place (figure 2). In the presence of ATP, RecA binds DNA (either single stranded or gapped duplex) to form a right-handed helical nucleoprotein-filament (West *et al.* 1980; Stasiak *et al.* 1981; Flory & Radding 1982; Stasiak & DiCapua 1982). Recent studies suggest that RecF,

RecO, RecR and SSB may facilitate the loading of RecA onto the initiating single strand (Madiraju & Clark 1990, 1991; Umezu *et al.* 1993) and may be considered, therefore, as accessory proteins for RecA. Electron microscopic observations of RecA filaments formed on duplex DNA, in the presence of ATP or a non-hydrolysable ATP-analogue (ATPγS), show that the DNA is underwound as the pitch of the helix is extended to approximately 95Å (Stasiak *et al.* 1981). Thus DNA is stretched from a 3.4Å axial rise per base pair (b.p.) in B-form DNA to a 5.1Å rise per b.p. in the RecA–DNA complex. A similar stretching occurs with single-stranded DNA. This extended and regular filament structure, which contains 6.2 RecA monomers per turn of DNA (18.6 b.p.) (DiCapua *et al.* 1982; Yu & Egelman 1990), represents the active form of RecA. A second, non-extended form of the RecA filament has been observed with single-stranded DNA in the absence of a nucleotide cofactor, though this structure is thought to be inactive (Yu & Egelman 1992; Egelman & Stasiak 1993; Ruigrok *et al.* 1993). The crystal structure of the RecA-helical polymer has been solved at a resolution of 2.3Å, and resembles the inactive filament (Story & Steitz 1992; Story *et al.* 1992; Egelman & Stasiak 1993).

The primary function of RecA is to bring two DNA molecules into close proximity within a single filament, so that the DNA sequences are aligned, ready for strand exchange and the formation of heteroduplex DNA (Howard-Flanders *et al.* 1984; Stasiak *et al.* 1984; West 1992). Pairing is thought to occur by means of multiple random contacts which are facilitated, at least *in vitro*, by the formation of large protein–DNA aggregates that serve to concentrate the DNA (Gonda & Radding 1986). It is likely that the two DNA molecules become interwound within the RecA filament in the form of a multi-stranded DNA helix (figure 2) (see also article by C. M. Radding). The

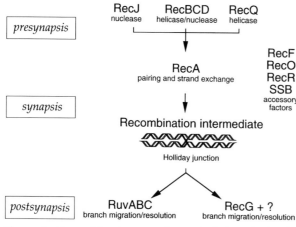

| *presynapsis* | RecJ
nuclease | RecBCD
helicase/nuclease | RecQ
helicase |

RecA
pairing and strand exchange

RecF
RecO
RecR
SSB
accessory
factors

synapsis

Recombination intermediate

Holliday junction

| *postsynapsis* | RuvABC
branch migration/resolution | RecG + ?
branch migration/resolution |

Figure 1. Recombination proteins and their roles in the recombination process. The RecBCD, RecJ and RecQ proteins utilize their nuclease and/or helicase functions to generate regions of single-stranded DNA which are recognized by RecA. The RecF, RecO, RecR and SSB proteins act as accessory proteins which facilitate the interaction between RecA and ssDNA. RecA forms helical nucleoprotein filaments which interact with other duplex DNA molecules leading to homologous pairing and strand exchange. Recombination intermediates, containing Holliday junctions made by RecA are then recognized by RuvAB or RecG, which catalyse branch migration and the formation of heteroduplex DNA. Finally, the Holliday junctions are resolved by RuvC (or an alternative resolvase activity), and the recombinant DNA molecules are repaired by DNA ligase. A number of the indicated proteins, including RecQ, RecA, RuvA and RuvB, are part of the sos response to DNA damage and induced by uv-irradiation. In addition to their role as general recombination proteins, they are likely to play a particularly important role during recombinational repair.

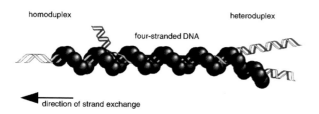

homoduplex   heteroduplex

four-stranded DNA

direction of strand exchange

Figure 2. Homologous pairing and strand exchange mediated by RecA protein. The DNA lies within the deep groove of the RecA filament and is stretched (axial rise = 5.1Å compared with 3.4Å in B-form DNA). The two interacting duplexes are proposed to be interwound within the RecA filament. Rotation of the filament along its longitudinal axis causes the naked duplex DNA to be spooled into the filament such that strand exchange occurs (although not shown, this corresponds to a 5′–3′ polarity relative to the single-stranded DNA on which filament formation was initiated). For simplicity, the RecA filament is drawn as only a few protein monomers, in reality it may be much longer. Similarly the diameter of the RecA filament (approximately 100Å) and the length of the DNA are underestimated for diagrammatic purposes. Watson-Crick b.p. and any additional bonds are not shown. Deproteinization of the four-stranded immediate would produce a classical Holliday junction.

reaction then proceeds into its next phase in which strands are exchanged to form heteroduplex DNA. Strand exchange occurs relatively slowly (2–10 b.p. per second), with a defined 5′–3′ polarity (Cox &

Lehman 1981; Kahn *et al.* 1981; West *et al.* 1981) and during the course of the reaction large amounts of ATP are hydrolysed by RecA (Kowalczykowski 1991; Roca & Cox 1990).

3. PROCESSING OF RECOMBINATION INTERMEDIATES

Recent work has led to significant advances in our understanding of the late steps of genetic recombination and related recombinational repair processes. It is now known that Holliday junctions made by RecA can be recognized by the RuvA and RuvB proteins which catalyse their movement along DNA (Tsaneva *et al.* 1992*b*). This process, known as branch migration, is required for the formation of heteroduplex DNA. The next step, resolution of the junction to allow the separation of recombinant duplexes that can be repaired by DNA ligase, is catalysed by RuvC protein, a Holliday junction-specific endonuclease (Dunderdale *et al.* 1991; Iwasaki *et al.* 1991; Bennett *et al.* 1993). Surprisingly, mutations in *ruvA*, *ruvB* or *ruvC* do not lead to a recombination defective phenotype (Lloyd 1991), thus providing evidence for the presence of a second pathway for Holliday-junction processing. This pathway is likely to involve RecG, an alternative branch migration protein which is functionally analogous to RuvAB (Lloyd & Sharples 1993*a*, 1993*b*; Whitby *et al.* 1993), and may require a second, as yet unidentified, Holliday-junction resolvase activity (Lloyd 1991).

(a) *Branch Migration Catalysed by RuvAB*

Electron microscopic visualization of deproteinized recombination intermediates made by RecA, shows that the two interacting DNA molecules are linked by a crossover or Holliday junction (DasGupta *et al.* 1981; West *et al.* 1983; Müller *et al.* 1992). The structure of this junction appears to be an integral component of subsequent processing reactions. *In vitro*, the RuvA (22 kDa) and RuvB (37 kDa) proteins have been shown to act upon synthetic Holliday junctions, or recombination intermediates made by RecA, and catalyse branch migration (Iwasaki *et al.* 1992; Parsons *et al.* 1992; Tsaneva *et al.* 1992a, 1992*b*; Müller *et al.* 1993*a*; Parsons & West 1993). The RuvB protein is a DNA-dependent ATPase (Iwasaki *et al.* 1989; Parsons & West 1993) which, in the presence of ATP and high concentrations of Mg^{2+} ($\geqslant$ 15 mM) can promote branch migration without the need for RuvA (Tsaneva *et al.* 1992*b*; Müller *et al.* 1993*a*). This result indicates that RuvB is the catalyst of the branch migration reaction, with high levels of Mg^{2+} required to overcome the low binding affinity that RuvB shows for DNA (Müller *et al.* 1993*b*). At lower Mg^{2+} concentrations ($\leqslant$ 10 mM), RuvB binds DNA weakly and branch migration shows an absolute requirement for RuvA (Müller *et al.* 1993*a*, 199*b*). Under these conditions, and in the presence of RuvA, the stoichiometric requirement for RuvB is reduced 50-fold, to about 20 RuvB monomers per junction (Müller *et al.* 1993*a*; Parsons & West 1993).

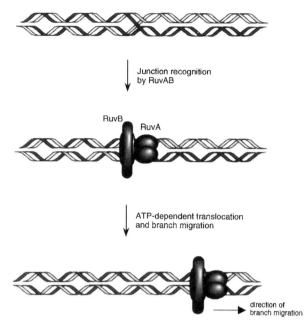

Figure 3. Model for branch migration catalysed by RuvA and RuvB. The RuvA protein specifically targets the RuvB ATPase to the Holliday junction. The RuvA protein is tetrameric while the RuvB protein is likely to take the form of a ring structure which encompasses the DNA. It is not at present known whether one or both DNA helices pass through the hollow cavity in the RuvB ring structure. Translocation of the RuvAB complex, coupled with DNA unwinding, is proposed to lead to the movement (branch migration) of the Holliday junction along DNA.

How does RuvA reduce the requirement for RuvB and thereby facilitate RuvB-mediated branch migration? The answer to this question was provided by band-shift assays which showed that RuvA, which interacts with RuvB in solution (Shiba *et al.* 1993), binds specifically to Holliday junctions (Parsons *et al.* 1992). Moreover, in the presence of a non-hydrolysable ATP analogue (ATPγS) it has been possible to detect stable [RuvAB]–Holliday junction complexes using this assay (Parsons & West 1993). In contrast, without RuvA, RuvB failed to bind the junction. Interestingly, the DNA-dependent ATPase of RuvB, which is normally quite low, is activated by the presence of RuvA (Shiba *et al.* 1991), and junction-specific ATPase activity has been detected (Parsons & West 1993). These results indicate that the primary role of RuvA is to target the RuvB enzyme to the site of the junction where it promotes ATP-dependent branch migration.

Until recently, little was known about the mechanics of RuvAB-mediated branch migration. However, a key observation was made recently when Stasiak *et al.* observed that RuvB protein formed doublet ring-like structures on relaxed circular duplex DNA in the presence of ATPγS and 15 mM Mg^{2+} (Stasiak *et al.* 1994). Scanning transmission electron microscopy and three-dimensional image reconstruction indicates that each ring contains six RuvB monomers. The dodecameric ring structure appears to surround the DNA which passes through a deep hollow core. As the RuvB ring structures were observed in the absence of RuvA, it is not, at present, clear whether this structure represents the active form of the protein involved in

branch migration. In fact, recent gel-filtration studies indicate that RuvA and RuvB associate in solution to form a structure made up of a RuvA tetramer with a RuvB hexamer (A. M. Mitchell & S. C. West, unpublished data), and further studies will be required to determine whether the active form of RuvB involves a single or a double ring.

A model for branch migration catalysed by RuvAB is presented in figure 3. It proposes that the high affinity binding shown by RuvA targets RuvB directly to the junction point. Here the RuvB ring structure is assembled, although it is not, at present, known whether the ring encompasses one DNA helix or two within its hollow core. RuvAB have been shown to exhibit DNA-helicase activity (5′–3′ relative to single-stranded DNA) (Tsaneva *et al.* 1983). Based on this fact, it is proposed that the helicase activity plays a direct role in branch migration since RuvB tracks along DNA and promotes strand separation followed by reannealing. It is also possible that ATP hydrolysis is directly coupled to DNA unwinding. Interestingly, recent work indicates that RuvAB can dissociate RecA protein from duplex DNA (Adams *et al.* 1994), possibly as a consequence of translocation. This result is consistent with the proposal that RuvAB act after RecA and it has been suggested that RuvAB may play an important role in recycling RecA protein (Adams *et al.* 1994).

(b) Holliday Junction Resolution by RuvC

Following branch migration, the production of mature recombination DNA molecules requires the resolution of Holliday junctions – this reaction is carried out by the 19 kDa RuvC protein (Connolly *et al.* 1991; Dunderdale *et al.* 1991; Iwasaki *et al.* 1991; Bennett *et al.* 1993). Band-shift assays show that RuvC forms a specific complex with a Holliday junction, indicating that recognition of the junction is structure-specific (Dunderdale *et al.* 1991; Bennett *et al.* 1993). The binding reaction occurs efficiently in the absence of Mg^{2+} (Bennett *et al.* 1993), a result which is surprising given that divalent cations are known to play an important role in the folding of a Holliday junction (see accompanying article by D. M. J. Lilley) (Duckett *et al.* 1990). The reason for this is that RuvC protein directs the folding of the junction upon binding, so that the initial folding-state of the junction is unimportant (R. J. Bennett & S. C. West, unpublished work).

Whereas junction binding is independent of co-factors, resolution requires the presence of Mg^{2+} (Bennett *et al.* 1993; Dunderdale *et al.* 1994) or Mn^{2+} (Shah *et al.* 1994). The cation is needed for nucleolytic activity rather than DNA folding, because it cannot be replaced by other divalent cations such as Ca^{2+} or Zn^{2+}. Resolution by RuvC occurs via the introduction of nicks into two strands of like-polarity (figure 4). The cuts are placed with perfect symmetry in each duplex, so that homologous product DNA molecules contain nicks that can be ligated by *E. coli* DNA ligase (Bennett *et al.* 1993; Dunderdale *et al.* 1994). Although binding of a Holliday junction by RuvC is structure-specific, the incision reaction exhibits sequence-specificity (Bennett

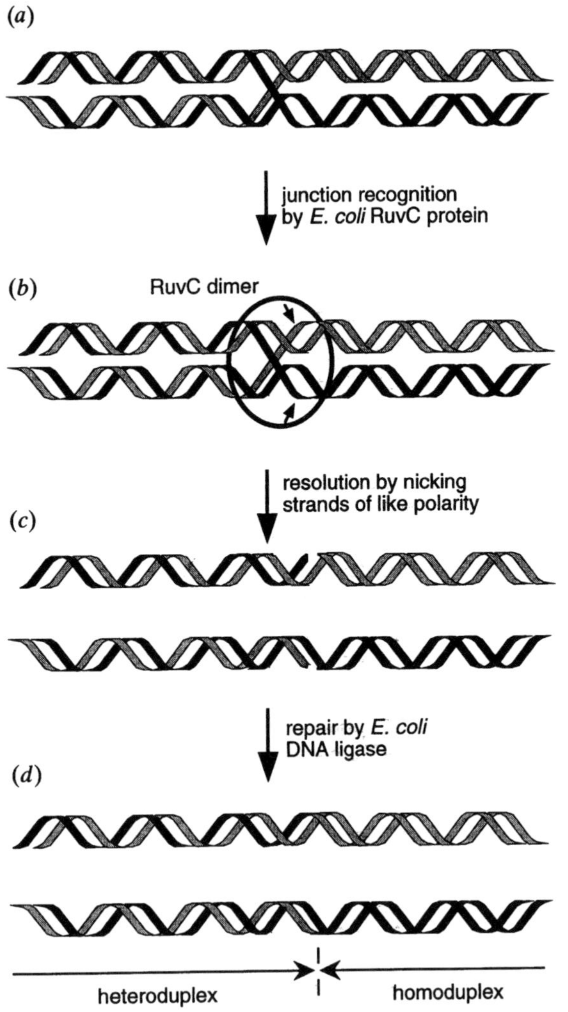

(a)

↓ junction recognition
by *E. coli* RuvC protein

(b)   RuvC dimer

↓ resolution by nicking
strands of like polarity

(c)

↓ repair by *E. coli*
DNA ligase

(d)

heteroduplex ← → homoduplex

Figure 4. Schematic diagram illustrating the basic features of Holliday junction resolution by RuvC. RuvC protein binds the Holliday junction via structure-specific contacts to form a RuvC-Holliday junction complex (b). Resolution occurs at specific DNA sequences such that nicks are introduced at the same sequence into two strands of like polarity (c). The nicked duplex products are repaired by DNA ligase (d).

et al. 1993; Shah *et al.* 1994). Which may, in part, be relaxed by the presence of Mn^{2+} ions (Shah *et al.* 1994). Although the precise sequences for cleavage are at present unknown, it is likely that branch migration to specific resolution hotspots is required for efficient RuvC-mediated cleavage. This may account for a number of genetic observations which imply a role for RuvAB in Holliday-junction resolution (Mandal *et al.* 1993). Future studies will be required to investigate possible protein–protein interactions between RuvAB and RuvC.

REFERENCES

Adams, D.E., Tsaneva, I.R. & West, S.C. 1994 Dissociation of RecA filaments from duplex DNA by the RuvAB branch migration protein. *Proc. natn. Acad. Sci. U.S.A.* **91**, 9901–9905.

Bennett, R.J., Dunderdale, H.J. & West, S.C. 1993 Resolution of Holliday junctions by RuvC resolvase: Cleavage specificity and DNA distortion. *Cell* **74**, 1021–1031.

Connolly, B., Parsons, C.A., Benson, F.E., Dunderdale, H.J., Sharples, G.J., Lloyd, R.G. & West, S.C. 1991 Resolution of Holliday junctions *in vitro* requires *Escherichia coli ruvC* gene product. *Proc. natn. Acad. Sci. U.S.A.* **88**, 6063–6067.

Cox, M.M. & Lehman, I.R. 1981 Directionality and polarity in RecA protein-promoted branch migration. *Proc. natn. Acad. Sci. U.S.A.* **78**, 6018–6022.

DasGupta. C., Wu, A.M., Kahn, R., Cunningham, R.P. & Radding, C.M. 1981 Concerted strand exchange and formation of Holliday structures by *E. coli* RecA protein. *Cell* **25**, 507–516.

DiCapua, E., Engel, A., Stasiak, A. & Koller, T. 1982 Characterization of complexes between RecA protein and duplex DNA by electron microscopy. *J. molec. Biol.* **157**, 87–103.

Duckett, D.R., Murchie, A.I.H. & Lilley, D.M.J. 1990 The role of metal ions in the conformation of the four-way junction. *EMBO J.* **9**, 583–590.

Dunderdale, H.J., Benson, F.E., Parsons, C.A., Sharples, G.J., Lloyd, R.G. & West, S.C. 1991 Formation and resolution of recombination intermediates by *E. coli* RecA and RuvC proteins. *Nature, Lond.* **354**, 506–510.

Dunderdale, H.J., Sharples, G.J., Lloyd, R.G. & West, S.C. 1994 Cloning, over-expression, purification and characterization of the *E. coli* RuvC Holliday junction resolvase. *J. biol. Chem.* **269**, 5187–5194.

Egelman, E.H. & Stasiak, A. 1993 Electron microscopy of RecA-DNA complexes: Two different states, their functional significance and relation to the solved crystal structure. *Micron.* **24**, 309–324.

Flory, J. & Radding, C.M. 1982 Visualization of RecA protein and its association with DNA: a priming effect of single-strand-binding protein. *Cell* **28**, 747–756.

Gonda, D.K. & Radding, C.M. 1986 The mechanism of the search for homology promoted by RecA protein. Facilitated diffusion within nucleoprotein networks. *J. biol. Chem.* **261**, 13087–13096.

Howard-Flanders, P., West, S.C. & Stasiak, A.J. 1984 Role of RecA spiral filaments in genetic recombination. *Nature, Lond.* **309**, 215–220.

Iwasaki, H., Shiba, T., Makino, K., Nakata, A. & Shinagawa, H. 1989 Overproduction, purification, and ATPase activity of the *Escherichia coli* RuvB protein involved in DNA repair. *J. Bact.* **171**, 5276–5280.

Iwasaki, H., Takahagi, M., Nakata, A. & Shinagawa, H. 1992 *Escherichia coli* RuvA and RuvB proteins specifically interact with Holliday junctions and promote branch migration. *Genes Dev.* **6**, 2214–2220.

Iwasaki, H., Takahagi, M., Shiba, T., Nakata, A. & Shinagawa, H. 1991 *Escherichia coli* RuvC protein is an endonuclease that resolves the Holliday structure. *EMBO J.* **10**, 4381–4389.

Kahn, R., Cunningham, R.P., DasGupta, C. & Radding, C.M. 1981 Polarity of heteroduplex formation promoted by *Escherichia coli* RecA protein. *Proc. natn. Acad. Sci. U.S.A.* **78**, 4786–4790.

Kowalczykowski, S.C. 1991 Biochemistry of genetic recombination: energetics and mechanism of DNA strand exchange. *A. Rev. Biophys. biophys. Chem.* **20**, 539–575.

Lloyd, R.G. 1991 Conjugal recombination in resolvase-deficient *ruvC* mutants of *Escherichia coli K12* depends on *recG*. *J. Bact.* **173**, 5414–5418.

Lloyd, R.G. & Sharples, G.J. 1993*a* Dissociation of synthetic Holliday junctions by *E. coli* RecG protein. *EMBO J.* **2**, 17–22.

Lloyd, R.G. & Sharples, G.J. 1993*b* Processing of recombination intermediates by the RecG and RuvAB proteins of *Escherichia coli*. *Nucl. Acids Res.* **21**, 1719–1725.

Lovett, S.T. & Kolodner, R.D. 1989 Identification and

purification of a single-stranded DNA-specific exonuclease encoded by the *recJ* gene of *Escherichia coli*. *Proc. natn. Acad. Sci. U.S.A.* **86**, 2627–2631.

Madiraju, M.V.V.S. & Clark, A.J. 1990 Use of recA803, a partial suppressor of *recF*, to analyze the effects of the mutant SSb (single-stranded DNA-binding) proteins *in vivo* and *in vitro*. *Mol. gen. Genet.* **224**, 129–135.

Madiraju, M.V.V.S. & Clark, A.J. 1991 Effect of RecF protein on reactions catalyzed by RecA protein. *Nucl. Acids Res.* **19**, 6295–6300.

Mandal, T.N., Mahdi, A.A., Sharples, G.J. & Lloyd, R.G. 1993 Resolution of Holliday intermediates in recombination and DNA repair: indirect suppression of *ruvA*, *ruvB* and *ruvC* mutations. *J. Bact.* **175**, 4325–4334.

Matson, S.W. & George, J.W. 1987 DNA helicase II of *E. coli*. Characterisation of the single stranded DNA dependent NTPase and helicase activities. *J. biol. Chem.* **262**, 2066–2076.

Mendonca, V.M., Kaiser-Rogers, K. & Matson, S.W. 1993 Double helicase II (*uvrD*)-helicase IV (*helD*) deletion mutants are defective in the recombination pathways of *Escherichia coli*. *J. Bact.* **175**, 4641–4651.

Müller, B., Burdett, I. & West, S.C. 1992 Unusual stability of recombination intermediates made by *E. coli* RecA protein. *Embo J.* **11**, 2685–2693.

Müller, B., Tsaneva, I.R. & West, S.C. 1993*a* Branch migration of Holliday junctions promoted by the *Escherichia coli* RuvA and RuvB proteins: I. Comparison of the RuvAB- and RuvB-mediated reactions. *J. biol. Chem.* **268**, 17179–17184.

Müller, B., Tsaneva, I.R. & West, S.C. 1993*b* Branch migration of Holliday junctions promoted by the *Escherichia coli* RuvA and RuvB proteins: II. Interaction of RuvB with DNA. *J. biol. Chem.* **268**, 17185–17189.

Parsons, C.A., Tsaneva, I., Lloyd, R.G. & West, S.C. 1992 Interaction of *Escherichia coli* RuvA and RuvB proteins with synthetic Holliday junctions. *Proc. natn. Acad. Sci. U.S.A.* **89**, 5452–5456.

Parsons, C.A. & West, S.C. 1993 Formation of a RuvAB-Holliday junction complex *in vitro*. *J. molec. Biol.* **232**, 397–405.

Roca, A.I. & Cox, M.M. 1990 The RecA protein: Structure and function. *Crit. Revs. Biochem. molec. Biol.* **25**, 415–456.

Ruigrok, R.W.H., Bohrmann, B., Hewat, E., Engel, A., Kellenberger, E. & DiCapua, E. 1993 The inactive form of RecA protein: the compact structure. *EMBO J.* **12**, 9–16.

Shah, R., Bennett, R.J. & West, S.C. 1994 Activation of RuvC Holliday junction resolvase *in vitro*. *Nucl. Acids Res.* **22**, 2490–2497.

Shiba, T., Iwasaki, H., Nakata, A. & Shinagawa, H. 1991 SOS-inducible DNA repair proteins, RuvA and RuvB, of *Escherichia coli*: Functional interactions between RuvA and RuvB for ATP hydrolysis and renaturation of the cruciform structure in supercoiled DNA. *Proc. natn. Acad. Sci. U.S.A.* **88**, 8445–8449.

Shiba, T., Iwasaki, H., Nakata, A. & Shinagawa, H. 1993 *Escherichia coli* RuvA and RuvB proteins involved in recombination repair: physical properties and interactions with DNA. *Molec. gen. Genet.* **237**, 395–399.

Smith, G.R. 1990 RecBCD enzyme. In *Nucleic Acids and Molecular Biology*, vol 4 (ed. F. Eckstein & D. M. Lilley), pp. 78–98. Berlin: Springer-Verlag.

Stasiak, A. & DiCapua, E. 1982 The helicity of DNA in complexes with RecA protein. *Nature, Lond.* **299**, 185–186.

Stasiak, A., DiCapua, E. & Koller, T. 1981 Elongation of duplex DNA of RecA protein. *J molec. Biol.* **151**, 557–564.

Stasiak, A., Stasiak, A.Z. & Koller, T. 1984 Visualization of RecA-DNA complexes involved in consecutive stages of an *in vitro* strand exchange reaction. *Cold Spring Harb. Symp. quant. Biol.* **49**, 561–570.

Stasiak, A., Tsaneva, I.R., West, S.C., Benson, C.J.B., Yu, X. & Egelman, E.H. 1994 The *E. coli* RuvB branch migration protein forms double hexameric rings around DNA. *Proc. natn. Acad. Sci. U.S.A.* **91**, 7618–7622.

Story, R.M. & Steitz, T.A. 1992 Structure of the RecA protein-ADP complex. *Nature, Lond.* **355**, 374–376.

Story, R.M., Weber, I.T. & Steitz, T.A. 1992 The structure of the *Escherichia coli* RecA protein monomer and polymer. *Nature, Lond.* **355**, 318–325.

Taylor, A.F. 1988 RecBCD enzyme of *Escherichia coli*. In *Genetic Recombination* (ed. R. Kucherlapati & G. R. Smith), pp. 231–264. Washington: American Society for Microbiology.

Tsaneva, I.R., Illing, G.T., Lloyd, R.G. & West, S.C. 1992*a* Purification and properties of the RuvA and RuvB proteins of *Escherichia coli*. *Molec. gen. Genet.* **235**, 1–10.

Tsaneva, I.R., Müller, B. & West, S.C. 1992*b* ATP-dependent branch migration of Holliday junctions promoted by the RuvA and RuvB proteins of *E. coli*. *Cell* **69**, 1171–1180.

Tsaneva, I.R., Müller, B. & West, S.C. 1993 The RuvA and RuvB proteins of *Escherichia coli* exhibit DNA helicase activity *in vitro*. *Proc. natn. Acad. Sci. U.S.A.* **90**, 1315–1319.

Umezu, K., Chi, N.W. & Kolodner, R.D. 1993 Biochemical interaction of the *Escherichia coli* RecF, RecO, and RecR proteins with RecA protein and single-stranded DNA binding protein. *Proc. natn. Acad. Sci. U.S.A.* **90**, 3875–3879.

Umezu, K., Nakayama, K. & Nakayama, H. 1990 *Escherichia coli* RecQ Protein is a DNA helicase. *Proc. natn. Acad. Sci. U.S.A.* **87**, 5363–5367.

West, S.C. 1992 Enzymes and molecular mechanisms of homologous recombination. *A. Rev. Biochem.* **61**, 603–640.

West, S.C. 1993 The nucleases of genetic recombination. In *Nucleases* (ed. S. M. Linn, R. S. Lloyd and R. J. Roberts), pp. 145–169. New York: Cold Spring Harbor Laboratory Press.

West, S. C. 1994 The processing of recombination intermediates: Mechanistic insights from studies of bacterial proteins. *Cell* **76**, 9–15.

West, S.C., Cassuto, E. & Howard-Flanders, P. 1981 Heteroduplex formation by RecA protein: Polarity of strand exchange. *Proc. natn. Acad. Sci. U.S.A.* **78**, 6149–6153.

West, S.C., Cassuto, E., Mursalim, J. & Howard-Flanders, P. 1980 Recognition of duplex DNA containing single-stranded regions by RecA protein. *Proc. natn. Acad. Sci. U.S.A.* **77**, 2569–2573.

West, S.C., Countryman, J.K. & Howard-Flanders, P. 1983 Enzymatic formation of biparental figure-8 molecules from plasmid DNA and their resolution in *Escherichia coli*. *Cell* **32**, 817–829.

Whitby, M.C., Ryder, L. & Lloyd, R.G. 1993 Reverse branch migration of Holliday junctions by RecG protein: A new mechanism for resolution of intermediates in recombination and DNA repair. *Cell* **75**, 341–350.

Wood, E.R. & Matson, S.W. 1987 Purification and characterisation of a new DNA-dependent ATPase with helicase activity from *Escherichia coli*. *J. biol. Chem.* **262**, 15269–15276.

Yu, X. & Egelman, E. H. 1990 Image analysis reveals that *Escherichia coli* RecA protein consists of two domains. *Biophys. J.* **57**, 555–566.

Yu, X. & Egelman, E. H. 1992 Structural data suggest that the active and inactive forms of the RecA filament are not simply interconvertible. *J molec. Biol.* **227**, 334–346.

4

Structure of the four-way DNA junction and its interaction with proteins

DEREK R. DUCKETT, ALASTAIR I. H. MURCHIE,
MARIE-JOSÈPHE E. GIRAUD-PANIS, J. RICHARD PÖHLER
AND DAVID M. J. LILLEY*

CRC Nucleic Acid Structure Research Group, Department of Biochemistry, The University, Dundee DD1 4HN, U.K.

SUMMARY

The four-way DNA junction is an important intermediate in recombination processes; it is, the substrate for different enzyme activities. In solution, the junction adopts a right-handed, antiparallel-stacked X-structure formed by the pairwise coaxial-stacking of helical arms. The stereochemistry is determined by the juxtaposition of grooves and backbones, which is optimal when the smaller included angle is 60°. The antiparallel structure has two distinct sides with major and minor groove-characteristics, respectively. The folding process requires the binding of metal cations, in the absence of which, the junction remains extended without helix–helix stacking. The geometry of the junction can be perturbed by the presence of certain base–base mispairs or phosphodiester discontinuities located at the point of strand exchange. The four-way DNA junction is selectively cleaved by a number of resolving enzymes. In a number of cases, these appear to recognize the minor groove face of the junction and are functionally divisible into activities that recognize and bind the junction, and a catalytic activity. Some possible mechanisms for the recognition of branched DNA structure are discussed.

1. INTRODUCTION

Recombination is of immense evolutionary importance, facilitating the provision of new combinations of genetic variants from which the best combinations may arise by natural selection. Homologous genetic recombination may occur between any two sections of DNA, provided that stretches of homology exist within them. By contrast, site-specific recombination occurs between well-defined target sequences, and is the basis of specific DNA rearrangements used by transposons and bacteriophage, and by higher organisms (for events such as immunoglobulin gene maturation). Recombination events entail the physical rearrangement of DNA molecules and are brought about by proteins that must recognize and manipulate DNA structure.

To recombine two DNA molecules, it is necessary to juxtapose the helices in some way, and then to carry out chemical reactions on the phosphodiester backbones that generate a new connectivity. A final resolution step may be required to recreate independent duplex molecules that may, or may not, be recombinant. The four-way DNA junction is believed to be an intermediate in homologous genetic recombination (Holliday 1964), and there is good evidence for its role in site-specific recombination of the integrase class (Hoess *et al.* 1987; Kitts & Nash 1987;

Nunes-Düby *et al.* 1987; Jayaram *et al.* 1988). Such branched DNA intermediates have rather precise three-dimensional structures and their manipulation will require the intervention of proteins that are largely structure-specific.

2. STRUCTURE OF THE FOUR-WAY DNA JUNCTION

The past five years has seen a substantial improvement in understanding of the structure of the four-way DNA junction. The junction undergoes a metal-ion-dependent conformational folding into a structure termed the 'stacked X-structure'. This structure is based on the pairwise coaxial-stacking of helices, and rotation into an overall X-shaped conformation. This structure is based upon evidence from a number of sources. Unfortunately, the four-way junction has been resistant to crystallization and is too large to be readily solved by nuclear magnetic resonance (NMR) methods, so it has been necessary to employ some relatively unconventional methods.

Gel electrophoresis has proved to be very powerful in the analysis of the structure of the branched DNA species. We showed that the creation of a four-way junction at the centre of a DNA fragment conferred abnormally low mobility in polyacrylamide (Gough & Lilley 1985), consistent with the introduction of a pronounced bend or kink at the position of the junction.

---

* To whom correspondence should be addressed.

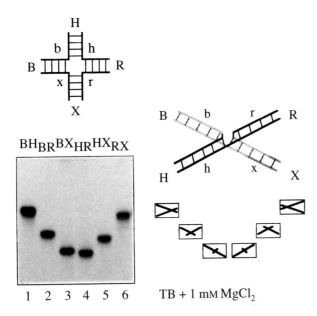

Figure 1. Gel electrophoretic analysis of the structure of a four-way DNA junction in the presence of magnesium ions. The relative configuration of the four arms was deduced by comparing the electrophoretic mobility of the six possible species in which two arms had been shortened by restriction enzyme cleavage. The junction (junction 3 from Duckett *et al.* (Duckett *et al.* 1988)) has four arms labelled B, H, R and X, and comprises four strands, labelled b, h, r and x as shown. The resulting species with two long and two short arms are indicated by their long arms, i.e. species BH has shortened R and X arms. These six long–short species have been electrophoresed on an 8% polyacrylamide gel in 90 mM Tris borate (pH 8.3) (TB buffer), 1 mM magnesium chloride. The slow-intermediate−fast-fast-intermediate-slow 2:2:2 pattern of mobilities is explained in terms of the X-shaped structure formed by coaxial stacking of B on X arms, and H on R arms as indicated. This leads to the formation of the six long–short species shown, interpreted in terms of the expectation that the mobility will be proportional to the size of the included angle between the long arms. Note that the chemical polarity of the continuous strands in this structure (i.e. strands h and x) is antiparallel, with the exchanging strands (strands b and r) turning around the small angle of the X. The relatively short distances between the ends of the B and H arms, and between the ends of the R and X arms, were further established by fluorescence resonance energy transfer experiments (Murchie *et al.* 1989; Clegg *et al.* 1992), thereby confirming the antiparallel character of the structure.

The electrophoretic mobility was found to be very dependent on the concentration and type of cation present (Diekmann & Lilley 1987), indicating a role for metal ions in the structure. Cooper & Hagerman (1987) developed a technique based on observation of the effect on the electrophoretic mobility of a four-way junction following the ligation of reporter arms. They concluded that the symmetry of the junction was lower than tetrahedral and that two of the strands were more severely bent than proposed in the model of Sigal & Alberts (1972).

We employed a related gel electrophoretic technique to compare the six isomeric junctions with two long and two short arms generated by pairwise restriction cleavage. We observed a pattern of two-fast, two-intermediate and two-slow (2:2:2 pattern) species in

the presence of added cations (figure 1) (Duckett *et al.* 1988). This suggested to us that the junction is X-shaped, formed by stacking the helical arms in coaxial pairs, followed by a rotation in the manner of opening a pair of scissors.

This arrangement generates a favourable increase in basepair stacking interactions, while reducing steric and electrostatic interaction between the stacked pairs of arms. The reduction to twofold symmetry divides the four strands of the junction into two classes: two strands (continuous) have continuous axes, while the other two strands (exchanging) pass between the two helical stacks at the point of strand exchange. This distinction between strands is consistent with probing of four-way DNA junctions using hydroxyl radicals (Churchill *et al.* 1988), where it was found that two strands were more protected than the other two.

Two isomers of the stacked X-structure are possible, depending on the choice of helical stacking partners. When we altered the sequence at the point of strand exchange, the electrophoretic pattern of our long–short arm junctions changed, consistent with an exchange of stacking partners (Duckett *et al.* 1988). This isomerization changes the nature of each strand in the structure; continuous strands become exchanging strands, and vice versa. The identity of the most stable isomer will be governed by the thermodynamics of the interactions at the point of strand exchange, probably mainly by the stacking interactions.

Electrophoretic mobility of DNA that is bent by curvature or bulge-kinking is proportional to end-to-end distance. If we use this as a basis for assigning the six long–short arm junction species, we conclude that the structure is approximately antiparallel, i.e. the two continuous strands run in opposite directions. This is in contrast to the normal depiction of Holliday junctions, and to the model of Sigal & Alberts (1972). We therefore sought alternative methods to test the structure, that were independent of any assumptions about the relative mobilities of different species in polyacrylamide gels, and turned to fluorescence resonance energy transfer (FRET) (Murchie *et al.* 1989; Clegg *et al.* 1992). The two short end-to-end distances that were observed were only consistent with an antiparallel structure and were in complete agreement with the stacking isomeric forms deduced from our earlier gel electrophoresis. All experimental results using a variety of other techniques indicate that the antiparallel structure is most stable in solution and there is none consistent with the parallel structure.

Of all the possible X-shaped structures, modelling indicates that a right-handed, antiparallel structure is likely to be most stable, as it permits a favourable alignment of strands and grooves that helps avoid steric clash between backbones (figure 2). This is most effective if the small angle is 60°. The right-handed configuration is consistent with FRET measurements of the handedness (Murchie *et al.* 1989). It is clearly a very natural way for DNA molecules to interact, as similar packing has been observed in a number of crystal structures of double-stranded oligonucleotides (Timsit *et al.* 1989; Lipanov *et al.* 1993). The strand–groove alignment leads to a localized protection

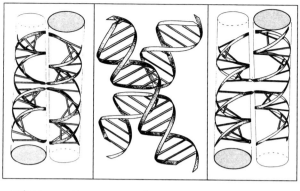

major groove side   face   minor groove side

Figure 2. Ribbon model of the right-handed, antiparallel stacked X-structure of the four-way DNA junction, observed from three points of view. Note the juxtaposition of the continuous strands in the major grooves of the opposing helices, which is optimal for a small angle of 60° for the helix crossing. Centre: face view, showing the X-shape of the folded junction: the two sides of the structure are not equivalent. On one side (left) the four basepairs at the point of strand exchange all present major groove edges, while on the other side (right) the minor groove edges are presented.

against cleavage by DNase I (Lu *et al.* 1989; Murchie *et al.* 1990). Coaxial stacking of DNA helices is consistent with the results of cleavage by *Mbo*II (Murchie *et al.* 1991).

One important aspect of the stereochemistry is that the antiparallel junction presents two dissimilar sides, as seen in figure 2 (Murchie *et al.* 1989; von Kitzing *et al.* 1990). The connectivity required to generate the four-way junction creates two sides of major- and minor-groove characteristics respectively, these are preserved upon folding into an antiparallel conformation. It may be seen, for example, that on the major groove side there is a continuous major groove that runs down one arm, passes through the point of strand exchange and continues on an arm of the opposite helical stack. This has important consequences for interaction with proteins.

3. ROLE OF METAL IONS IN FOLDING THE FOUR-WAY DNA JUNCTION

Metal ions play a critical role in the structure of the four-way DNA junction. In the absence of added cations, the junction cannot fold into the stacked X-structure, and remains extended with unstacked arms. Gel electrophoretic experiments (figure 3) indicate that under low-salt conditions, the junction adopts a structure with approximately square symmetry (Duckett *et al.* 1988, 1990), which is confirmed by FRET experiments (Clegg *et al.* 1993). This suggests that the folding of the junction into the stacked X-structure creates close phosphate juxtaposition that is destabilizing unless reduced by ion screening.

Folding the four-way junction into its stacked form reflects a balance between the favourable interactions stabilizing the folded form, particularly helix–helix stacking interactions and destabilization due to electrostatic repulsion (figure 4). A variety of ions are able

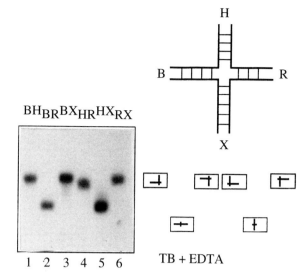

TB + EDTA

Figure 3. Gel electrophoretic analysis of the structure of a four-way junction in the absence of added metal ions. Long–short arm analysis of a junction in 90 mM Tris borate (pH 8.3), 0.1 mM EDTA (Duckett *et al.* 1988). Under these conditions, junctions of any sequence exhibit a 4: pattern of mobility in the order slow, fast, slow slow, fast, slow. This is consistent with a square configuration of helical arms, giving four species where the long arms subtend approximately 90° (slow species), and two with angles of approximately 180° (faster species). The four strands are equivalent in this structure. The extended, square configuration of arms has been confirmed by FRET measurements (Clegg *et al.* 1993), and is consistent with the reactivity of thymine bases at the point of strand exchange to osmium tetroxide at low salt concentrations (Duckett *et al.* 1988).

to bring about the folding, with differing efficiencies (Duckett *et al.* 1990). The balance between stacking and electrostatic interactions was revealed by experiments in which selected phosphate groups were replaced by electrically neutral methyl phosphonates; different stacking isomers resulted, depending on which phosphates were replaced (Duckett *et al.* 1990). A high-affinity ion-binding site at the point of strand exchange in the junction has recently been revealed using uranyl photocleavage (Møllegaard *et al.* 1994).

Thus metal ions are an integral part of the folded conformation of the DNA junction. This should not come as a surprise. DNA is a highly charged polyelectrolyte, the folding of which is likely to generate repulsive interactions that must be screened. Critical ion interactions are likely to play important roles in the folding of many functionally significant nucleic acids.

4. PERTURBATION OF THE STRUCTURE OF THE FOUR-WAY DNA JUNCTION

The right-handed, antiparallel stacked X-structure may be distorted by a variety of influences. While the angle subtended between the pairs of coaxially stacked helices is normally about 60°, this can probably be distorted relatively easily. Kimball *et al.* (1990) showed that it was possible to force a junction into a parallel configuration by restraining the distances between the ends of given arms with a molecular tether. The

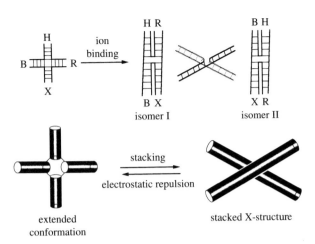

Figure 4. The cation-induced folding of the four-way DNA junction. In the absence of added cations, electrostatic repulsion outweighs the free energy available from coaxial helical stacking, and the junction remains extended. Upon addition of cations (e.g. $> 80\ \mu M\ Mg^{2+}$), the junction folds into the stacked X-structure. The folding generates a site of high affinity for metal ions, which is located at the point of strand exchange (Møllegaard *et al.* 1994). There are two possible stacking isomers of the folded conformation; for most sequences one isomer is significantly more stable than the other, and the relative stability of the isomeric forms is determined by the sequence at the point of strand exchange.

successful construction of molecules containing two four-way junctions supports the ability of a relatively flexible junction to be conformable (Fu & Seeman 1993).

Imperfections in homology between recombining sequences will lead to the introduction of non-Watson–Crick base mismatches at the four-way junction. The inclusion of such mismatches may have a very destabilizing effect on the folded structure (Duckett & Lilley 1991). In general, the effects of mismatches were dependent both on the nature of the mismatch and its context. Most junctions, even those containing severely destabilizing mismatches, could be persuaded to fold into the stacked X-structure by increasing cation concentrations, supporting the concept of a balance between stacking and electrostatic interactions.

Junctions containing covalent interruptions in the phosphodiester backbone (nicks) at a single location may be created either by a unitary strand exchange process, or by enzymic cleavage of an intact junction. We found that single nicks have a significant influence on the conformation of the junction in the presence of added metal ions (Pöhler *et al.* 1994). We obtained gel electrophoretic patterns suggesting that while coaxial helix–helix stacking was retained, the angle between the helices changes to be closer to 90° (figure 5). This suggests that the additional conformational flexibility permits the helices to disengage from the close backbone–groove juxtaposition and swing around to a perpendicular arrangement that lowers overall electrostatic repulsion. To observe the change in conformation, the nick was required to be immediately at the point of strand exchange. Interestingly, the stacking isomer was determined by the position of the strand break, in order to place the nick on the

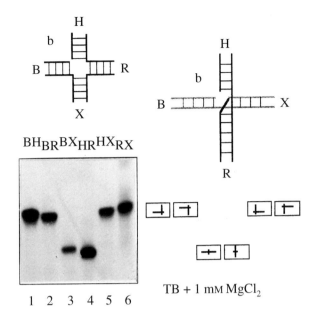

Figure 5. Effect of introducing a nick into one strand of the four-way DNA junction at the point of strand exchange. Gel electrophoretic analysis of a junction containing a nick on the b-strand, in the presence of 1 mM magnesium ions. The long–short arm analysis was carried out as before (see figure 1). The pattern of mobilities was clearly different from the 2:2:2 pattern of the intact junction in magnesium, indicating that the configuration of arms had changed. Four slow and two fast species were observed, but the pattern was slow, slow, fast, fast, slow, slow, in contrast to that observed for the intact junction in the absence of added metal cations (compare with figure 3). This suggests that coaxial pairwise helical stacking is retained, but that the angles included between the arms are close to 90° as shown. When the nick was placed on the x-strand, we observed an isomerization of the junction such that B on H stacking now occurred (Pöhler *et al.* 1994). The result of this is that the nick is once again located on an exchanging strand.

exchanging strand. Clearly, the relaxation of the structure lowered the free energy of the junction by more than the difference between stacking isomers.

5. INTERACTION WITH JUNCTION RESOLVING ENZYMES

Four-way DNA junctions are substrates for resolving enzymes, a class of structure-specific nucleases (reviewed in Duckett *et al.* 1992). Such activities have been isolated from a wide variety of sources from bacteriophage to mammals, and are probably ubiquitous enzymes for the manipulation of branched DNA. In addition, there are proteins that selectively bind DNA junctions without resulting in nucleolysis (Elborough & West 1988; Bianchi *et al.* 1989; Parsons *et al.* 1992). Some of these proteins are largely specific for certain branched DNA structures, whereas others exhibit some sequence selectivity. Some proteins interact specifically with the four-way junction, whereas others, exemplified by T4 endonuclease VII, cleave a variety of branched DNA structures.

Endonuclease VII of bacteriophage T4 (Kemper & Garabett 1981) is a well-characterized junction-resolving enzyme. The enzyme cleaves four-way DNA

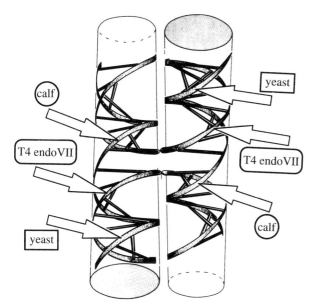

Figure 6. Cleavage sites for three different junction-resolving enzymes on the minor groove side of the four-way DNA junction. While T4 endonuclease VII cleaves the exchanging strands of a junction 3′ to the point of strand exchange, analysis of the cleavage sites of related junctions by an endo X1 from yeast (West *et al.* 1987) and an enzyme from calf thymus (Elborough & West 1990) show that these cleave the continuous strands, 5′ and 3′ respectively to the point of strand exchange. While these sets of cleavage positions appear to be quite unrelated at first sight, when they are placed onto the model of the stacked X-structure they are all found to be located on the minor groove face.

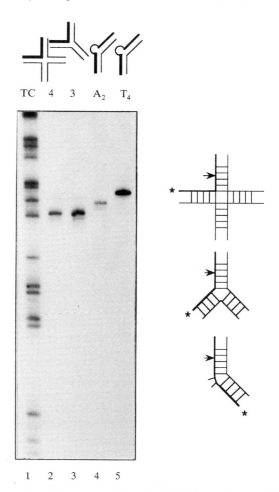

Figure 7. Cleavage of branched DNA species by T4 endonuclease VII. A four-way junction was radioactively [5′-^{32}P] labelled on one strand and incubated with T4 endonuclease VII. Cleavage at virtually a single phosphodiester bond may be seen on the sequencing gel. Three other branched DNA species of closely related sequence were examined. The same radioactive strand was incorporated into a three-way junction, and two bulged species, containing A$_2$ and a T$_4$ bulges respectively, each of which were based on the same sequence. These species were cleaved in a manner that was virtually identical to that on the four-way junction (the shift in the position of the bands on the bulged species is due to the insertion of the bulge bases).

junctions (Duckett *et al.* 1988; Mueller *et al.* 1988) and cruciform structures in supercoiled DNA (Mizuuchi *et al.* 1982; Lilley & Kemper 1984). It cleaves the exchanging strands of the junction, two or three bases 3′ to the point of strand exchange. The scissile bonds are located symmetrically on the minor-groove side of the stacked X-structure (figure 6), suggesting that the enzyme interacts selectively with this face of the junction. This is consistent with regions of the junction protected by the enzyme against hydroxyl radical cleavage (Parsons *et al.* 1990; Bhattacharyya *et al.* 1991). The minor-groove side is also the apparent target for junction resolving enzymes isolated from yeast (West *et al.* 1987) and calf thymus (Elborough & West 1990) (figure 6). This suggests that the three enzymes bind the junction in a related manner, despite their wide evolutionary separation. However, although all three enzymes appear to interact with the same face of the junction, the actual cleavage positions differ in each case. This suggests that the proteins might be functionally divisible into binding and catalytic parts, which are oriented in different ways in the various enzymes.

T4 endonuclease VII responds primarily to DNA structure. The cleavages are located primarily on the exchanging strands and upon stacking isomerization, due to local sequence changes, cleavage sites are found on the new exchanging strands (Duckett *et al.* 1988). To prove this point rigorously, a junction of constant sequence was constrained to exist in one or other stacking isomer by means of tethering (Kimball *et al.*

1990), whence cleavage by T4 endonuclease VII was restricted to the exchanging strands of each isomer (Bhattacharyya *et al.* 1991).

This raises the question of what are the critical structural features of the DNA junction that are recognized by the resolving enzyme. Two general possibilities exist:

1. *Recognition of local conformation* Clearly, the strand trajectory that generates the strand exchange in the junction leads to some unusual stereochemical features. These might be recognized by the enzyme: for example, the junction contains a high-affinity binding site for a number of intercalators (Guo *et al.* 1989). Perhaps then, an aromatic sidechain might probe the DNA structure in a similar manner to these compounds. Modelling the structure of the four-way junction indicates that local widening of grooves is required (von Kitzing *et al.* 1990), and could generate another recognizable feature.

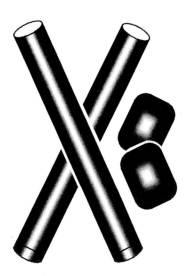

Figure 8. Schematic to show the interaction between T4 endonuclease VII and the minor groove side of the junction. It might be anticipated that the dimeric enzyme has complementarity of surface shape, such that the discrimination of the angle of helical inclination in the junction is an element in the structural selectivity of the resolving enzyme.

2. *Global recognition* The stacked X-structure provides a number of faces at which there is a precise relative inclination of the two pairs of coaxially stacked DNA helices. If two subunits of the enzyme make precise contacts with these two helices, protein–protein interactions could generate selectivity for the angle of inclination of the DNA (Bhattacharyya *et al.* 1991).

There is no completely convincing evidence for either of these models and any suggestion can only presently be regarded as a working model which may turn out to be wrong. Enzymes such as T4 endonuclease VII cleave a variety of DNA structures, including four-way and three-way junctions and bulged DNA molecules. We have shown (Bhattacharyya *et al.* 1991) that these are cleaved in a related way (figure 7). The common feature amongst these species is a mutual inclination of two DNA helices (for a discussion see Lilley & Clegg 1993), and it seems feasible that this aspect is important in the recognition process. T4 endonuclease VII exists as a dimer in solution (Kosak & Kemper 1990), and the two subunits could be oriented so as to interact most effectively with two DNA helices that are mutually inclined at 120° (shown schematically in figure 8). The nuclease activity might become activated when the included angle falls within certain limits. This idea is supported by the observation that T4 endonuclease VII cleaves bulged molecules fastest when they have particular numbers of bulged bases (e.g. two adenines) (Bhattacharyya *et al.* 1991), which might generate a degree of axial kinking that is optimal for interaction with the enzyme. Further substrates for T4 endonuclease VII are A-tract curved DNA, which becomes nicked one base to the 3′ side of each A-tract (Bhattacharyya *et al.* 1991), and DNA containing a single site of modification by *cis*-diamminedichloroplatinum (II) (Murchie & Lilley 1993), which creates a local kinking of DNA (Rice *et al.* 1988). The cleavage positions in the platinated DNA do not

suggest a simple location of the enzyme on the inner face of the kink, but a kinked duplex has a rather different geometry from a stacked X-structure junction, and exact equivalence should not be expected. Some junction-resolving enzymes (such as RuvC (Connolly *et al.* 1991) perhaps) may be rather more specific for four-way junctions, when compared to the phage enzymes, although the sequence-specificity for the cleavage reaction generates greater discrimination than binding (Benson & West 1994).

6. INTERACTION OF T7 ENDONUCLEASE I WITH FOUR-WAY JUNCTIONS

T7 endonuclease I cleaves four-way DNA junctions in a manner that is different from the enzymes discussed above in that all four strands become cleaved at positions very close to the point of strand exchange (Duckett *et al.* 1988). The cleavage positions do not appear to have the same two-fold symmetric relationship that is exhibited by resolving enzymes like T4 endonuclease VII. This might suggest a different manner of junction-protein interaction. Nevertheless, like the other resolving enzymes, T7 endonuclease I is highly selective for branched DNA species and must therefore, be capable of structure-selective interaction with DNA.

To explore this further we have taken a genetic approach, based on the isolation of catalytically non-functional mutants of T7 endonuclease I (Duckett *et al.* 1995). Overexpression of T7 endonuclease I in *E. coli* leads to severe toxicity; we used this as a basis for the selection of mutant resolving enzymes. The gene for T7 endonuclease I was subjected to random chemical mutagenesis, reinserted into the expression site of a plasmid and transformed into a strain of *E. coli* lacking the LacI repressor required to repress the P_{lac} promoter. Under these conditions, the level of wild-type T7 endonuclease I produced is lethal; any surviving colonies are likely to express mutant protein. Sequencing a series of such T7 endonuclease I genes revealed in each case that the amino acid sequence of the protein had suffered one or two changes. The mutant proteins were expressed with histidine-tags for ease of manipulation and their DNA-binding properties were analysed. In each case we found that the mutant proteins bound very well to four-way DNA junctions, giving a well defined retarded species on polyacrylamide gel electrophoresis (PAGE) (figure 9*a*). Moreover, the binding to the junction could not be out-competed by a thousand-fold excess of linear DNA of the same sequence (figure 9*b*). Clearly these mutant proteins retained their full structure-selectivity for the four-way junction, whilst having lost all ability to cleave the phosphodiester backbone of the DNA. This is consistent with a functional divisibility of structure-selective binding and catalysis for this enzyme. When we analysed the positions in which the catalytically inactive proteins had suffered mutation, we found that all the amino acid changes clustered into the second quarter of the protein sequence. Interestingly, this part of the sequence shares some sequence similarity with T4 endonuclease VII, suggesting that these regions

(a)

[endo I E65K]

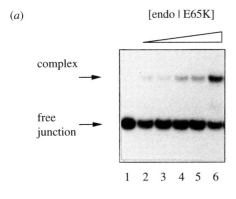

complex

free
junction

1 2 3 4 5 6

(b)

[duplex]

100   1000   ratio
10   500   duplex/junction

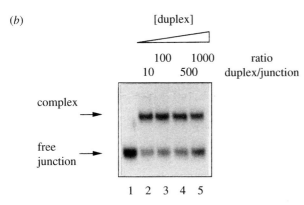

complex

free
junction

1 2 3 4 5

Figure 9. Structure-selective binding of T7 endonuclease I to the four-way DNA junction. (a) Electrophoretic retardation of the complex formed between [^{32}P] radioactively labelled DNA junction and an inactive E65K mutant of T7 endonuclease I in 90 mM Tris borate (pH 8.3), 200 μM MgCl$_2$. Track 1, junction without added protein; tracks 2–6, junction incubated with increasing concentrations of the mutant resolving enzyme. (b) Competition between four-way junction and duplex for binding E65K mutant T7 endonuclease I. Radioactive junction was incubated with E65K endonuclease I in 90 mM Tris borate (pH 8.3), 200 μM MgCl$_2$, either alone (track 1), or with an increasing molar ratio of unlabelled competitor duplex DNA (tracks 2–5). Note that even a 1000-fold excess of linear duplex fails to displace a significant fraction of the complex between the resolving enzyme and the four-way junction.

might provide amino acids important in the active site of the resolving enzymes.

One of these catalytically inactive mutants of T7 endonuclease I was used to explore the shape of the complex bound to the four-way junction, using the gel electrophoretic analysis of junctions with the permutations of two-long and two-short arms discussed for the isolated junction above. We can observe modulation of the electrophoretic mobility of the six long–short species as a complex with the mutant T7 endonuclease I (figure 10). Although the difference in mobility between the fastest and slowest species is much less than that for the pure DNA further down the gel, it appears that the pattern of mobilities is different for the complex compared to free DNA junction. Although some caution is necessary in the interpretation of this result, due to possible effects on mobility of the presence of the protein itself, it appears that there has been a conformational change in the configuration of

(a)

junction +
junction alone   endo I E65K

BH$_{BR}$BX$_{HR}$HX$_{RX}$BH$_{BR}$BX$_{HR}$HX$_{RX}$

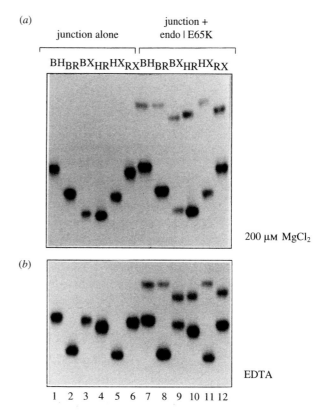

200 μM MgCl$_2$

(b)

EDTA

1 2 3 4 5 6 7 8 9 10 11 12

Figure 10. Gel electrophoretic analysis of the complex between a four-way junction and E65K mutant T7 endonuclease I. (a) The six double-restriction digests of junction 3 (see figure 1) were incubated with E65K endonuclease I in 90 mM Tris borate (pH 8.3), 200 μM MgCl$_2$. These were analysed by gel electrophoresis (tracks 6–12), in comparison with the same species in the absence of protein (tracks 1–6). Note the pattern of mobilities of the retarded species formed in the presence of the protein are different from that of the free DNA. (b) The equivalent experiment in 90 mM Tris borate (pH 8.3), 1 mM EDTA. Note that the pattern of retarded species is exactly the same as that found in the presence of magnesium ions.

the arms of the junction. The pattern of the shifted species does not appear to be a fast, intermediate, slow 2:2:2 pattern, but is more similar to the slow, slow, fast, fast, slow, slow pattern of the nicked junction (Pöhler *et al.* 1994) (see above). This suggests that in the presence of the resolving enzyme, the arms might remain coaxially stacked but alter their relative juxtaposition – thereby changing the angles between arms from the 60°/120° of the free junction to something more like 90°. We observe exactly the same pattern of mobilities whether the gel is run in the presence of magnesium or EDTA, indicating that the protein can itself induce folding of the junction on binding.

7. RECOGNITION OF BRANCHED DNA STRUCTURES BY PROTEINS

DNA junctions are manipulated by proteins that recognize DNA three-dimensional structure. An ability to recognize mutually inclined DNA helices might be a general way of recognizing certain DNA structures. This facility could be important in DNA repair and T4 endonuclease VII and T7 endonuclease I are best classified as repair enzymes. DNA may be damaged by a variety of agents (Reardon & Sancar 1991). A fairly common feature at the site of damage may be axial kinking, as is found in the case of a cisplatin adduct, for example (Visse *et al.* 1991). This could generate a feature that is recognizable by certain proteins. We might, therefore, class together a series of proteins that recognize DNA structure and manipulate it in some way – including topoisomerases and proteins that manipulate DNA structure in a variety of cellular processes (such as IHF). The HMG1 domain (Bianchi *et al.* 1989) and HU protein (Pontiggia *et al.* 1993) selectively bind DNA junctions and might therefore be classified in the same way.

It seems probable that enzymes that are required to manipulate DNA junctions will be functionally divisible into two activities: recognition of and selective binding to the structure of the junction, and catalysis of some reaction. The binding and catalytic activities of the phage-resolving enzymes appear to be functionally divisible. These proteins might, therefore, be thought of as analogous to a missile, requiring a delivery vehicle that can locate the target and a warhead that fulfils its function when delivered to the target site. At least two different activities are required for the manipulation of the four-way DNA junction in recombination, branch migration and resolution. In *E. coli* they are catalysed respectively by RuvAB (Iwasaki *et al.* 1992; Tsaneva *et al.* 1992) and RuvC (Connolly *et al.* 1991; Iwasaki *et al.* 1991; Sharples & Lloyd, 1991). For resolution, it is clear that the catalytic activity required is a nuclease. In the case of the proteins that facilitate branch migration the catalyst is less obvious. Measured rates of spontaneous branch migration are low, especially in the presence of magnesium ions (Panyutin & Hsieh 1994), where the junction is tightly folded into the stacked X-structure. In order to catalyse the process, a protein that can destabilize the structure is required and this turns out to be a helicase. Thus in the case of RuvAB, it is the B subunit that performs catalysis, while the A subunit directs the complex to the four-way DNA junction (Tsaneva *et al.* 1993). In the case of RecG (Lloyd & Sharples 1993), the two functions are combined within one protein.

The division of recombination enzymes into binding and catalytic functions is supported by experimental data from a number of different systems: (i) comparisons of the cleavage sites for junction resolving enzymes from phage T4, yeast and calf thymus (discussed above); (ii) the demonstration that the sequence-specificity of RuvC resides at the level of catalysis, and that binding and catalysis are separable (Bennett *et al.* 1993); (iii) although yeast endo X2 exhibits some sequence-specificity, four-way junctions that could not be cleaved could nevertheless bind the enzyme and served as a competitive inhibitor of cruciform cleavage (Evans & Kolodner 1988); (iv) a fusion of T7 endonuclease I to the *lac* repressor (Panayotatos & Backman 1989) cleaved DNA adjacent to *lac* operator sites, indicating that the nuclease function of the resolving enzyme could function with a new DNA binding domain; and (v) mutants of T7 endonuclease I bind four-way junctions without cleav-

age (discussed above). A mutant of RuvC with equivalent properties has been reported (Sharples & Lloyd 1993). Although the recognition processes are unlikely to be identical between different enzymes, we suspect that they will be similar in principle for all these proteins whatever their source. Recombination is likely to be mediated by proteins that recognize and manipulate the structure of folded DNA, and understanding the DNA structure is an important element of understanding the overall mechanism.

We thank our collaborators Dr R. M. Clegg and Dr N. E. Møllegaard for many valuable discussions and the Cancer Research Campaign for financial support.

REFERENCES

Bennett, R.J., Dunderdale, H.J. & West, S.C. 1993 Resolution of Holliday junctions by RuvC resolvase: cleavage specificity and DNA distortion. *Cell* **74**, 1021–1031.

Benson, F.E. & West, S.C. 1994 Substrate specificity of the *Escherichia coli* RuvC protein – resolution of three- and four-stranded recombination intermediates. *J. biol. Chem.* **269**, 5195–5201.

Bhattacharyya, A., Murchie, A.I.H., von Kitzing, E., Diekmann, S., Kemper, B. & Lilley, D.M.J. 1991 A model for the interaction of DNA junctions and resolving enzymes. *J. molec. Biol.* **221**, 1191–1207.

Bianchi, M.E., Beltrame, M. & Paonessa, G. 1989 Specific recognition of cruciform DNA by nuclear protein HMG1. *Science, Wash.* **243**, 1056–1059.

Churchill, M.E., Tullius, T.D., Kallenbach, N.R. & Seeman, N.C. 1988 A Holliday recombination intermediate is twofold symmetric. *Proc. natn. Acad. Sci. U.S.A.* **85**, 4653–4656.

Clegg, R.M., Murchie, A.I.H., Zechel, A., Carlberg, C., Diekmann, S. & Lilley, D.M.J. 1992 Fluorescence resonance energy transfer analysis of the structure of the four-way DNA junction. *Biochemistry, Wash.* **31**, 4846–4856.

Clegg, R.M., Murchie, A.I.H., Zechel, A. & Lilley, D.M.J. 1993 The solution structure of the four-way DNA junction at low salt concentration; a fluorescence resonance energy transfer analysis. *Biophys. J.* **66**, 99–109.

Connolly, B., Parsons, C.A., Benson, F.E., Dunderdale, H.J., Sharples, G.J., Lloyd, R.G. & West, S.C. 1991 Resolution of Holliday junctions *in vitro* requires the *Escherichia coli ruvC* gene product. *Proc. natn. Acad. Sci. U.S.A.* **88**, 6063–6067.

Cooper, J.P. & Hagerman, P.J. 1987 Gel electrophoretic analysis of the geometry of a DNA four-way junction. *J. molec. Biol.* **198**, 711–719.

Diekmann, S. & Lilley, D.M.J. 1987 The anomalous gel migration of a stable cruciform: temperature and salt dependence, and some comparisons with curved DNA. *Nucl. Acids Res.* **14**, 5765–5774.

Duckett, D.R., Giraud Panis, M.-J.E. & Lilley, D.M.J. 1995 Binding of the junction-resolving enzyme T7 endonuclease I to DNA; separation of binding and catalysis by mutation. *J. Molec. Biol.* (In the Press.)

Duckett, D.R. & Lilley, D.M.J. 1991 Effects of base mismatches on the structure of the four-way DNA junction. *J. molec. Biol.* **221**, 147–161.

Duckett, D.R., Murchie, A.I.H., Bhattacharyya, A., Clegg, R.M., Diekmann, S., von Kitzing, E. & Lilley, D.M.J. 1992 The structure of DNA junctions, and their interactions with enzymes. *Eur. J. Biochem.* **207**, 285–295.

Duckett, D.R., Murchie, A.I.H., Diekmann, S., von Kitzing, E., Kemper, B. & Lilley, D.M.J. 1988 The structure of the Holliday junction and its resolution. *Cell* **55**, 79–89.

Duckett, D.R., Murchie, A.I.H. & Lilley, D.M.J. 1990 The role of metal ions in the conformation of the four-way junction. *EMBO J.* **9**, 583–590.

Elborough, K. & West, S. 1988 Specific binding of cruciform DNA structures by a protein from human extracts. *Nucl. Acids Res.* **16**, 3603–3614.

Elborough, K.M. & West, S.C. 1990 Resolution of synthetic Holliday junctions in DNA by an endonuclease from calf thymus. *EMBO J.* **9**, 2931–2936.

Evans, D.H. & Kolodner, R. 1988 Effect of DNA structure and nucleotide sequence on Holliday junction resolution by a *Saccharomyces cerevisiae* endonuclease. *J. molec. Biol.* **201**, 69–80.

Fu, T.J. & Seeman, N.C. 1993 DNA double-crossover molecules. *Biochemistry, Wash.* **32**, 3211–3220.

Gough, G.W. & Lilley, D.M.J. 1985 DNA bending induced by cruciform formation. *Nature, Lond.* **313**, 154–156.

Guo, Q., Seeman, N.C. & Kallenbach, N.R. 1989 Site-specific interaction of intercalating drugs with a branched DNA molecule. *Biochemistry, Wash.* **28**, 2355–2359.

Hoess, R., Wierzbicki, A. & Abremski, K. 1987 Isolation and characterisation of intermediates in site-specific recombination. *Proc. natn. Acad. Sci. U.S.A.* **84**, 6840–6844.

Holliday, R. 1964 A mechanism for gene conversion in fungi. *Genet. Res.* **5**, 282–304.

Iwasaki, H., Takahagi, M., Nakata, A. & Shinagawa, H. 1992 *Escherichia coli* RuvA Protein and RuvB Protein specifically interact with Holliday junctions and promote branch migration. *Genes Dev.* **6**, 2214–2220.

Iwasaki, H., Takahagi, M., Shiba, T., Nakata, A. & Shinagawa, H. 1991 *Escherichia coli* RuvC protein is an endonuclease that resolves the Holliday structure. *EMBO J.* **10**, 4381–4389.

Jayaram, M., Crain, K.L., Parsons, R.L. & Harshey, R.M. 1988 Holliday junctions in FLP recombination: Resolution by step-arrest mutants of FLP protein. *Proc. natn. Acad. Sci. U.S.A.* **85**, 7902–7906.

Kemper, B. & Garabett, M. 1981 Studies on T4 head maturation. 1. Purification and characterisation of gene-49-controlled endonuclease. *Eur. J. Biochem.* **115**, 123–131.

Kimball, A., Guo, Q., Lu, M., Cunningham, R.P., Kallenbach, N.R., Seeman, N.C. & Tullius, T.D. 1990 Construction and analysis of parallel and antiparallel Holliday junctions. *J. biol. Chem.* **265**, 6544–6547.

Kitts, P.A. & Nash, H.A. 1987 Homology-dependent interactions in phage λ site-specific recombination. *Nature, Lond.* **329**, 346–348.

Kosak, H.G. & Kemper, B.W. 1990 Large-scale preparation of T4 endonuclease VII from over-expressing bacteria. *Eur. J. Biochem.* **194**, 779–784.

Lilley, D.M.J. & Clegg, R.M. 1993 The structure of branched DNA species. *Q. Rev. Biophys.* **26**, 131–175.

Lilley, D.M.J. & Kemper, B. 1984 Cruciform-resolvase interactions in supercoiled DNA. *Cell* **36**, 413–422.

Lipanov, A., Kopka, M.L., Kaczor-Grzeskowiak, M., Quintana, J. & Dickerson, R.E. 1993 Structure of the B-DNA decamer C-C-A-A-C-I-T-T-G-G in two different space groups: conformational flexibility of B-DNA. *Biochemistry, Wash.* **32**, 1373–1389.

Lloyd, R.G. & Sharples, G.J. 1993 Dissociation of synthetic Holliday junction by *E. coli* RecG protein. *EMBO J.* **12**, 17–22.

Lu, M., Guo, Q., Seeman, N.C. & Kallenbach, N.R. 1989 DNaseI cleavage of branched DNA molecules. *J. biol. Chem.* **264**, 20851–20854.

Mizuuchi, K., Kemper, B., Hays, J. & Weisberg, R.A. 1982 T4 endonuclease VII cleaves Holliday structures. *Cell* **29**, 357–365.

Møllegaard, N.E., Murchie, A.I.H., Lilley, D.M.J. & Nielsen, P.E. 1994 Uranyl photoprobing of a four-way DNA junction: Evidence for specific metal ion binding. *EMBO J.* **13**, 1508–1513.

Mueller, J.E., Kemper, B., Cunningham, R.P., Kallenbach, N.R. & Seeman, N.C. 1988 T4 endonuclease VII cleaves the crossover strands of Holliday junction analogs. *Proc. natn. Acad. Sci. U.S.A.* **85**, 9441–9445.

Murchie, A.I.H., Carter, W.A., Portugal, J. & Lilley, D.M.J. 1990 The tertiary structure of the four-way DNA junction affords protection against DNaseI cleavage. *Nucl. Acids Res.* **18**, 2599–2606.

Murchie, A.I.H., Clegg, R.M., von Kitzing, E., Duckett, D.R., Diekmann, S. & Lilley, D.M.J. 1989 Fluorescence energy transfer shows that the four-way DNA junction is a right-handed cross of antiparallel molecules. *Nature, Lond.* **341**, 763–766.

Murchie, A.I.H. & Lilley, D.M.J. 1993 T4 endonuclease VII cleaves DNA containing a cisplatin adduct. *J. molec. Biol.* **233**, 77–85.

Murchie, A.I.H., Portugal, J. & Lilley, D.M.J. 1991 Cleavage of a four-way DNA junction by a restriction enzyme spanning the point of strand exchange. *EMBO J.* **10**, 713–718.

Nunes-Düby, S.E., Matsomoto, L. & Landy, A. 1987 Site-specific recombination intermediates trapped with suicide substrates. *Cell* **50**, 779–788.

Panayotatos, N. & Backman, S. 1989 A site-targeted recombinant nuclease probe of DNA structure. *J. biol. Chem.* **264**, 15070–15073.

Panyutin, I.G. & Hsieh, P. 1994 The kinetics of spontaneous DNA branch migration. *Proc. natn. Acad. Sci. U.S.A.* **91**, 2021–2025.

Parsons, C.A., Kemper, B. & West, S.C. 1990 Interaction of a four-way junction in DNA with T4 endonuclease VII. *J. biol. Chem.* **265**, 9285–9289.

Parsons, C.A., Tsaneva, I., Lloyd, R.G. & West, S.C. 1992 Interaction of *Escherichia coli* RuvA and RuvB proteins with synthetic Holliday junctions. *Proc. natn. Acad. Sci. U.S.A.* **89**, 5452–5456.

Pöhler, J.R.G., Duckett, D.R. & Lilley, D.M.J. 1994 Structure of four-way DNA junctions containing a nick in one strand. *J. molec. Biol.* **238**, 62–74.

Pontiggia, A., Negri, A., Beltrame, M. & Bianchi, M.E. 1993 Protein HU binds specifically to kinked DNA. *Molec. Microbiol.* **7**, 343–350.

Reardon, J. & Sancar, A. 1991 The repair of uv-damaged DNA. In *Nucleic Acids and Molecular. Biology*, vol. 5 (ed. F. Eckstein, D. M. J. Lilley), pp 54–71. Heidelberg: Springer-Verlag.

Rice, J.A., Crothers, D.E., Pinto, A.L. & Lippard, S.J. 1988 The major adduct of the antitumor drug *cis*-diamminedichloroplatinum (II) with DNA bends the duplex by ∼ 40° towards the major groove. *Proc. natn. Acad. Sci. U.S.A.* **85**, 4158–4161.

Sharples, G.J. & Lloyd, R.G. 1991 Resolution of Holliday junctions in *E. coli*: Identification of the *ruvC* gene product as a 19 kDa protein. *J. Bact.* **173**, 7711–7715.

Sharples, G.J. & Lloyd, R.G. 1993 An *E. coli* RuvC mutant defective in cleavage of synthetic Holliday junctions. *Nucl. Acids Res.* **21**, 3359–3364.

Sigal, N. & Alberts, B. 1972 Genetic recombination: the nature of crossed strand-exchange between two homologous DNA molecules. *J. molec. Biol.* **71**, 789–793.

Timsit, Y., Westhof, E., Fuchs, R.P.P. & Moras, D. 1989 Unusual helical packing in crystals of DNA bearing a mutation hot spot. *Nature, Lond.* **341**, 459–462.

Tsaneva, I.R., Muller, B. & West, S.C. 1992 ATP-dependent branch migration of Holliday junctions promoted by the RuvA and RuvB proteins of *E. coli. Cell* **69**, 1171–1180.

Tsaneva, I.R., Muller, B. & West, S.C. 1993 RuvA and RuvB proteins of *Escherichia coli* exhibit DNA helicase activity in vitro. *Proc. natn. Acad. Sci. U.S.A.* **90**, 1315–1319.

Visse, R., de Ruijter, M., Brouwer, J., Brandsma, J.A. & van de Putte, P. 1991 Uvr excision repair protein complex of *Escherichia coli* binds to the convex side of a cisplatin-induced kink in the DNA. *J. biol. Chem.* **266**, 7609–7617.

von Kitzing, E., Lilley, D.M.J. & Diekmann, S. 1990 The stereochemistry of a four-way DNA junction: a theoretical study. *Nucl. Acids Res.* **18**, 2671–2683.

West, S.C., Parsons, C.A. & Picksley, S.M. 1987 Purification and properties of a nuclease from *Saccharomyces cerevisiae* that cleaves DNA at cruciform junction. *J. biol. Chem.* **262**, 12752–12758.

5

Site-specific recombination and circular chromosome segregation

DAVID J. SHERRATT, LIDIA K. ARCISZEWSKA, GARRY BLAKELY,
SEAN COLLOMS, KAREN GRANT*, NICK LESLIE
AND RICHARD McCULLOCH‡

Microbiology Unit, Department of Biochemistry, University of Oxford, South Parks Road, Oxford OX1 3QU, U.K.

SUMMARY

The Xer site-specific recombination system functions in *Escherichia coli* to ensure that circular plasmids and chromosomes are in the monomeric state prior to segregation at cell division. Two recombinases, XerC and XerD, bind cooperatively to a recombination site present in the *E. coli* chromosome and to sites present in natural multicopy plasmids. In addition, recombination at the natural plasmid site *cer*, present in ColE1, requires the function of two additional accessory proteins, ArgR and PepA. These accessory proteins, along with accessory DNA sequences present in the recombination sites of plasmids are used to ensure that recombination is exclusively intramolecular, converting circular multimers to monomers. Wild-type and mutant recombination proteins have been used to analyse the formation of recombinational synapses and the catalysis of strand exchange *in vitro*. These experiments demonstrate how the same two recombination proteins can act with different outcomes, depending on the organization of DNA sites at which they act. Moreover, insight into the separate roles of the two recombinases is emerging.

1. INTRODUCTION

In site-specific recombination, recombinase proteins catalyse conservative break–join reactions at specific sites in DNA. Site-specific recombination is involved in a range of programmed DNA rearrangements in microbes. These include the integration and excision of viruses into and out of the bacterial chromosome, inversion gene switches that control the expression of bacterial cell-surface proteins and phage tail proteins, the processing of transposition intermediates and the copy-number control and stable segregation of plasmids (reviewed in Stark *et al.* 1992).

The physical state of circular chromosomes, unlike linear chromosomes, can be changed by homologous recombination. Any number of homologous recombinational exchanges between sister, or homologous, linear chromosomes will generate linear chromosomes of the same size as the parents (assuming the parents are of the same length and have the same gene organization). In contrast, odd numbers of homologous recombinational exchanges between sister, or homologous, circular chromosomes will lead to circles in which two chromosomes-worth of DNA are present in a single dimeric DNA molecule (Figure 1).

The Xer site-specific recombination system appears to function in *Escherichia coli* to convert circular dimers

of the *E. coli* chromosome and of multicopy plasmids to monomers, thereby helping chromosome and plasmid segregation at cell division. This system requires two related recombinase proteins, XerC and XerD, en-

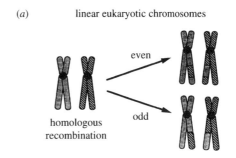

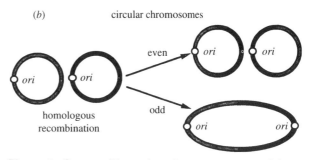

Figure 1. Cartoon illustrating the consequences of homologous recombination on (*a*) linear and (*b*) circular chromosomes. Note that on linear chromosomes, homologous exchanges can occur between homologues (shown) or between sister chromosomes.

* Present address: Wellcome Molecular Parasitology Unit, Anderson College, Church Street, Glasgow G11 5JS, U.K.
‡ Present address: Netherlands Cancer Institute, Antoni Van Leeuwenhoek Huis, Plesmanlaan 121, 1066 CX Amsterdam, The Netherlands.

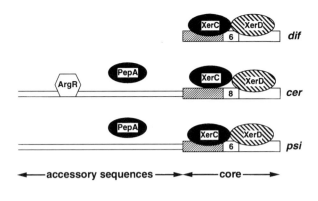

Figure 2. Xer recombination sites. The top panel provides a cartoon of the *dif*, *cer* and *psi* recombination sites while the bottom panel shows the sequence of a number of core recombination sites. A functional *dif* site consists of just a recombination core of XerC and XerD binding sites separated by 6 b.p. A functional *cer* site is about 220 b.p. ArgR binds about 100 b.p. upstream of the core site. We do not yet know if PepA binds DNA and/or interacts with one of the other recombination proteins. *psi* (present in plasmid pSC101; Cornet & Louarn 1994) has accessory sequences that do not interact with ArgR. PepA is required for its recombination, which shows resolution selectivity. Note that in *cer* the XerC binding site is 2 b.p. removed from the XerD binding site when compared to *dif*. This will result in increased spacing and approximate 72° rotation in relative position between the two binding sites.

	XerC	central region	XerD
cer	GGTGCGTACAA	TTAAGGGA	TTATGGTAAAT
psi	GGTGCGCGCAA	GATCCA	TTATGTTAAAC
clf	GGTACCGATAA	GGGATG	TTATGGTAAAT
cer 8-1	GGTGCGTACAA	TTGGGATG	TTATGGTAAAT
cer 6-1	GGTGCGTACAA	GGGATG	TTATGGTAAAT
dif	GGTGCGCATAA	TGTATA	TTATGTTAAAT
dif 8	GGTGCGCATAA	TTTGTATA	TTATGTTAAAT
dif 1-1	GGTGCGCATAA	TCTAGA	TTATGTTAAAT

consensus   GG$_{GA}^{TGC}$C$_{CGGC}^{GTAT}$AA   TTATG$_T^G$TAAA$_C^T$

coded at 4024 kb.p. and 3050 kb.p. on the *E. coli* chromosome respectively. Each recombinase is co-expressed with at least two other proteins that appear not to have a role in Xer recombination (Colloms *et al.* 1990; Blakely *et al.* 1993). XerC and XerD contain amino acid residues conserved in the integrase family of site-specific recombinases. Recombination at sites present in natural multicopy plasmids (for example, the 220 b.p. *cer* site in plasmid ColE1) requires two additional proteins, ArgR and PepA (Stirling *et al.* 1988, 1989), and is exclusively intramolecular (i.e. it shows resolution selectivity). In contrast a 32 b.p. sequence, *dif*, normally present in the replication terminus region of the *E. coli* chromosome and required for normal chromosomal segregation, recombines both inter- and intramolecularly when inserted into a plasmid recombination substrate (Blakely *et al.* 1991). Recombination at *dif* requires XerC and XerD but not ArgR and PepA. These and other results indicate that ArgR and PepA act as accessory proteins and are involved in determining resolution selectivity (Summers

1989; Blakely *et al.* 1993). Similarly 190 b.p. of the 220 b.p. *cer* site are accessory sequences that function in resolution selectivity, whilst the remaining 30–32 b.p. constitute the recombination core, that is similar in sequence to the 32 b.p. *dif* site (see figure 2; Blakely *et al.* 1993).

Current experiments are aimed at understanding: (i) how the interactions of the recombination proteins with recombination sites generate a functional recombination synapse that may (*cer*) or may not (*dif*) show resolution selectivity during recombination; (ii) the catalytic mechanism of recombination; and (iii) how, precisely, recombination at *cer* and *dif* leads to stable circular replicon segregation at cell division.

2. RESULTS AND DISCUSSION

(a) *Interaction of XerC and XerD with* cer *and* dif *recombination core sites*

In figure 2 the overall structure of functional *cer* and *dif* sites are cartooned, and the DNA sequences of the core recombination sites of *cer*, *dif* and some related derivatives are shown. XerC binds to the left half of the core sites and XerD to the right half of the core sites (Blakely *et al.* 1993). The affinity of XerC for its half site is lower than that of XerD for its half site. Binding of both XerC and XerD is highly cooperative, with the affinity of each protein for its half site being 40–160-fold higher when the other recombinase is already bound (Blakely *et al.* 1993). Note that the *cer* core site and *dif* have 8 b.p. and 6 b.p. respectively in their central regions that separate the XerC and XerD binding sites. This difference results in reduced overall binding of XerC/XerD to *cer* when compared to *dif*, and a different overall geometry to the protein/DNA complex for the complexes with *cer* and *dif* (Blakely *et al.* 1993), so that the XerC/XerD complex with *cer* migrates more slowly than the equivalent complex with *dif* (Blakely *et al.* 1993).

Because the core *cer* site differs from *dif* not only in the length of the overlap region but in residues involved in XerC and XerD binding, a *dif* derivative containing 8 b.p. in its central region was constructed by inserting the dinucleotide TT to the 5′ end of the central region (see figure 2, which shows there is a one nucleotide difference in the XerD-binding site and a two nucleotide difference in the XerC-binding site). *dif8* has similar properties to *cer*; it is inactive as a core recombination site but when supplied with accessory sequences and the accessory proteins ArgR and PepA, as well as XerC and XerD, intramolecular resolution occurs *in vivo* with a plasmid containing two directly repeated sites.

The affinities of XerC/XerD to *dif8* and the overall geometry of the protein/DNA complex are more similar to that of the complex with *cer* than to the complex between wild-type *dif* and XerC/XerD. Similarly, a *cer* derivative containing only 6 b.p. in its central region (*cer6-1*) has the recombination properties of *dif*, recombining inter- and intramolecularly without accessory sequences and accessory proteins. Taken together, these observations show that the different recombination properties of *cer* and *dif* (i.e. exclusive intramolecular recombination compared to both inter- and intramolecular recombination respectively) and their different recombination requirements can be determined simply by changing the relative spacing of the XerC and XerD binding sites. Note, however, that recombination properties and requirements can also be changed by alterations to the XerC binding site. For example, *psi* and *clf* sites (see figure 2) have only a 6 b.p. central region. Nevertheless, they require accessory proteins and accessory sequences for recombination, which is exclusively intramolecular. *dif* differs from the *cfl* core site only in the XerC-binding site and central region and therefore these differences must determine the different recombination requirements and outcomes for these sites.

We have proposed (Blakely *et al.* 1993) that resolution selectivity can arise when recombinase–core site interactions and recombinase–recombinase interactions are too weak to allow stable recombination synapse formation. In systems where such interactions are strong enough to allow functional synapse formation, recombination can occur without additional proteins and DNA sequences and will show no selectivity for a particular configuration of recombination sites (e.g. recombination at *dif*, *cer6-1*; with FLP at *frt* sites and with Cre at *loxP* sites). We propose that sites with weaker recombinase interactions need additional DNA sequences and accessory proteins that interact with these sequences to form a functional recombinational synapse (e.g. *cer*, *dif8-1*, *psi*, *clf*; *res* and *gix* (the sites at which Tn3 resolvase and Gin invertase interact, respectively)). The complexity of such a nucleoprotein structure and the fact that the DNA will follow a highly defined path through such a complex, provides a mechanism for resolution selectivity (see Stark *et al.* 1989) that has been well documented for the Tn3 resolvase and Gin invertase systems.

(b) *Recombination at the chromosomal site* dif *and chromosome segregation*

E. coli dif is located in the replication terminus region of the chromosome (see figure 3) (Blakely *et al.* 1991; Kuempel *et al.* 1991). Deletion of *dif* with about 2 kb of flanking DNA results in cells that filament and show abberant chromosome segregation, a phenotype indistinguishable to that of XerC⁻ and XerD⁻ cells. Reinsertion of a 33 b.p. fragment containing the *dif* core site into the deleted region results in cells that appear to divide and segregate their chromosomes normally. This same fragment is a competent recombination site *in vivo* when inserted into a plasmid. Reinsertion of *dif* into either of two ectopic sites (close to *oriC* and within *lacZ*) of chromosomes deleted for normally located *dif*, does not suppress the filamentation-abberant segregation phenotype, despite the fact that such sites are competent for Xer recombination – as judged by their ability to recombine with *dif* sites present in a plasmid. As yet we do not understand why *dif* does not allow normal chromosomal segregation when inserted at these ectopic sites.

Since recombination at *dif*, at least when inserted in a plasmid, does not show resolution selectivity, how

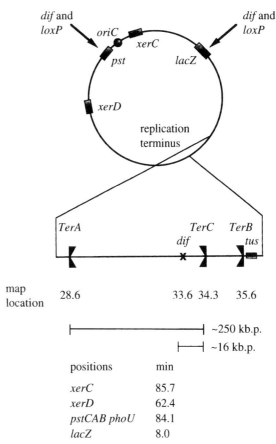

Figure 3. A diagrammatic map of the *E. coli* chromosome indicating the normal position of *dif* in the replication terminus region and two ectopic positions (constructed in a strain deleted for its normal *dif* site). The *loxP* site was also inserted at these positions. Neither *dif* nor *loxP* allowed normal chromosome segregation when inserted ectopically.

positions	min
xerC	85.7
xerD	62.4
pstCAB phoU	84.1
lacZ	8.0

does such recombination ensure that chromosomes are monomeric prior to cell division? We have proposed two models (Sherratt 1993). In the first, rapid Xer-mediated exchanges occur after *dif* is replicated, so that rapid interconversion of monomers to dimers occurs. The partition mechanism will then have an opportunity to segregate monomers. In the second model, one pair of Xer-mediated strand exchanges occurs and generates Holliday junction irrespective of whether the completely replicated chromosomes are destined to be monomers or dimers. As the partition mechanism begins to separate the joined chromosomes, a second pair of exchanges occurs in the direction that will ensure monomer segregation. The second model is attractive because of its economy and the possible separate control of the two pairs of strand exchanges in this system, but we have no direct experimental evidence to support it.

(c) *The role of the two recombinases, XerC and XerD, in Xer site-specific recombination*

The best characterized site-specific recombination systems (e.g. lambda Int, FLP, Cre) use a single recombinase to mediate the recombination event. Why then does the Xer system require two? Earlier experiments (Blakely *et al.* 1993) have demonstrated

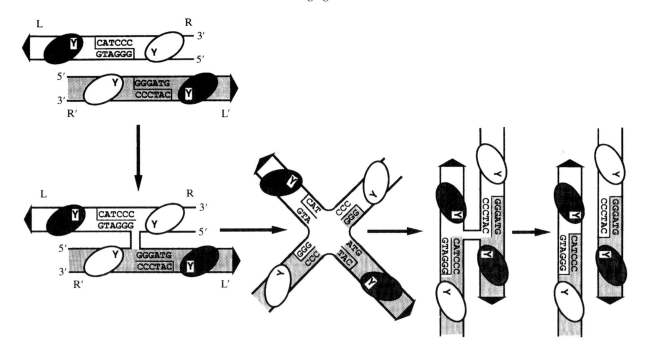

Figure 4. Cartoon showing a 'classical' view of the integrase family recombination mechanism as applied to the Xer system. XerC molecules are represented as unfilled ovoids while XerD molecules are shaded dark. The central region is that of *cer6.1*. After synapsis (here arbitrarily indicated in the antiparallel configuration) a pair of XerC-mediated strand exchanges give a Holliday junction containing intermediate. Branch migration/isomerization move the exchange point to where the XerD-mediated exchanges would be expected to occur. After such exchanges recombinant product forms.

that the asymmetry introduced into core recombination sites by having separate half-sites binding different recombinases (see figure 2), is used to ensure that only correctly aligned sites are recombined in the Xer system. In contrast, correct alignment is ensured in single recombinase systems by either using asymmetry outside of the core recombination site (e.g. with Tn3 *res*, Bednarz *et al.* 1990; Stark *et al.* 1992) or asymmetry at the centre of the core site in the region flanked by the strand exchanges (lambda Int, Gin; see Stark *et al.* 1992). We believe that the need for correct alignment does not provide the major reason for using two recombinases, since *dif* and *cer* sites contain symmetry in their central regions that in principle could be used to ensure that only correctly aligned sites recombine. We suspect, therefore, that the prime requirement for two recombinases is to be able to control the two pairs of strand exchanges differentially. Our data are consistent with each recombinase catalysing one pair of strand exchanges (Blakely *et al.* 1993). By having two recombinases, each pair of strand exchanges is potentially under separate biochemical and genetic control, thus allowing the production and resolution of Holliday junction intermediates to be functionally separated. How this relates to the biological role of this system remains unclear, though as indicated earlier, we have previously suggested how such functional separation of the pairs of strand exchanges could function in chromosome segregation (Sherratt 1993). Experimental evidence from both *in vivo* and *in vitro* experiments supports such functional separation. For example, Xer recombination between two directly repeated *cer* sites in a plasmid substrate *in vivo* in an *E. coli* strain, RM40, in which XerC

expression is under the stringent control of the *lac* promoter, can lead to the production of XerC-mediated Holliday junction-containing intermediates that persist over several hours after induction of XerC expression (McCulloch *et al.* 1994), despite the fact that such cells are *xerD+*. Similarly, *in vitro* assays using any of three different recombination substrates have demonstrated XerC-mediated strand exchanges in the absence of XerD-mediated exchanges in reactions that require the presence of both recombinases (see below). Nevertheless, both XerC and XerD mediated cleavages can be observed *in vitro* (see below), and have been inferred to occur *in vivo* (Blakely *et al.* 1993). Taken together, these results indicate that subtle changes in recombination site sequence and the structure of the complexes with recombination proteins can influence the outcome of the recombination reaction.

The separation of the XerC and XerD coding sequences on the *E. coli* chromosome, and the co-expression with other genes may also point to the importance of the functional separation of the XerC and XerD activity, though the genes co-expressed with XerC and XerD remain a bizarre collection with no apparent relation to the recombinase function: XerD is co-expressed with DsbC (previously XprA, see Lovett & Kolodner 1991) a periplasmic disulphide isomerase (Missiakas *et al.* 1994) and *RecJ*, a 5′ exonuclease involved in homologous recombination (Lovett & Kolodner 1991). XerC is co-expressed with a DapF (diaminopimelate epimerase) and two genes of unknown function (Richaud *et al.* 1987; Colloms *et al.* 1990). The functions of none of these other genes are essential for Xer recombination at *cer* or *dif* (our unpublished data).

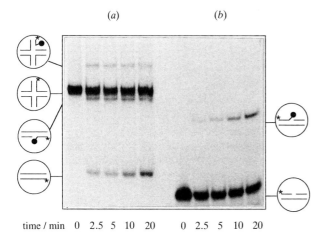

(a) *(b)*

time / min   0 2.5 5 10 20   0 2.5 5 10 20

Figure 5. Xer site-specific recombination *in vitro* on Holliday junction substrates *(a)* and linear suicide substrates *(b)*. Substrates contained the *cer6.1* core site and were incubated with purified XerC and XerD. The Holliday junctions were constructed as described in the text. The suicide substrates were constructed by annealing three oligonucleotides as shown in the diagram. The nick is between the third (G) and the fourth (A) nucleotide of the central region. XerC-mediated cleavage releases a trinucleotide and generates a stable covalent protein DNA intermediate ($\underline{\bullet}$) between XerC and recombinase. In panel *(a)*, the positions of duplex products and covalent intermediates are indicated. The gel is 4% polyacrylamide in TBE+0.16% SDS. Visualization was by autoradiography. The position of ³²P atoms is indicated (*).

(d) The Xer site-specific recombination strand exchange mechanism

The classical view of integrase family-mediated site-specific recombination when applied to the Xer system is cartooned in figure 3. Two recombinase molecules (one each of XerC and XerD in the Xer system) bind specifically to each core site. Recombinase–recombinase interactions now lead to recombination synapse formation. In systems using no additional accessory sequences or accessory proteins (e.g. FLP, Cre, Xer recombination at *dif*) recombinase–DNA and recombinase–recombinase interactions lead to synapsis which occurs irrespectively of the configuration of the recombination partners (i.e. whether on separate molecules or in either direct or inverted configuration on the same molecule). Within synaptic complexes, phosphodiester bond activation followed by two transesterifications (using a recombinase tyrosine nucleophile and a 5′ OH nucleotide nucleophile, respectively) lead to the completion of one pair of strand exchanges. Holliday junction branch migration/isomerization now place the intermediate ready for the second pair of transesterifications (see figure 3).

In order to test this model for the Xer system and in particular to determine the functional roles of the two recombinases, we constructed synthetic Holliday junction molecules containing the *cer6-1* core recombination site. We reasoned that such structures would avoid the need for a potentially rate-limiting synapsis step and should be good candidates for *in vitro* recombination substrates. The *cer6-1* sequence was chosen because it can recombine with or without accessory sequences

and accessory proteins. The initial substrates were produced by annealing four synthetic oligonucleotides of 76, 2×84 and 92 nucleotides. The resulting four-way junction could potentially branch migrate throughout the whole core region (but not beyond it) and each of the four arms has diagnostic restriction sites to allow product analysis. Subsequent substrates have had the junction position constrained to particular regions of the core by using heterology to block branch migration.

Recombinant product with any of these substrates requires that both XerC and XerD be present. In the presence of both proteins, recombinant products are observed (see figure 4, panel *a*). The products have the size expected for an XerC-mediated strand exchange (assuming XerC activates and cleaves the phosphodiester adjacent to its binding site, see figure 2). No evidence of XerD-mediated cleavage or substrates containing the *cer6-1* or *cer* cores sites has been observed for reasons we do not understand. The majority product from Xer-mediated cleavage is complete duplex in which both pairs of strand exchanges have been completed. Significant amounts of covalent complex between XerC recombinase and both duplex product and Holliday junction substrate were also observed. This has allowed mapping of the Xer-mediated cleavages in these intermediates (cleavage occurs between the last nucleotide of the XerC-binding site and the first nucleotide of the central region, see figure 2) and has allowed the demonstration that it is XerC rather than XerD that becomes covalently bound to DNA (by using fusion protein derivatives of both XerC and XerD that have different sizes to the parental protein, data not shown). By using mutants of XerC and XerD that are defective in their presumptive active site tyrosine nucleophile (Y converted to F) or defective in their presumptive activation domain (R converted to Q) or defective in both activation and nucleophile (Blakely *et al.* 1993), we have observed normal levels of XerC-mediated recombinant product when XerD is defective in nucleophile or activation domain, or both domains, as long as XerC is wild-type (though note that XerD protein needs to be present for reaction to occur). In contrast, mutation in either nucleophile or activation domain of XerC abolishes recombinant product formation on this substrate, confirming that XerC is mediating the catalysis we observed. We have observed no functional complementation between XerC and XerD mutant proteins. Moreover in mixtures containing XerD along with XerC^{YF} and XerC^{RQ} proteins we have observed no functional complementation between the XerC mutants (as measured by covalent complex production). All of these mutant proteins bind their cognate core recombination half-sites and can interact cooperatively. We therefore have found no evidence to support the fractional active site hypothesis of Jayaram and co-workers (Chen *et al.* 1992; Jayaram 1994) which suggests that for FLP recombinase, two recombinase protomers cooperate to form a catalytically-active molecule in which a single-strand exchange is mediated by the activation domain of one protomer and the nucleophile of the other protomer acting in *trans*. Certainly our data are inconsistent with the 'trans-diagonal' and 'trans-horizontal' models of Jayaram and co-workers as applied to Holliday junction resolution in the Xer system; moreover, we can find no support for their 'trans-vertical' model in our system. We therefore favour the idea that on a Holliday junction substrate a single XerC molecule promotes both phosphodiester activation and nucleophilic attack at that activated phosphodiester.

We find essentially the same results with a 'suicide' substrate (see figure 5b). In this linear substrate a recombinase-mediated cleavage leads to the diffusion away of a trinucleotide (Pargellis *et al.* 1987), thus stabilizing the recombinase–DNA covalent intermediate. With such substrates we have observed XerC but not XerD-mediated catalysis. Attempts at complementation have yielded the same results as for the Holliday junction substrate.

In other experiments (data not shown), we have used supercoiled substrates containing two directly repeated *cer* sites or two directly repeated *psi* sites (see figure 2). Addition of two recombinases and appropriate accessory proteins leads to recombinant product formation. The recombinants have a unique topology, confirming our ideas about resolution selectivity. With the *cer* substrate, the products are Holliday junction-containing supercoils in which XerC-mediated catalysis has occurred. In contrast, the *psi* substrate undergoes both pairs of strand exchanges. This preliminary result further confirms how subtle changes in recombination sites can effect the outcome of Xer recombination.

We thank our many colleagues for help and useful discussions. Particularly, we thank Jenny Stephens for preparing the manuscript, Mary Burke for technical assistance and Marshall Stark for advice and ideas. The work was supported by the MRC, SERC and the Wellcome Trust.

REFERENCES

Bednarz, A.L., Boocock, M.R. & Sherratt, D.J. 1990 Determinants of correct *res* site alignment in site-specific recombination by Tn3 resolvase. *Genes Dev.* **4**, 2366–2375.

Blakely, G., Colloms, S., May, G., Burke, M. & Sherratt, D.J. 1991 *Escherichia coli* XerC recombinase is required for chromosomal segregation at cell division. *New Biol.* **8**, 789–798.

Blakely, G., May, G., McCulloch, R., Arciszewska, L.K. 1993 Two related recombinases are required for site-specific recombination at *dif* and *cer* in E. coli K12. *Cell* **75**, 351–361.

Chen, J.-W., Lee, J. & Jayaram, M. 1992 DNA cleavage in trans by the active site tyrosine during FLP recombination: switching protein partners before exchanging strands. *Cell*, **69**, 647–658.

Colloms, S.D., Sykora, P., Szatmari, G. & Sherratt, D.J. 1990 Recombination at ColE1 *cer* requires the *Escherichia coli xerC* gene product, a member of the Lambda integrase family of site-specific recombinases. *J. Bact.* **172**, 6973–6980.

Jayaram, M. 1993 Phosphoryl transfer in Flp recombination: a template for strand transfer mechanisms. *Trends Biochem. Sci.* **19**, 78–82.

Kuempel, P.L., Henson, J.M., Dircks, L., Tecklenburg, M. & Lim, D.F. 1991 *dif*, a recA-independent recombination site in the terminus regions of the chromosome of *Escherichia coli. New Biol.* **3**, 799–811.

Lovett, S.T. & Kolodner, R.D. 1991 Nucleotide sequence of the *Escherichia coli* recJ chromosomal region and construction of RecJ-overexpression plasmids. *J. Bact.* **173**, 353–364.

McCulloch, R., Coggins, L.W., Colloms, S.D. & Sherratt, D.J. 1994 Xer-mediated site-specific recombination at *cer* generates Holliday junctions *in vivo. EMBO J.* **13**, 1844–1855.

McCulloch, R., Burke, M.E. & Sherratt, D.J. 1994 Peptidase activity of *Escherichia coli* aminopeptidase A is not required for its role in Xer site-specific recombination. *Molec. Microbiol.* **12**, 241–251.

Missiakas, D., Georgopoulos, C. & Raina, S. 1994 The *Escherichia coli dsbC* (*xprA*) gene encodes a periplasmic protein involved in disulfide bond formation. *EMBO J.* **13**, 2013–2020.

Richaud, C., Higgins, W., Mengin-Lecreulx, D. & Stragier, P. 1987 Molecular cloning, characterization, and chromosomal localization of *dapF*, the *Escherichia coli* gene for diaminopimelate epimerase. *J. Bact.* **169**, 1454–1459.

Stark, W.M., Boocock, M.R. & Sherratt, D.J. 1989 Site-specific recombination by Tn3 resolvase. *Trends Genet.* **5**, 304–309.

Stark, W.M., Boocock, M.R., Sherratt, D.J. 1992 Catalysis by site-specific recombinases. *Trends Genet.* **8**, 432–439.

Stirling, C.J., Stewart, G. & Sherratt, D.J. 1988 Multicopy plasmid stability in *Escherichia coli* requires host-encoded functions that lead to plasmid site-specific recombination. *Mol. gen. Genet.* **214**, 80–84.

Stirling, C.J., Szatmari, G., Stewart, G., Smith, M.C.M. & Sherratt, D.J. 1988 The arginine repressor is essential for plasmid-stabilizing site-specific recombination at the ColE1 *cer* locus. *EMBO J.* **7**, 4389–4395.

Stirling, C.J., Colloms, S., Collins, J.F., Szatmari, G. & Sherratt, D.J. 1989 *xerB*, an *Escherichia coli* gene required for plasmid ColE1 site-specific recombination is identical to *pepA*, encoding aminopeptidase A, a protein with substantial similarity to bovine lens leucine aminopeptidase. *EMBO J.* **8**, 1623–27.

Summers, D.K. & Sherratt, D.J. 1988 Resolution of ColE1 dimers requires a DNA sequence implicated in the three-dimensional organization of the *cer* site. *EMBO J.* **7**, 851–858.

Sherratt, D.J. 1993 Site-specific recombination and the segregation of circular chromosomes. *Nucl. Acids mol. Biol.* **7**, 202–216.

6

Steps along the pathway of V(D)J recombination

MARTIN GELLERT AND J. FRASER McBLANE

Laboratory of Molecular Biology, National Institute of Diabetes and Digestive and Kidney Diseases, Building 5, Room 241, National Institutes of Health, Bethesda, Maryland 20892, U.S.A.

SUMMARY

The mechanism of lymphoid-specific gene rearrangement (V(D)J recombination) is discussed, with a focus on the existence of broken DNA intermediates. Older evidence in support of this idea includes the sequence alterations at the recombined junctions and the presence of aberrant recombinants. More recently, broken DNA molecules have been directly detected in recombinationally active cells. The signal sequence ends have normal blunt-ended DNA breaks, but the coding ends have a hairpin (self-joined) structure that provides an explanation for the self-complementary P nucleotide insertions often found after V(D)J joining in the antigen receptor genes.

1. INTRODUCTION

During the development of lymphoid cells, a series of DNA rearrangements puts functional immunoglobulin and T-cell receptor genes together from the gene fragments existing in germline DNA. Because of the many possible choices of the V, D, and J segments that are joined, these DNA rearrangements are responsible for generating much of the diversity of the immune system (Tonegawa 1983; Blackwell & Alt 1988; Gellert 1992; Kallenbach *et al.* 1992). This article will compare the reaction, which is generally called V(D)J recombination, with other recombination systems for the purpose of gaining some insights about its mechanism.

V(D)J joining always occurs at the boundaries between a pair of coding segments and the recombination signal sequences that adjoin them. These signal sequences are made up of conserved heptamer and nonamer motifs (their consensus sequences are CACAGTG and ACAAAAACC), separated by a spacer of 12 or 23 (±1) base pairs (b.p.) of non-conserved sequence. Joining is efficient only when the two signals have different spacer lengths (the 12/23 rule). The coding segments become fused in a structure called a coding joint, and the signals are joined by fusing heptamer to heptamer (a signal joint). Because the coding side of the recombination site is not specifically recognized (almost any sequence can be used), a coding joint looks much like random-sequence DNA, and could not be identified as resulting from V(D)J recombination unless one knew its history.

2. SIGNIFICANCE OF INEXACT JOINING

Some clues about the reaction come from the structures of the recombined junctions. Although signal joints are normally precise fusions of the two signal sequences, V(D)J coding joints are remarkably imprecise. Often a few bases from one or both ends have been lost, and

several bases of non-germline DNA have been inserted. It is well known that these alterations are responsible for a large share of immune system diversity because the sequence around the junction forms part of the antigen binding site in both immunoglobulins and T-cell receptors. By contrast, most types of site-specific recombination (such as those catalysed by the integrase and resolvase enzymes) exchange DNA strands precisely, without loss or gain of nucleotides.

The imprecision of coding joints gives indications about the reaction mechanism. It means that there cannot be close coupling (by protein–DNA bonds or other means) of the beginning and end of the process. At some time in between, the ends of the coding sequence must be available for modification. Furthermore, as a result of the increasing number of sequenced junctions, it is now possible to distinguish two types of insertions, one non-templated and one whose sequence depends on the attached coding end. Non-templated sequences up to 15 nucleotides long (called N regions) are added by the enzyme terminal deoxynucleotidyl transferase (TdT), which is expressed mainly in the early lymphoid cells where V(D)J recombination occurs. In situations where TdT is not expressed, such as fibroblasts where V(D)J recombination is activated by expression of the *RAG1* and *RAG2* genes, coding joints are formed without N regions, but the recombination process is otherwise normal (Kallenbach *et al.* 1992). Similarly, in mice with a disruption of the *TdT* gene, V(D)J joining proceeds normally except that N regions are absent (Gilfillan *et al.* 1993; Komori *et al.* 1993).

A second class of templated insertions is more enlightening; it adds DNA with a sequence related to the attached coding end. It was noted that commonly one or two nucleotides complementary to the last base(s) of the coding end are added but occasionally longer, complementary inserts of 3 to 5 nucleotides are found (Lafaille *et al.* 1989; McCormack *et al.* 1989).

These 'P nucleotide' insertions (P for palindromic) have been useful in clarifying the reaction mechanism. Most or all of them are attached to coding ends that have not lost any nucleotides, implying that the addition occurred early in the recombination process, before any removal of bases. Furthermore, complementary insertions are most likely to result from the resolution of a DNA hairpin precursor; as is discussed below, these DNA structures have actually been observed.

3. DNA WITH DOUBLE-STRAND BREAKS

The variability of coding joints implies that DNA with double-strand breaks might well be an intermediate in the reaction. Support for this idea also comes from a class of aberrant products of V(D)J recombination, in which a signal sequence becomes attached to the coding segment that originally flanked its partner signal. It seems that the recombining pieces are at the same time available for joining in either a correct or an incorrect configuration. These 'hybrid joints' (Lewis *et al.* 1988; Morzycka-Wroblewska *et al.* 1988) can represent more than 20% of all the recombination events in some artificial substrates.

A search for broken DNA associated with V(D)J recombination was thus plausible, and recently such broken molecules have been detected in mouse lymphoid cells, at the TCRδ locus (Roth *et al.* 1992), at the immunoglobulin loci (Schlissel *et al.* 1993), and at the TCRβ locus (J. F. McBlane, unpublished results). An initially puzzling result was that all of the broken DNA at TCRδ in cells of normal mice corresponded to signal ends only, although each primary breakage should liberate both a signal and a coding end. The puzzle of the missing coding ends was solved when DNA from *scid* mice was looked at. Mice with the *scid* defect lack mature B or T cells, and only occasionally have correct V(D)J rearrangements in their antigen receptor genes (Schuler *et al.* 1986; Bosma & Carroll 1991). In *scid* lymphoid cell lines, a defect in V(D)J recombination can readily be shown, and it is apparent that the two types of junctions are very differently affected. Although signal joints are made at a normal rate, very few coding joints are completed (Lieber *et al.* 1988; Blackwell *et al.* 1989). Thus it must still be possible to initiate V(D)J recombination in *scid* cells, but a later step in the pathway to coding joints is apparently blocked.

In DNA from *scid* cells, it is found that both the broken coding end and signal end resulting from cleavage at the same site are detectable (Roth *et al.* 1992). One presumes this is because the coding ends in *scid* cells are prevented from joining and thus have a longer life. In fact, coding ends and signal ends are present in comparable amounts.

4. HAIRPIN DNA IN V(D)J RECOMBINATION

The striking result is that the coding ends have the hairpin DNA structure anticipated from the presence of P nucleotides; they are closed back on themselves,

apparently with the 5′ end at the break joined to the 3′ end of the complementary strand (Roth *et al.* 1992) (see figure 1). Broken coding ends have been detected at three sites in the TCRδ locus, and in each case they are covalently sealed in this way. Hairpins are strange structures to be recombination intermediates, because they cannot take part in joining without first being re-broken, but the presence of P nucleotides provides compelling evidence for this pathway. Figure 1 shows in more detail how the off-centre nicking of a hairpin, followed by fill-in of the shorter strand, would naturally result in adding complementary bases to the coding end. Studies of the structure of hairpin DNA have shown that a hairpin cannot be double-stranded all the way to its tip, because of the constraint of turning the chain back on itself. In a fully self-complementary DNA, at least two and more probably four bases have to be unpaired, and may then be recognized and nicked, perhaps off-centre, by a single-strand-specific nuclease. This model was originally suggested to explain the self-complementary insertions (quite simi-

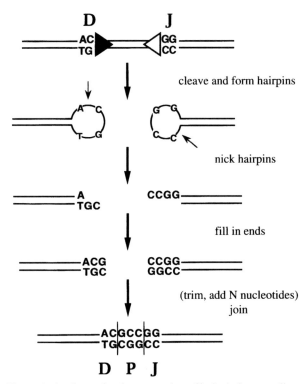

Figure 1. A scheme for the processing of hairpin intermediates to generate self-complementary insertions. The drawing shows the joining of two coding segments labelled D and J. In the top panel, the last two base pairs of D and the first two base pairs of J are shown. The DNA is cleaved at both signal/coding borders, leaving a hairpin structure with four unpaired bases on each coding end. A nick on one side of each hairpin, one base from the terminus on the left and two bases on the right (at the sites marked by the small arrows), leaves single-stranded tails whose last one or two nucleotides are complementary to the original end. If the normal convention is used that the top strand reads 5′ to 3′ from left to right, the ends as drawn can be filled in by a DNA polymerase. Later nucleotide removal by an exonuclease or addition by TdT could occur before joining, but is not shown here. To simplify the figure, the signal ends are not shown after breakage. The self-complementary (P nucleotide) insertion is indicated in the bottom panel.

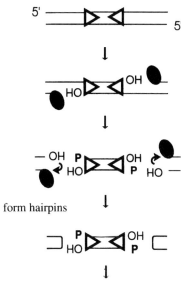

form hairpins

cleave hairpins, join coding ends
join signal ends

Figure 2. A possible scheme for V(D)J recombination involving a covalent protein–DNA intermediate. The triangles represent the signal sequences, and the dark ellipses indicate bound protein molecules. As drawn, the first nick at each signal/coding border attaches a protein to the 5′ end of the coding DNA and leaves a free 3′ end on the signal. A nick on the other strand then results in a blunt end on the signal and yields a 3′-hydroxyl end on the coding DNA that is capable of attacking the protein–DNA bond, displacing the protein and generating a hairpin end.

lar to P nucleotides) found after the excision of transposable elements in plants (Coen *et al.* 1986). The hairpin processing may not always leave a P nucleotide trace, because the nick can also be in the exact centre of the hairpin and leave no overhang. Alternatively, a P nucleotide tract initially formed could be trimmed off during later processing of the end.

How might hairpins be formed? A number of known biochemical reactions can couple cleavage of a DNA bond with rejoining to the same DNA or a new DNA partner. This is the well-known activity of topoisomerases, and a speculative model based on this class of enzymes is presented below. All topoisomerases share the same basic mode of operation. While breaking DNA, the protein attaches to one broken end, usually through a phosphoryl-tyrosine bond, and then this protein–DNA bond activates the DNA end for rejoining to either the same or a different partner DNA. Some of these enzymes and their close relatives (for instance the nicking-joining enzyme of vaccinia virus (Reddy & Bauer 1989) and the A* protein of phage φX174 (van der Ende *et al.* 1981)) are known to be capable of generating DNA hairpins. Hairpins can also result from the reaction of the topoisomerase-like phage λ Int or yeast Flp recombinases, when they act at damaged recombination sites (Nash & Robertson 1989; Chen *et al.* 1992).

In the hypothetical scheme (Roth *et al.* 1993) shown in figure 2, the protein that nicks at the signal-coding border ends up attached to the coding DNA. A subsequent nick (without protein attachment) on the other strand leaves a DNA end capable of attacking the

protein–DNA bond, making a hairpin and liberating the bound protein. This scheme is preferred to an alternative involving a second protein–DNA bond that, by chemical symmetry, would leave a bound protein on one strand of the signal end. The preference derives from recent experiments probing the structure of broken signal ends in more detail. These experiments have shown that the signal ends have the simplest possible structure: almost all of them are cut at the border of the signal sequence and at the same position on both strands, leaving blunt ends. Furthermore, the ends are available for ligation to (non-phosphorylated) adapter fragments of DNA, and so must be free of any interfering protein fragments, the exposed 5′ ends carrying a phosphoryl group (Roth *et al.* 1993; Schlissel *et al.* 1993).

This is by no means the only possible mechanism. Another class of DNA strand–transfer enzymes, typified by the phage Mu transposase, can activate and transfer a DNA end without covalent linkage at any stage (Mizuuchi 1992). Such a process would avoid the need for an unsymmetrical reaction posed by the scheme shown in figure 2.

Until now we have discussed the formation of hairpin ends, but we also have to inquire how they are processed once made. One starting point is to ask why hairpins accumulate in *scid* cells. It is possible that the *scid* defect arrests the normal processing of hairpin DNA, blocking the pathway leading to coding joints at this stage. An observation consistent with this idea is that among the rare coding joints found in *scid* cells, some contain P nucleotide tracts much longer than those in normal cells, with up to 15 added nucleotides perfectly complementary to the adjoining coding sequence (Kienker *et al.* 1991; Schuler *et al.* 1991). In rare cases, this hairpin processing defect might be bypassed by a random nick further from the tip, leading to a junction with a long stretch of P nucleotides. However, the observation that hairpin-ended DNA transfected into *scid* cells is rejoined with normal efficiency (Lewis 1994) does not agree with this model, leaving only the possible reservation that transfected DNA may be subject to different processing from DNA resident in the nucleus.

The exact role of the *scid* factor in V(D)J recombination is still unknown. However, it has become clear that the *scid* factor operates more generally in DNA repair. It is widely expressed, as shown by the fact that non-lymphoid *scid* cell lines are hypersensitive to X-rays and defective in DNA double-strand break repair (Fulop & Phillips 1990; Biedermann *et al.* 1991; Hendrickson *et al.* 1991). The role of a general repair function in V(D)J joining is made more plausible by recent observations that mutations in several other DNA repair genes also induce a defect in V(D)J recombination (Pergola *et al.* 1993; Taccioli *et al.* 1993; Taccioli *et al.* 1994). One class of these mutations has now been shown to affect the Ku protein that is known to preferentially bind to DNA ends (Getts & Stamato 1994; Rathmell & Chu 1994).

Double-strand breaks can be initiating events in homologous recombination. In those cases, the broken ends invade the unbroken DNA partner leading, eventually, to the formation of a Holliday junction. In V(D)J recombination there is no partner capable of donating a homologous sequence bridging the final junction, so that the usage of the broken molecules must be quite different. Because they carry no recognition sites, the coding ends in particular may plausibly be joined by a process with many features common to the repair of double-strand breaks resulting from DNA damage. This could account for the linkage to multiple repair functions. In this context, the DNA hairpin intermediates remain enigmatic. It would be surprising if damaged DNA commonly passed through a hairpin stage on its way to repair, so it is unclear how the hairpins generated by the V(D)J process become engaged with the repair machinery. However, the possibility that hairpin structures are used in the repair of some forms of DNA damage has not been systematically tested, and may be worth pursuing.

We are grateful to the members of our laboratory for many valuable discussions.

REFERENCES

Biedermann, K.A., Sun, J.R., Giaccia, A.J., Tosto, L.M. & Brown, J.M. 1991 *scid* mutation in mice confers hypersensitivity to ionizing radiation and a deficiency in DNA double-strand break repair. *Proc. natn. Acad. Sci. U.S.A.* **88**, 1394–1397.

Blackwell, K., Malynn, B., Pollock, R., *et al.* 1989 Isolation of scid pre-B cells that rearrange kappa light chain genes: formation of normal signal and abnormal coding joins. *EMBO J.* **8**, 735–742.

Blackwell, T.K. & Alt, F.W. 1988 Immunoglobulin genes. In *Molecular immunology* (ed. B. D. Hames & D. M. Glover), pp. 1–60. Oxford: IRL Press.

Bosma, M.J. & Carroll, A.M. 1991 The scid mouse mutant: definition, characterization, and potential uses. *A. Rev. Immunol.* **9**, 323–344.

Chen, J.-W., Lee, J. & Jayaram, M. 1992 DNA cleavage in trans by the active site tyrosine during Flp recombination: switching protein partners before exchanging strands. *Cell* **69**, 647–658.

Coen, E.S., Carpenter, R. & Martin, C. 1986 Transposable elements generate novel spatial patterns of gene expression in *Antirrhinum majus*. *Cell* **47**, 285–296.

Fulop, G.M. & Phillips, R.A. 1990 The *scid* mutation in mice causes a general defect in DNA repair. *Nature, Lond.* **347**, 479–482.

Gellert, M. 1992 Molecular analysis of V(D)J recombination. *A. Rev. Genet.* **22**, 425–446.

Getts, R.C. & Stamato, T.D. 1994 Absence of a Ku-like DNA end binding activity in the *xrs* double-strand DNA repair-deficient mutant. *J. biol. Chem.* **269**, 15981–15984.

Gilfillan, S., Dierich, A., Lemeur, M., Benoist, C. & Mathis, D. 1993 Mice lacking TdT: Mature animals with an immature lymphocyte repertoire. *Science, Wash.* **261**, 1175–1178.

Hendrickson, E.A., Qin, X.-Q., Bump, E.A., Schatz, D.G., Oettinger, M.A. & Weaver, D.T. 1991 A link between double-strand break-related repair and V(D)J recombination: the *scid* mutation. *Proc. natn. Acad. Sci. U.S.A.* **88**, 4061–4065.

Kallenbach, S., Doyen, N., Fanton d'Andon, M. & Rougeon, F. 1992 Three lymphoid-specific factors account for all junctional diversity characteristic of somatic assembly of T-cell receptor and immunoglobulin genes. *Proc. natn. Acad. Sci. U.S.A.* **89**, 2799–2803.

Kienker, L.J., Kuziel, W.A. & Tucker, P.W. 1991 T cell receptor γ and δ gene junctional sequences in SCID mice: excessive P nucleotide insertion. *J. exp. Med.* **174**, 769–773.

Komori, T., Okada, A., Stewart, V. & Alt, F.W. 1993 Lack of N regions in antigen receptor variable region genes of TdT-deficient lymphocytes. *Science, Wash.* **261**, 1171–1175.

Lafaille, J.J., DeCloux, A., Bonneville, M., Takagaki, Y. & Tonegawa, S. 1989 Junctional sequences of T cell receptor gamma delta genes: implications for gamma delta T cell lineages and for a novel intermediate of V-(D)-J joining. *Cell* **59**, 859–870.

Lewis, S.M. 1994 P nucleotide insertions and the resolution of hairpin DNA structures in mammalian cells. *Proc. natn. Acad. Sci. U.S.A.* **91**, 1332–1336.

Lewis, S.M., Hesse, J.E., Mizuuchi, K. & Gellert, M. 1988 Novel strand exchanges in V(D)J recombination. *Cell* **55**, 1099–1107.

Lieber, M.R., Hesse, J.E., Lewis, S., *et al.* 1988 The defect in murine severe combined immune deficiency: Joining of signal sequences but not coding segments in V(D)J recombination. *Cell* **55**, 7–16.

McCormack, W.T., Tjoelker, L.W., Carlson, L.M., *et al.* 1989 Chicken IgL gene rearrangement involves deletion of a circular episome and addition of single nonrandom nucleotides to both coding segments. *Cell* **56**, 785–791.

Mizuuchi, K. 1992 Transpositional recombination: Mechanistic insights from studies of Mu and other elements. *A. Rev. Biochem.* **61**, 1011–1051.

Morzycka-Wroblewska, E., Lee, F.E.H. & Desiderio, S.V. 1988 Unusual immunoglobulin gene rearrangement leads to replacement of recombinational signal sequences. *Science, Wash.* **242**, 261–263.

Nash, H.A. & Robertson, C.A. 1989 Heteroduplex substrates for bacteriophage lambda site-specific recombination: cleavage and strand transfer products. *EMBO J.* **8**, 3523–3533.

Pergola, F., Zdzienicka, M.Z. & Lieber, M.R. 1993 V(D)J recombination in mammalian cell mutants defective in DNA double-strand break repair. *Molec. Cell. Biol.* **13**, 3464–3471.

Rathmell, W.K. & Chu, G. 1994 A DNA end-binding factor involved in double-strand break repair and V(D)J recombination. *Molec. Cell. Biol.* **14**, 4741–4748.

Reddy, M.K. & Bauer, W.R. 1989 Activation of the vaccinia virus nicking-joining enzyme by trypsinization. *J. biol. Chem.* **264**, 443–449.

Roth, D.B., Menetski, J.P., Nakajima, P.B., Bosma, M.J. & Gellert, M. 1992 V(D)J recombination: broken DNA molecules with covalently sealed (hairpin) coding ends in scid mouse thymocytes. *Cell* **70**, 983–991.

Roth, D.B., Nakajima, P.B., Menetski, J.P., Bosma, M.J. & Gellert, M. 1992 V(D)J recombination in mouse thymocytes: double-strand breaks near T cell receptor δ rearrangement signals. *Cell* **69**, 41–53.

Roth, D.B., Zhu, C. & Gellert, M. 1993 Characterization of broken DNA molecules associated with V(D)J recombination. *Proc. natn. Acad. Sci. U.S.A.* **90**, 10788–10792.

Schlissel, M., Constantinescu, A., Morrow, T., Baxter, M. & Peng, A. 1993 Double-strand signal sequence breaks in V(D)J recombination are blunt, 5′-phosphorylated, RAG-dependent, and cell-cycle-regulated. *Genes Dev.* **7**, 2520–2532.

Schuler, W., Ruetsch, N.R., Amsler, M. & Bosma, M.J. 1991 Coding joint formation of endogenous T cell receptor genes in lymphoid cells from scid mice: unusual P-nucleotide additions in VJ-coding joints. *Eur. J. Immun.* **21**, 589–596.

Schuler, W., Weiler, I.J., Schuler, A., *et al.* 1986 Rearrangement of antigen receptor genes is defective in mice with severe combined immune deficiency. *Cell* **46**, 963–972.

Taccioli, G.E., Cheng, H.L., Varghese, A.J., Whitmore, G. & Alt, F.W. 1994 A DNA repair defect in Chinese hamster ovary cells affects V(D)J recombination similarly to the murine scid mutation. *J. biol. Chem.* **269**, 7439–7442.

Taccioli, G.E., Rathbun, G., Oltz, E., Stamato, T., Jeggo, P.A. & Alt, F.W. 1993 Impairment of V(D)J recombination in double-strand repair mutants. *Science, Wash.* **260**, 207–210.

Tonegawa, S. 1983 Somatic generation of antibody diversity. *Nature, Lond.* **302**, 575–581.

van der Ende, A., Langeveld, S., Teertstra, R., van Arkel, G. & Weisbeek, P.J. 1981 Enzymatic properties of the bacteriophage φX174 A* protein on superhelical φX174 DNA. *Nucl. Acids Res.* **9**, 2037–2053.

7

Regulation and mechanisms of gene amplification

KATHLEEN A. SMITH[1], MUNNA L. AGARWAL[2],
MICHAIL V. CHERNOV[2], OLGA B. CHERNOVA[2], YUTAKA DEGUCHI[2],
YUKIHITO ISHIZAKA[2], THOMAS E. PATTERSON[2],
MARIE-FRANCE POUPON[3] AND GEORGE R. STARK[2]

[1] *Imperial Cancer Research Fund, 44 Lincoln's Inn Fields, London WC2A 3PX, U.K.*
[2] *Department of Molecular Biology, Research Institute, The Cleveland Clinic Foundation, 9500 Euclid Avenue, Cleveland, Ohio 44195, U.S.A.*
[3] *CNRS URA 620, Institut Curie – Section de Biologie, 26, rue d'Ulm, F-75231 Paris, Cedex 05, France*

SUMMARY

Amplification in rodent cells usually involves bridge-breakage-fusion (BBF) cycles initiated either by end-to-end fusion of sister chromatids, or by chromosome breakage. In contrast, in human cells, resistance to the antimetabolite N-(phosphonacetyl)-L-aspartate (PALA) can be mediated by several different mechanisms that lead to overexpression of the target enzyme <u>c</u>arbamyl-P synthetase, <u>a</u>spartate transcarbamylase, <u>d</u>ihydro-orotase (CAD). Mechanisms involving BBF cycles account for only a minority of CAD amplification events in the human fibrosarcoma cell line HT 1080. Here, formation of a 2p isochromosome and overexpression of CAD by other types of amplification events (and even without amplification) are much more prevalent.

Broken DNA is recognized by mammalian cells with intact damage-recognition pathways, as a signal to arrest or to die. Loss of these pathways by, for example, loss of p53 or pRb tumour suppressor function, or by increased expression of *ras* and *myc* oncogenes, causes non-permissive rat and human cells to become permissive both for amplification and for other manifestations of DNA damage. In cells that are already permissive, amplification can be stimulated by overexpressing oncogenes such as c-*myc* or *ras*, or by damaging DNA in a variety of ways. To supplement genetic analysis of amplification in mammalian cells, an amplification selection has been established in *Schizosaccharomyces pombe*. Selection with LiCl yields cells with amplified *sod2* genes in structures related to those observed in mammalian cells. The effect on amplification in *S. pombe* can now be tested for any mutation in a gene involved in repair of damaged DNA or in normal cellular responses to DNA damage.

1. INTRODUCTION

Overexpression, through amplification of oncogenes and of genes that contribute to drug resistance, are important aspects of tumour development (Schwab 1990; Schwab & Amler 1990). Amplified DNA is a prominent manifestation of genetic instability in mammalian cells and is related, in origin, to several other abnormal forms of DNA (deletions, broken chromosomes, etc.) through the common participation of DNA strand breaks (for a review, see Stark *et al.* 1989, 1990; Windle & Wahl 1992; Stark 1993). Formation of broken DNA during the process of amplification stimulates regulation through damage-control mechanisms that recognize and respond to broken DNA in normal mammalian cells and that are defective in most tumours and cell lines. These defence mechanisms lead to the arrest or death of cells in which DNA damage persists and involve important tumour suppressor genes such as p53 and pRb. In this article, we discuss current information on amplification mechanisms in rodent and human cells, especially from the point of view of how the consequences of different mechanisms of amplification may be recognized and dealt with in normal cells.

2. MECHANISMS OF AMPLIFICATION
(a) Rodent cells

Most work on mechanisms of amplification has been done in cells of Syrian hamster, Chinese hamster and mouse, and has been reviewed recently by one of us (Stark 1993). Briefly, evidence from several laboratories reveals that dicentric chromosomes are a common intermediate and that bridge-breakage-fusion (BBF) is a common process in many – probably most – amplifications in rodent cells. Two BBF cycles are shown in figure 1, where it can be seen that asymmetric breakage of the DNA that lies between the two centromeres of a dicentric chromosome leads to unequal distribution of the intercentromere DNA into the two daughter cells. One daughter receives two copies of some intercentromere markers and the other

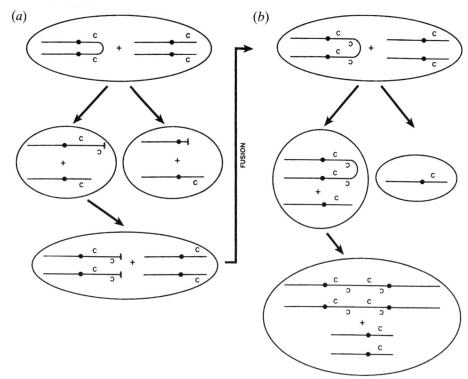

Figure 1. Two bridge-breakage-fusion (BBF) cycles follow the initial formation of a dicentric chromosome, caused by fusing two telomeres of sister chromatids. Note that in the mitotic cell at the top of (*b*), the dicentric chromatid will appear to be a pair of monocentric sister chromatids, whereas after a process such as segregation without breakage (b, bottom), a dicentric sister chromatid (as shown in figure 2) will become apparent. C, a marker gene such as CAD; ●, the centromeres.

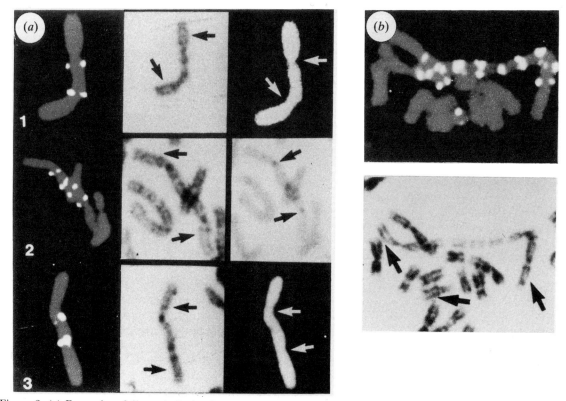

Figure 2. (*a*) Examples of dicentric Syrian hamster chromosomes with amplified CAD genes, present soon after the initial event. The columns (left to right) show *in situ* hybridization, G-banding (arrows point to B9q; the normal location of CAD is on B9p), and for example 2 only, C-banding (arrows point to centromeres). (*b*) A dicentric chromosome containing many amplified CAD genes, present many cell generations after the initial event (arrows point to B9q).

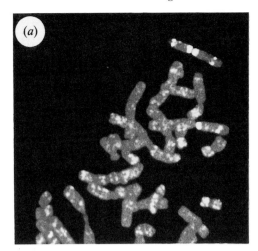

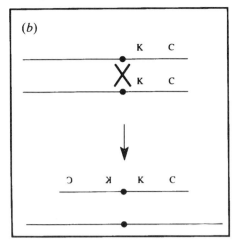

Figure 3. An isochromosome 2p in PALA-resistant HT1080 cells. (*a*) The uppermost chromosome has been derived from human chromosome 2 by centromeric fusion. A normal chromosome 2 can be seen below. The marker chromosome has two p arms with CAD (C) near the telomeres and the V_k gene cluster (K) near the centromere. (*b*) The proposed primary event, involving recombination through the centromeres of sister chromatids. The two centromeres are identical. One has two 'right' portions and the other two 'left' portions. It is important that the recombined centromere on the chromosome bearing CAD retains functions. (Figure and legend reproduced, with permission, from Stark (1993).)

receives none, so that the same basic process leads both to amplification and to deletion. Continuation of BBF events through additional cell cycles can lead to accumulation of multiple copies of a target gene in some of the daughter cells (see figure 1*b*), in arrays that are consistent with the amplified structures seen by *in situ* hybridization analyses of drug-resistant rodent cells (for examples, see figure 2). It is important to note that broken DNA will be present in every daughter cell of a BBF family until some process, such as loss of the broken chromosome before replication, or healing of the broken end through acquisition of telomeric sequences, occurs. Thus any regulatory process that recognizes broken DNA will still be in force many cell generations after initiation of a BBF cycle. It is also important to recognize that BBF cycles can be initiated in two very different ways. (i) fusion first, as illustrated at the top of figure 1*a*. Formation of a dicentric chromosome might result from loss of the repeat sequence TTAGGG from telomeres of cells that lack telomerase activity, as discussed in depth by Stark (1993); or (ii) breakage first (not illustrated). Following replication of a broken chromosome, the adjacent broken ends of two sister chromatids can fuse to form the first dicentric chromosome and initiate BBF cycles.

(b) Human cells

Relatively little has been done so far to study gene amplification in human cells. Recent work by Schaefer *et al.* (1993) in SV40-infected IMR-90 cells has revealed that, in contrast to rodent cells, human cells can achieve resistance to PALA through formation of an isochromosome 2p and through accumulation of extra copies of chromosome 2. We too have observed an isochromosome 2p in PALA-resistant HT1080 fibrosarcoma cells (see figure 3, K. A. Smith & G. R. Stark, unpublished data, cited in Stark 1993) and have also found additional mechanisms of resistance to PALA in

these cells. Thirty-one PALA-resistant HT1080 clones were selected, using a protocol (Smith *et al.* 1990) that insures that the clones result from recent and independent amplification events. Upon analysis by *in situ* hybridization, only two out of 31 clones showed the ladder-like structures commonly seen for amplified CAD genes in Syrian hamster cells (see figure 2*b*) and were presumed to have arisen via BBF cycles. In nine out of 31 cases, isochromosomes 2p were apparent (see figure 3 for an example and explanation). Here, the CAD gene-copy number increases, from the normal two per cell to only three per cell. This modest increase leads to more than a proportional increase in resistance to PALA, accounting for the ability of the cells to survive a selective concentration of drug. In 20 out of 31 cases, analysis by *in situ* hybridization did not reveal any amplified CAD genes. Three of these cases were investigated further: in all three, the specific activity of CAD was about twice as high as in control HT1080 cells, accounting for their resistance to PALA. In two out of three cases, quantitative Southern analysis, using internal normalization with a probe for a single-copy sequence, revealed no significant increase in CAD gene copy number, in agreement with the *in situ* results and suggesting that resistance to PALA was achieved through an increase in CAD transcription or translation, or through stabilization of the CAD mRNA or protein. In the third case, the increase in the specific activity of CAD was accompanied by a comparable increase in gene-copy number. As the extra copies were not seen by *in situ* analysis of fixed metaphase chromosomes in this clone, extrachromosomal amplified DNA may be involved.

In summary, at least five different mechanisms of PALA resistance have been seen in HT1080 and SV40-infected IMR-90 human cells (amplifications as ladders, amplification not as ladders (presumed to be extrachromosomal), isochromosomes 2p, extra chromosomes 2, and increases in the specific activity of CAD without amplification). As discussed next, PALA resistance has not been observed in cells with intact pathways of response to DNA damage, raising the question of how regulation of so many different mechanisms of resistance can be achieved in normal human cells.

3. PERMISSIVITY

(a) Non-permissive cell strains and cell lines

Observations made in several laboratories show that normal human or rodent cell strains fail to give drug-resistant colonies containing amplified DNA when selected with PALA, methotrexate or hydroxyurea (Lücke-Huhle et al. 1987; Lücke-Huhle 1989; Wright et al. 1990; Tlsty 1990). Virtually all cell lines do give clones containing amplified DNA, at frequencies typically in the range 10^{-4} to 10^{-6}. A very useful exception is the rat cell line REF52, which does not give colonies containing amplified CAD or dihydro-folate reductase (DHFR) genes upon selection with PALA or metrotrexate (Perry et al. 1992b). The frequency is now known to be less than 10^{-8} (M. Commane, O. B. Chernova & G. R. Stark, unpublished results). A non-permissive human cell line would be extremely useful for comparative experiments because a much wider range of resistance mechanisms is seen in human cells. Yin et al. (1992) worked with non-permissive human cells derived from the Li-Fraumeni line MDAH041 (lacking functional p53) by introduction of wild-type p53 cDNA under control of a constitutive promoter. Unfortunately, these cells, which express p53 in an unregulated manner, have not proved to be stable. We have recently succeeded in preparing a stable non-permissive human cell line from the same MDAH041 parental cells by introducing a construct (kindly provided by Peter Chumakov, Engelhardt Institute of Molecular Biology, Russian Academy of Sciences, Moscow) in which expression of wild-type human p53 cDNA is regulated by the normal human p53 promoter (Archana Agarwal, M. L. Agarwal & G. R. Stark, unpublished results). The parental permissive cells give PALA-resistant colonies at a frequency of 3×10^{-5}, whereas no colonies were obtained from 6×10^6 transfected cells. Both selections were done at $3 \times$ LD$_{50}$ for PALA. These cells can now be used to determine which mechanisms of resistance are observed when the cells are made permissive in different ways.

(b) Involvement of p53, pRb, ras, and myc

The presence of normal p53 in human and mouse cells correlates well with an inability to give rise to colonies with amplified CAD DNA, and loss of p53 from these cells allows them to become permissive for amplification. (Livingstone et al. 1992; Yin et al. 1992). Both of these groups also found that the presence of wild-type p53 correlated well with the ability to arrest in the G1 phase of the cell cycle in response to the pyrimidine deprivation caused by PALA. These results are readily understood in view of the discussion above, showing that broken DNA often accompanies amplification, and that p53 is a major element in regulating

the response of normal cells to DNA damage (for an example, see Nelson & Kastan 1994). The reason for the regulatory effect of p53 on mechanisms of PALA resistance that do *not* involve broken DNA is unclear at present.

Non-permissive REF52 cells have been used to introduce genes that affect permissivity. Not surprisingly, introduction of SV40 large T-antigen, which binds to both p53 and pRb, converts REF52 cells to a permissive state (Perry et al. 1992b). The effect of T-antigen on REF52 cells results from the loss of p53 because introduction of the dominant negative C141Y mutant of human p53 also permits REF52 cells to achieve resistance to PALA, at a frequency of 7×10^{-5} (O. B. Chernova, M. V. Chernov & G. R. Stark, unpublished results). Conversely, expression of an adenovirus 5 E1A protein, which binds to pRb but not to p53, does not convert REF52 cells to permissivity (Perry et al. 1992b). Recent work with the E7 oncoprotein of human papillomavirus type 16 (which also binds to pRb) has shown that the ability to arrest growth in G1 in normal human cells in response to DNA damage can be lost in the presence of wild-type p53 (Demers et al. 1994; White et al. 1994). Although PALA-resistant colonies could be obtained from cells expressing E7, they exhibited polyploidy rather than amplification through rearrangement of DNA (White et al. 1994). This result differs from that obtained by Perry et al. (1992b) with REF52 cells expressing E1A where no PALA-resistant clones were observed.

It is clear that the presence of wild-type p53 is necessary but not sufficient to maintain a non-permissive state. Perry et al. (1992b) found that, although neither a mutant form of *ras* nor the adenovirus E1A gene alone was capable of converting REF52 cells to permissivity, the combination did so readily, without loss of p53. Similarly, Livingstone et al. (1992) found that two cell lines with wild-type p53 were nevertheless permissive.

Overexpression of *myc* genes alone can also convert REF52 cells to permissivity. Introduction of a construct constitutively expressing mouse c-*myc* gives PALA-resistant colonies at a frequency of 5×10^{-5} at $3 \times$ LD$_{50}$, and introduction of human N-*myc* gives an even higher frequency, 3×10^{-4} (Y. Ishizaka, O. B. Chernova, M. V. Chernov & G. R. Stark, unpublished results). Coamplification of CAD and N-*myc*, which lie very near each other on rat chromosome 6 and human chromosome 2, accounts for the observation that pretreatment of non-permissive REF52 or human MDAH041 (wild-type p53) cells with a low concentration of PALA ($1.5 \times$ LD$_{50}$) for three days, converts them to a state permissive for CAD gene amplification, whereas pretreatment with a comparable concentration of methotrexate has no effect on permissivity (O. B. Chernova, M. V. Chernov, M. L. Agarwal & G. R. Stark, unpublished results). In an intermediate level of PALA, the cells can divide slowly, for up to ten days, but the stress of replicating DNA under conditions of severe starvation for the deoxypyrimidine triphosphate precursors of DNA may lead to DNA strand breaks and thus to amplification. Since CAD and N-*myc* are near neighbours, they are likely to be

Table 1. *Incorporation of BrdU into new PALA^R colonies shifted to a non-permissive temperature*

(Rat REF52 cells expressing the temperature-sensitive SV40 large T-antigen mutant tsA58 were used. Selection at 33 °C for 26 days yielded colonies of 100–300 cells. These colonies were shifted to 39.5 °C for 13 days. The pulse of BrdU was for 3 h.)

PALA^R colonies examined	BrdU$^+$ cells/colony			
	0	1–3	4–10	> 10
22	13	7	0	2

coamplified; increased expression of N-*myc* leads to permissivity and increased expression of CAD to PALA resistance.

(c) Manipulation of permissivity

The role of p53 in regulating the cellular response to broken DNA present early in an amplification sequence was investigated by using temperature-sensitive (ts) SV40 large T-antigen to inactive p53 in REF 52 cells (Y. Ishizaka & G. R. Stark unpublished results). Although SV40 large T-antigen binds other cellular proteins as well, we know that inactivation of p53 alone is sufficient to make REF52 cells permissive for amplification (see the previous section). The tsA58 mutant was used. At 33 °C, PALA-resistant colonies were readily observed but not at 40 °C, as expected, because T antigen is not present at this temperature. The independent, new colonies that formed at 33 °C were shifted to 40 °C. When 'late' colonies of *ca.* 10^6 cells were shifted, there was no growth arrest and *ca.* 60 % of the colonies were labelled with a 3 h pulse of BrdU. Conversely, when 'early' colonies of *ca.* 100 cells were shifted to 40 °C, growth was arrested and only a few cells in under half the colonies were labelled with a pulse of BrdU (see table 1). We interpret these results to indicate that, soon after an amplification event has been initiated, the broken DNA present in most cells triggers growth arrest in the presence of wild-type p53. In time, the broken DNA is lost or the broken ends are healed in most cells; for example, very few dicentric chromosomes carrying amplified CAD genes are seen in PALA-resistant Syrian hamster cells at the 10^6-cell stage (Smith *et al.* 1990). Therefore, despite the fact that the 'late' non-permissive REF52 cells still contain amplified DNA, their growth is no longer regulated by wild-type p53.

4. PROBABILITY OF AMPLIFICATION

(a) Amplificator cells

The probability of amplification can be increased in permissive cells in a variety of ways. The effects of transient treatment with DNA-damaging agents or metabolic inhibitors are well established and are discussed further below. It is also possible, however, to alter stably the probability of amplification. Selection of permissive cells simultaneously with two drugs gives 'amplificator' clones with rates of amplification that are generally increased, up to 25-fold (Giulotto *et al.* 1987). Furthermore, treatment of permissive cells with 5-aza-2'-deoxycytidine (which leads to extensive and relatively stable demethylation of DNA) increases the rate of amplification substantially (Perry *et al.* 1992 *a*). The amplificator phenotype is dominant in cell fusion experiments (Rolfe *et al.* 1988), leading to the hypothesis that overexpression of one or more genes can affect rates of amplification. Two such 'amplificator' genes have already been identified. Denis *et al.* (1991) showed that regulated overexpression of human c-*myc* increased the frequency of DHFR amplification in a permissive rat embryo fibroblast cell line by at least tenfold and similar results have been obtained by Lücke-Huhle (1989) in Chinese hamster cells. More recently, Wani *et al.* (1994) showed that regulated overexpression of a mutant human Ha-ras protein increased the frequency of both DHFR and CAD gene amplification in permissive NIH 3T3 cells, again by a substantial factor. From the above set of observations, it is clear that one may be able to clone 'amplificator' genes by using an expression strategy in which cloned DNA is introduced into a cell line with a low rate of amplification and then recovered from cells that have a high rate of amplification. These experiments are difficult and laborious in practice, as only a small fraction of cells carrying such an amplificator clone will actually amplify a gene such as CAD, allowing their selection. Despite these difficulties, we have isolated a genomic clone from a Syrian hamster amplificator cell line that stimulates amplification of CAD in monkey cells; we are presently characterizing the responsible gene (Y. Deguchi & G. R. Stark, unpublished results).

How might amplificator genes act? Our ideas have expanded with the realization that cells (especially human cells) may achieve drug resistance through a variety of mechanisms and also that permissivity may be enforced by different means, depending on the mechanism of resistance. Clearly, we expect any activity that increases the probability of forming dicentric chromosomes to stimulate amplification. For example, any activity that increases the probability of breaking DNA or of fusing the ends of sister chromatids should increase the rates of amplification through the BBF pathway shown in figure 1. In human cells, we would also expect to increase the rate of CAD amplification by expressing activities that stimulate excision of interstitial DNA. This, in turn, creates extrachromosomal elements capable of autonomous replication that increase either the rate of isochromosome formation through recombination of centromeric DNA, or the rate of chromosome non-disjunction. Finally, if some pathways are permitted in a particular cell line and some are not, an amplificator gene could open one or more forbidden pathways by making the cell tolerant of the resulting genomic change. On the face of it, such activities might be expected of oncogenes such as *myc* and *ras*. Isolation and characterization of new amplificator genes can shed further light on both the mechanisms and the regulation of amplification, possibly with important implications for understanding other manifestations of genomic instability as well.

Table 2. *Effect of pre-exposure to drugs on rates of amplification in baby hamster kidney (BHK) cells*

pre-treatment (6 days)	selective drug (ca. 28 days)	amplification rate ($\times 10^5$)
none	20 μM PALA	7.6
	200 μM PALA	< 0.01
	100 nM methotrexate	3.0
	200 nM methotrexate	0.2
20 μM PALA	200 μM PALA	0.9
	100 nM methotrexate	5.4
	200 nM methotrexate	2.3
100 nM methotrexate	200 μM PALA	0.5

(b) Effects of treatment with DNA damaging agents or metabolic inhibitors

It has been well appreciated for some time that DNA damage and inhibition of DNA synthesis can transiently increase the rate of amplification in permissive cells (reviewed by Stark & Wahl 1984; Schimke 1988). The effect of DNA damage is readily understood if damage leads to an increased probability of forming a dicentric chromosome or of excising an acentric chromosomal element capable of autonomous replication. Arrest of DNA replication, for example, by starvation for deoxynucleoside triphosphates, can also lead to transient stimulation of amplification. Recent experiments in our laboratory (M.-F. Poupon & G. R. Stark, unpublished results) have shown that pretreating *permissive* baby hamster kidney (BHK) cells with PALA or methotrexate can lead to an increased rate of gene amplification (see table 2). Pretreating BHK cells with 20 μM PALA leads to an increase of about tenfold in the rate at which the cells become resistant to 200 nM methotrexate and, conversely, pretreating the cells with 100 nM methotrexate allows colonies resistant to 200 μM PALA to be observed, whereas no colonies are observed without pretreatment. This result differs markedly from the effect of PALA pretreatment on the ability of the non-permissive REF52 cells to tolerate DNA damage (see above), where there is no effect of methotrexate pretreatment on resistance to PALA, or vice versa, and where coamplification of CAD and N-*myc* is responsible for the effect. In the BHK experiment (see table 2), we propose that starvation for deoxypyrimidine triphosphates (in PALA) or dTTP and deoxypurine triphosphates (in methotrexate) leads to DNA damage, stimulating formation of dicentric chromosomes and possibly other mechanisms of amplification.

5. AMPLIFICATION IN SCHIZOSACCHAROMYCES POMBE

We are studying amplification in this fission yeast to take advantage of the fact that genetic and biochemical experimentation can be carried out with relative ease because an extensive collection of mutants are available for use. L-Methionine sulfoximine is used to select for increased expression of *gln1*[+], which codes for glutamine

synthetase (Barel *et al.* 1988), and LiCl is used to select for increased expression of *sod2*[+], which codes for an Na[+](Li[+])/H[+] antiporter (Jia *et al.* 1992). As shown in figure 4, our physical mapping of these two genes indicates that they are located on the same arm of chromosome I: *gln1*[+] maps to *Not*I fragment D in the middle of the arm; *sod2*[+] maps telomere-proximal to *rad8*[+] on *Not*I fragment L, within *ca.* 160 kilobases (kb) of the 'left' telomere (Hoheisel *et al.* 1993).

Spontaneous amplification of *sod2*[+] is exceedingly rare (*ca.* 2.5×10^{-8}), but can be induced by irradiation with 254 nm ultraviolet (UV) light to 50% survival (T. E. Patterson & G. R. Stark, unpublished results). Under these conditions, the frequency of amplification is *ca.* 3×10^{-7} per cell. The level of amplification is variable; one to ten extra copies have been detected. In two independent strains that have been characterized further, the average amplicon size is 50 to 75 kb. Amplification of *sod2*[+] results in at least two structures: in one, the amplified sequences are found on an expanded *Not*I fragment L, in the other, the telomere-containing *Not*I fragment M of chromosome II is also involved (see figure 4). We are currently analysing the amplified DNA at *sod2*[+] for the presence of inverted repeats to learn more about the mechanism.

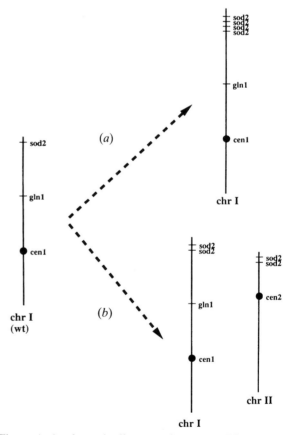

Figure 4. A schematic diagram of gene amplification in *S. pombe*. The two genes studied are located on the same arm of chromosome I, *sod2* near the telomere and *gln1* near the middle of the arm. No amplification of *gln1* has been found. However, *sod2* amplification is found easily. Two cases have been examined in detail. (*a*) the extra copies are found as a tandem array at or near the normal position of *sod2*. (*b*) The extra copies are found near the normal position of *sod2* and also near one telomere of chromosome II.

Although we can detect amplification of *sod2⁺*, under identical conditions we have not detected amplification of *gln1⁺* (frequency less than 2×10^{-9}). Therefore the UV-induced amplification frequency of *gln1⁺* is at least 140-fold lower than that of *sod2⁺*. The organization of these two genes suggests that proximity to a telomere might be an important determinant of amplification in *S. pombe*. To address this issue, we have constructed a strain in which the chromosomal locations of *sod2⁺* and *gln1⁺* have been exchanged reciprocally, the influence of chromosomal location on the frequency of amplification is now being tested.

We are also taking a genetic approach to understand mechanisms and regulation of gene amplification by screening known mutations in genes that are involved in responses to DNA damage, chromatin metabolism, etc., for their effects on the frequency of gene amplification. Candidates include previously identified *S. pombe* mutations, as well as genes identified in mammalian systems. Preliminary results indicate that a mutation in the cell cycle checkpoint control gene *rad9* (al-Khodairy & Carr 1992), involved in regulating cell cycle arrest in response to DNA damage, leads to a 100-fold increase in the frequency of UV-induced amplification of *sod2⁺*. This finding reinforces the idea, first generated from studies using mammalian systems, that the ability to progress through the cell cycle in the presence of damaged DNA is linked to the ability to amplify DNA.

6. CONCLUSIONS AND FUTURE DIRECTIONS

Recent work in which gene amplification has been studied in human cells has made it clear that multiple mechanisms are responsible. A major challenge for the future is to determine which specific mechanisms are affected by each treatment or agent that stimulates amplification in permissive cells. Another challenge is to relate the very different consequences of the genomic derangements that accompany different amplification mechanisms to specific regulatory pathways that govern permissivity. It is hard to imagine that the cell responds to abnormalities as different as dicentric chromosomes, isochromosomes or aneuploidy through the same regulatory pathway. Therefore, when a non-permissive cell is rendered permissive by introduction of either c-*myc* on or mutant p53, we do not necessarily expect that the drug-resistant cells will have become permissive in the same way. A detailed investigation of the mechanistic consequences of stimulating or permitting amplification in different ways is likely to yield information of broad interest.

REFERENCES

al-Khodairy, F. & Carr, A.M. 1992 DNA repair mutants defining G₂ checkpoint pathways in *Schizosaccharomyces pombe*. *EMBO J.* **11**, 1343–1350.

Barel, I., Bignell, G., Simpson, A. & McDonald, D. 1988 Isolation of a DNA fragment which complements glutamine synthetase deficient strains of *S. pombe*. *Curr. Genet.* **13**, 487–494.

Demers, G.W., Foster, S.A., Halbert, C.L. & Halloway, D.A. 1994 Growth arrest by induction of p53 in DNA damaged keratinocytes is bypassed by human papillomavirus 16 E7. *Proc. natn. Acad. Sci. U.S.A.* **91**, 4382–4386.

Denis, N., Kitzis, A., Kruh, J., Dautry, F. & Corcos, D. 1991 Stimulation of methotrexate resistance and dihydrofolate reductase gene amplification by c-*myc*. *Oncogene* **6**, 1453–1457.

Giulotto, E., Knights, C. & Stark, G.R. 1987 Hamster cells with increased rates of DNA amplification, a new phenotype. *Cell* **48**, 837–845.

Hoheisel, J.D., Maier, E., Mott, R., *et al.* 1993 High resolution cosmid and P1 maps spanning the 14 Mb genome of the fission yeast *S. pombe*. *Cell* **73**, 109–120.

Jia, Z.P., McCullough, N., Martel, R., Hemmingsen, S. & Young, P.G. 1992 Gene amplification at a locus encoding a putative Na⁺/H⁺ antiporter confers sodium and lithium tolerance in fission yeast. *EMBO J.* **11**, 1631–1640.

Livingstone, L.R., White, A., Sprouse, J., Livanos, E., Jacks, T. & Tlsty, T.D. 1992 Altered cell cycle arrest and gene amplification potential accompany loss of wild-type p53. *Cell* **70**, 923–935.

Lücke-Huhle, C., Hinrichs, S. & Speit, G. 1987 DHFR gene amplification in cultured skin fibroblasts of ataxia telangiectasia patients after methotrexate selection. *Carcinogenesis* **8**, 1801–1806.

Lücke-Huhle, C. 1989 Gene amplification – a cellular response to genotoxic stress. *Molec. Toxicol.* **2**, 237–253.

Nelson, W.G. & Kastan, M.B. 1994 DNA strand breaks: the DNA template alterations that trigger p53-dependent DNA damage response pathways. *Molec. Cell Biol.* **14**, 1815–1823.

Perry, M.E., Rolfe, M., McIntyre, P., Commane, M. & Stark, G.R. 1992*a* Induction of gene amplification by 5-aza-2′-deoxycytidine. *Mutat. Res.* **276**, 189–197.

Perry, M.E., Commane, M. & Stark, G.R. 1992*b* Simian virus 40 large tumor antigen alone or two cooperating oncogenes convert REF52 cells to a state permissive for gene amplification. *Proc. natn. Acad. Sci. U.S.A.* **89**, 8112–8116.

Rolfe, M., Knights, C. & Stark, G.R. 1988 Somatic cell genetic studies of amplificator cell lines. In *Cancer cells 6/eukaryotic DNA replication*, (ed. T. Kelly & B. Stillman), pp. 325–328. Cold Spring Harbor, New York: Cold Spring Harbor Laboratories.

Schaefer, D.I., Livanos E.M., White, A.E. & Tlsty T.D. 1993 Multiple mechanisms of *N*-phosphonoacetyl-L-aspartate drug resistance in SV40-infected precrisis human fibroblasts. *Cancer Res.* **53**, 4946–4951.

Schimke, R.T. 1988 Gene amplification in cultured cells. *J. biol. Chem.* **263**, 5989–5992.

Schwab, M. 1990 Oncogene amplification in neoplastic development and progression of human cancers. *CRC crit. Rev. Oncogen.* **2**, 35–51.

Schwab, M. & Amler, L.C. 1990 Amplification of cellular oncogenes: a predictor of clinical outcome in human cancer. *Genes Chromosomes Cancer* **1**, 181–193.

Smith, K.A., Gorman, P.A., Stark, M.B., Groves, R.P. & Stark, G.R. 1990 Distinctive chromosomal structures are formed very early in the amplification of CAD genes in Syrian hamster cells. *Cell* **63**, 1219–1227.

Stark, G.R. & Wahl, G.M. 1984 Gene amplification. *A. Rev. Biochem.* **53**, 447–491.

Stark, G.R., Debatisse, M., Giulotto, E. & Wahl, G.M. 1989 Recent progress in understanding mechanisms of mammalian DNA amplification. *Cell* **57**, 901–908.

Stark, G.R., Debatisse, M., Wahl, G.M. & Glover, D.M. 1990 DNA amplification in eukaryotes. In *Gene rearrange-*

ment (ed. B. D. Hames & D. M. Glovers), pp. 99–149. Oxford, U.K: IRL Press.

Stark, G.R. 1993 Regulation and mechanisms of mammalian gene amplification. *Adv. Cancer Res.* **61**, 87–113.

Tlsty, T.D. 1990 Normal diploid human and rodent cells lack a detectable frequency of gene amplification. *Proc. natn. Acad. Sci. U.S.A.* **87**, 3132–3136.

White A.E., Livanos E.M. & Tlsty T.D. 1994 Differential disruption of genomic integrity and cell cycle regulation in normal human fibroblasts by the HPV oncoproteins. *Genes Dev.* **8**, 666–677.

Windle, B.E. & Wahl, G.M. 1992 Molecular dissection of mammalian gene amplification: new mechanistic insights revealed by analyses of very early events. *Mutat. Res.* **276**, 199–224.

Wani, M.A., Xu, X. & Stambrook, P.J. 1994 Increased methotrexate resistance and *dhfr* gene amplification as a consequence of induced Ha-*ras* expression in NIH 3T3 cells. *Cancer Res* **54**, 2504–2508.

Wright, J.A., Smith, H.S., Watt, F.M., Hancock, M.C., Hudson, D.L. & Stark, G.R. 1990 *Proc. natn. Acad. Sci. U.S.A.* **87**, 1791–1795.

Yin, Y., Tainsky, M.A., Bischoff, F.Z., Strong, L.C. & Wahl, G.M. 1992 Wild-type p53 restores cell cycle control and inhibits gene amplification in cells with mutant p53 alleles. *Cell* **70**, 937–48.

8

Enzymes acting at strand interruptions in DNA

TOMAS LINDAHL, MASAHIKO S. SATOH AND GRIGORY DIANOV

Imperial Cancer Research Fund, Clare Hall Laboratories, South Mimms, Hertfordshire EN6 3LD, U.K.

SUMMARY

Endogenous and environmental DNA-damaging agents often generate single-strand interruptions in DNA. The lesions trigger a complex set of cellular reactions. In most eukaryotic cells, cellular poly(ADP-ribose) formation is the most acute response to such damage. Recently, such events have been amenable to study with soluble cell-free extracts of human cells. These investigations clarify the modulating role on DNA repair by poly (ADP-ribose), and suggest that the primary function of this unusual polymer is to act as an antirecombinant agent. Similar biochemical studies of subsequent repair events have revealed a branched pathway for the ubiquitous DNA base excision-repair process. The alternative pathway provides the cell with back-up functions for individual steps in this essential form of DNA repair.

1. INTRODUCTION

Ionizing radiation and chemicals such as bleomycin and neocarzinostatin that generate oxygen free-radicals, cause the formation of single-strand breaks in DNA. These strand interruptions have diverse and complex terminal structures, usually resulting from destruction of the deoxyribose residue at the 3′ or 5′ end of the break. Consequently, only a very small proportion of radiation-induced single-strand breaks can be rejoined directly by DNA ligase. The sensitive biophysical methods often employed to measure strand breaks in DNA have the inherent weakness of not being able to distinguish between breaks with different end groups, although various types of strand interruptions are repaired with marked differences in efficiency (Satoh *et al.* 1993). Thus one reason why rare double-strand breaks in DNA have often been implicated as the most important lethal lesions in radiological research may simply be they are easier to measure than a particular form of cytotoxic single-strand break.

Prior to their rejoining by complex excision-repair processes, oxygen radical-induced strand breaks in DNA elicit a cellular alarm response that leads to inhibition of DNA replication, apparently through unknown factors that cause elevation and stabilization of p53 protein levels (Lu & Lane 1993; Nelson & Kastan 1994). Two abundant DNA-binding nuclear enzymes are activated by strand interruptions in DNA: DNA-dependent protein kinase (Gottlieb & Jackson 1993; Anderson 1994) and poly(ADP-ribose) polymerase (de Murcia & de Murcia 1994). It is conceivable that one or both of these proteins may be involved in cellular signalling in response to DNA damage. The main role for poly(ADP-ribose) polymerase, however, appears to be to act as an antirecombinogenic factor that prevents instability of densely packed tandem-repeat sequences in chromatin. In addition, DNA-binding and activation of poly(ADP-ribose) polymerase modulates DNA repair (Satoh *et al.* 1994).

2. POLY(ADP-RIBOSE) SYNTHESIS

DNA strand interruptions that occur as reaction intermediates during lagging-strand DNA replication and nucleotide excision-repair processes are protected by multi-protein complexes and consequently are not accessible to poly(ADP-ribose) polymerase (Eki & Hurwitz 1991; Molinete *et al.* 1993; Satoh *et al.* 1993). In contrast, chain breaks generated directly by DNA-damaging agents, or appearing as intermediates in base excision-repair, elicit rapid binding and extensive automodification by poly(ADP-ribose) polymerase. This protein is abundant in cell nuclei (more than 10^5 molecules per cell, except in terminally differentiated cells) and is tightly attached to the nuclear matrix. NAD is the precursor of poly(ADP-ribose) and polymer formation is product-inhibited by nicotinamide analogues such as 3-aminobenzamide. Many investigations of poly(ADP-ribose) synthesis in response to DNA damage have been performed *in vivo* (reviewed in Cleaver & Morgan 1991) and recently the main features of the reaction have been reproduced with human cell-free extracts (Satoh & Lindahl 1992; Satoh *et al.* 1993, 1994; Smulson *et al.* 1994). DNA-free extracts of human cells (Manley *et al.* 1983) were incubated with plasmid DNA containing a single-strand break generated by ionizing radiation as well as deoxynucleoside triphosphates ATP and NAD. DNA repair was measured either by following the conversion of the nicked plasmid to a covalently closed form by agarose gel electrophoresis in the presence of ethidium bromide, or by measuring DNA repair replication by autoradiography on inclusion of a radioactively labelled deoxynucleoside triphosphate in the reaction mixture. Concurrent poly(ADP-ribose) synthesis was monitored by incorporation of ^{32}P-labelled NAD followed by gel electrophoresis and autoradiography. Within 30 seconds at 30 °C, long chains (more than 50 residues) of poly(ADP-ribose) are synthesized (Satoh *et al.* 1994). These remain attached to poly(ADP-ribose)

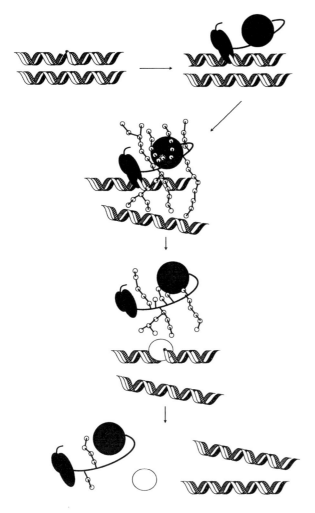

Figure 1. Poly(ADP-ribose) as an antirecombinogenic agent. Two homologous DNA sequences are shown, packed close together in the cellular chromatin. An accidental single-strand interruption generated by a DNA-damaging agent is prevented from triggering a recombination event by tight binding of poly(ADP-ribose) polymerase. Automodification of the enzyme generates negatively charged polymer chains which repel adjacent DNA sequences and prevent aligning of homologous stretches, prior to dissociation of the auto-modified enzyme from DNA and subsequent DNA repair. Poly(ADP-ribose) polymerase has a DNA-binding domain and a separate catalytic domain united by a short auto-modification region; repair enzymes are shown schematically as an open oval.

polymerase. The heavily modified enzyme, which has multiple acceptor sites, is released from DNA. Subsequently, the polymer chains are degraded by a specific poly(ADP-ribose) glycohydrolase. Very little DNA repair occurs during the first 2 min of incubation, so poly(ADP-ribose) synthesis precedes processing and rejoining of strand breaks by repair enzymes. This programme of events explains the observation of strong inhibition of DNA repair when NAD is excluded from reaction mixtures or when 3-aminobenzamide is included. The tight binding of unmodified poly(ADP-ribose) polymerase to DNA strand breaks interferes with DNA repair, but automodification of the enzyme serves as a release mechanism. If, prior to use, reaction mixtures are depleted of poly(ADP-ribose) polymerase by affinity chromatography, DNA repair proceeds

efficiently even in the absence of NAD (Satoh & Lindahl 1992). These data on the *in vitro* system have been extended recently by Smulson *et al.* (1994), who employed cell extracts depleted of endogenous poly-(ADP-ribose) polymerase but supplemented with mutationally altered poly(ADP-ribose) polymerase expressed in bacteria. Enzyme molecules with deletions in the N-terminal DNA-binding region were unable to suppress DNA repair. However, mutations in the C-terminal catalytic region resulted in poly(ADP-ribose) polymerase molecules that interfered with DNA repair in such a way that inhibition could not be alleviated by addition of NAD. The latter results agree well with the finding by Molinete *et al.* (1993) that expression *in vivo* of the subcloned DNA-binding domain of poly(ADP-ribose) polymerase sensitizes cells to DNA damage. Interestingly, in the experiments by Smulson's group, poly(ADP-ribose) polymerase with intact DNA-binding and catalytic domains, but a deletion in the automodification domain, behaved as a mutant with the catalytic domain deleted, *i.e.* DNA repair was inhibited and the reaction was insensitive to NAD. This mutated form of poly(ADP-ribose) polymerase had retained its capacity for low-level modification of other proteins, but such events did not affect DNA repair.

The amazingly elaborate polymer synthesis and automodification of poly(ADP-ribose) polymerase triggered by DNA strand breaks is unlikely to be required to induce a conformational change in the protein itself, which is often the function of more discrete modification events such as phosphorylation or mono(ADP-ribosyl)ation. Instead, the interaction between nuclear macromolecules could be modulated in this fashion. Short chains of poly(ADP-ribose) at multiple acceptor sites in the automodified enzyme are sufficient for its release from strand interruptions in DNA (Satoh *et al.* 1994). Such relatively persistent short chains, which normally result from partial degradation of initially-formed long poly(ADP-ribose) chains by poly(ADP-ribose) glycohydrolase, apparently serve to prohibit rapid reattachment of poly(ADP-ribose) polymerase to DNA strand breaks, allowing time for DNA repair to proceed. Thus, the overall effect of poly(ADP-ribose) polymerase on repair of DNA strand interruptions, resulting in a slight delay of DNA rejoining, does not appear to be the primary reason for the synthesis of long chains of poly(ADP-ribose), but a secondary consequence. A number of scenarios have been proposed to explain the occurrence of polymer synthesis, such as wilful depletion of cellular NAD pools (Berger 1985), inhibition of DNA topoisomerase I (Ferro *et al.* 1984), or histone rearrangements in chromatin (Panzeter *et al.* 1993), but none of these models seems particularly convincing. Interestingly, in lower eukaryotes, there seems to be a marked correlation between the occurrence of poly(ADP-ribose) polymerase and its accompanying poly(ADP-ribose) glycohydrolase with the abundance of repeated DNA sequences in the cellular genome (Satoh *et al.* 1994). For example, dinoflagellates, which belong to the protozoa, have almost one-half of their DNA in the form of interspersed repeated DNA sequences and have a poly(ADP-ribose) polymerase (but no histones), whereas *Saccharomyces cerevisiae* has very little repeated DNA of this type and apparently lacks poly(ADP-ribose) polymerase. Large numbers of complex sequence repeats must be a major challenge to mechanisms that serve to retain genomic stability, especially if a DNA strand interruption accidentally occurs in such a region of the chromatin to generate a potential hot spot for homologous recombination. The biochemical properties of poly(ADP-ribose) polymerase seem admirably suited to prevent this problem. The protein binds very rapidly and tightly to nicks in DNA and protects them from repair and recombination enzymes such as exonucleases. The subsequent slight delay in DNA repair seems a small price to pay for this efficient shielding. The automodification of the bound enzyme with multiple long branched chains of poly(ADP-ribose) results in a zone of high negative charge around the strand break and will effectively repel any immediately adjacent DNA sequences in tightly packed chromatin and prevent them from aligning as potential partners in homologous recombination events. A model is shown in figure 1. In apparent agreement with this scheme of events, several reports have appeared on the stimulation of homologous recombination, gene amplification and sister chromatid exchange by inhibition of poly(ADP-ribose) synthesis (Oikawa *et al.* 1980; Natarajan *et al.* 1981; Ferro *et al.* 1984; Waldman & Waldman 1991; Smulson *et al.* 1994). More definite experimental tests of the model in cell-free systems (Kawasaki *et al.* 1994) should now be possible however, cell lines or transgenic mice lacking poly (ADP-ribose) polymerase might be required to confirm finally the physiological roles of this enzyme.

3. DNA BASE EXCISION-REPAIR

The most common fate of a DNA lesion in *E. coli*, or in human cells, is its removal by 'excision-repair'. This general term covers two entirely different pathways employing different enzymes and DNA reaction intermediates. These pathways have been called base excision-repair versus nucleotide excision-repair, the semantic problems with this nomenclature have been discussed by Friedberg (1985). In addition, DNA mismatch correction occurs by a third route of excision-repair. Bulky DNA lesions that cause major helix distortion, e.g. the major lesions induced by ultraviolet light, are handled by nucleotide excision-repair, which is discussed elsewhere in this Volume. Base excision-repair is largely employed to correct potentially mutagenic or toxic lesions that only cause minor distortion of the DNA double helix; these include many lesions (including strand interruptions) generated by spontaneous DNA hydrolysis, oxygen free-radicals and methylating agents. Thymine residues in G·T mismatches in the DNA of mammalian cells are also removed by this pathway (Neddermann & Jiricny 1993).

Following a similar strategy to that employed for our

studies on nucleotide excision-repair (Wood *et al.* 1988) and poly(ADP-ribose) formation during DNA repair (Satoh & Lindahl 1992), base excision-repair has been investigated in DNA-free soluble cell extracts supplemented with a defined DNA substrate (Dianov *et al.* 1992). In this case, we have used double-stranded oligonucleotides containing a single, centrally located dUMP residue opposite a dGMP residue. Such oligonucleotides are repaired very efficiently by cell extracts of *E. coli* or human cells, with close to 100% replacement of the dUMP with a dCMP residue after 10–20 min incubation at 37 °C. The repair process apparently comprises five steps. A schematic outline of the process, with candidate human enzymes involved, is shown in figure 2. The first two steps are well-known and supported by a large body of biochemical and genetic data: the dUMP residue is cleaved by a DNA glycosylase that catalyses the release of free uracil, an apurinic/apyrimidinic (AP) endonuclease then hydrolyses the phosphodiester bond on the 5′ side of the base-free site. Several other distinct DNA lesions are dealt with in an analogous way, employing different DNA glycosylases. After removal of an altered base, the AP site remains well accommodated in the double-helix and causes surprisingly little distortion (Withka *et al.* 1991), although such an informationless residue in the DNA template acts as a partial block to replication. After incision next to the AP site, however, the hydrophilic deoxyribose-phosphate residue, which does not form hydrogen bonds with the base in the complementary strand, would be expected to swing out into an extra-helical position. The one-nucleotide gap in the double helix is then filled in by a DNA polymerase. In 80–90% of the repair events, no further polymerization takes place, so that DNA repair replication is confined to the replacement of a single nucleotide (Dianov *et al.* 1992). Occasionally, however, repair replication covers several additional nucleotides. The factors that regulate such additional synthesis are unclear at present, but in mammalian cells could simply depend on which DNA polymerase first encounters the gap. The longer repair patches may reflect a minor, back-up pathway for this particular step in the repair process, employing enzymes also used for late steps in lagging-strand DNA replication and nucleotide excision-repair. Several observations on a heterogenous mode of gap-filling during base excision-repair have been made *in vivo* (Snyder & Regan 1982; DiGiuseppe & Dresler 1989) and *in vitro* (Price & Lindahl 1991; Matsumoto & Bogenhagen 1991; Satoh *et al.* 1993). In the single nucleotide replacement route, the displaced deoxyribose-phosphate residue is excised as such, and candidate enzymes catalysing this step have been described in human cells (Price & Lindahl 1991) and in *E. coli* (Graves *et al.* 1992; Dianov *et al.* 1994). In the bacterial system, the RecJ protein (Lovett & Kolodner 1989) is the only enzyme found, so far, with the ability to release a 5′ terminal deoxyribose-phosphate residue in DNA by hydrolysis of the phosphodiester bond on its 3′ side. However, the Fpg protein, as well as basic proteins and polyamines, can promote a β-elimination event to liberate the sugar-phosphate and similarly generate a one-nucleotide

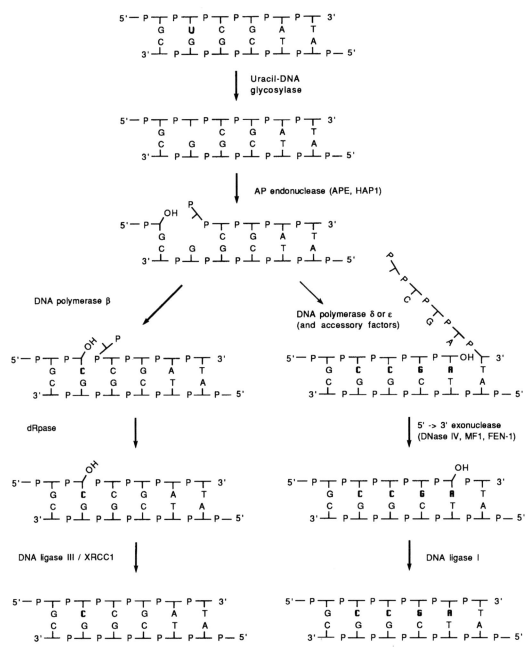

Figure 2. Branched pathway of DNA base excision-repair, resulting in heterogeneity of repair patch sizes. The human enzymes that tentatively account for each separate step are indicated.

gap. The $5' \rightarrow 3'$ exonuclease function of *E. coli* DNA polymerase I is totally unable to catalyse this particular event, but it can slowly release a 5′-terminal deoxy-ribose-phosphate residue as part of a small oligo-nucleotide (Price 1992). A mammalian exonuclease with biochemical properties and apparent physiological roles very similar to those of the $5' \rightarrow 3'$ exonuclease function of *E. coli* DNA polymerase I acts in an identical fashion in this regard. This mammalian $5' \rightarrow 3'$ exonuclease, which is not covalently bound to a DNA polymerase, was initially called DNase IV (Lindahl 1971 *a, b*; Price & Lindahl 1991) but has been renamed several times by various authors on rediscovery. DNase IV is the only known $5' \rightarrow 3'$ exonuclease acting on double-stranded DNA in mammalian cell nuclei; the other major exonuclease, DNase III, acts in the $3' \rightarrow 5'$ direction and preferentially degrades single-stranded DNA (Lindahl 1971 *b*). Thus,

DNase IV appears to be identical to the $5' \rightarrow 3'$ exonuclease that is an essential component of lagging-strand DNA replication (Ishimi *et al.* 1988; Kenny *et al.* 1988), as well as the related cca/exo activity (Goulian *et al.* 1990), the replication factor MF1 (Waga *et al.* 1994), the FEN-1 endonuclease (Harrington & Lieber 1994), and the $5' \rightarrow 3'$ exonuclease associated with DNA polymerase ϵ (Murante *et al.* 1994).

The occurrence of a branched pathway of base excision-repair (see figure 2) may provide increased versatility after inhibition of replication as a consequence of DNA damage, when the alternative pathway in figure 2 involving replication factors such as DNA polymerase δ (or ϵ) and associated components in replisomes may not be operative. The main pathway involving DNA polymerase β allows for effective excision-repair of DNA damage caused by ionizing radiation or alkylating agents even in the absence of replication factors. Moreover, the forked pathway offers a possible explanation for the unexpected finding that two different DNA ligases in mammalian cells (reviewed by Lindahl & Barnes 1992) are involved in base excision-repair. Simple S_N2 alkylating agents such as methyl methanesulphonate (MMS) and dimethyl sulphate induce the formation of 7-methylguanine and 3-methyladenine in DNA; the former lesion is not miscoding and remains in DNA for long periods. In contrast, the cytotoxic and mutagenic 3-methyladenine lesion is excised very rapidly by a DNA glycosylase, which acts in a fashion analogous to that of uracil-DNA glycosylase. DNA repair of MMS-induced damage consequently occurs by base excision-repair (Figure 2). There is now strong genetic evidence for a role of both DNA ligase I and DNA ligase III in this process. DNA ligase I is required for the efficient joining of Okazaki fragments during DNA replication (Li *et al.* 1994; Prigent *et al.* 1994; Waga *et al.* 1994.) A human cell line derived from an immunodeficient patient of stunted growth, 46BR, encodes a malfunctioning DNA ligase I with an amino acid substitution within a conserved region. This cell line is anomalously hypersensitive to MMS and exhibits altered repair with excessive DNA repair synthesis at repair patches (Prigent *et al.* 1994). DNA ligase III occurs as a heterodimer composed of the ligase catalytic subunit and the regulatory XRCC-1 protein (Caldecott *et al.* 1994; Ljungquist *et al.* 1994). In the absence of the XRCC-1 protein, the DNA ligase III catalytic subunit exhibits strongly reduced activity. Mammalian cell mutants deficient in the XRCC-1 protein are tenfold more sensitive to MMS than normal cells, strongly implying a defect in base excision-repair in these cells. It now seems possible that the major branch of base excision-repair, with replacement of only a single nucleotide, might depend on the DNA ligase III/XRCC-1 protein complex for efficient rejoining, whereas repair involving longer patches would require the same DNA ligase as lagging-strand DNA replication and nucleotide excision-repair, i.e. DNA ligase I.

DNA base excision-repair is likely to emerge as the most common DNA repair process in all cells (Lindahl 1993). Whereas loss of the nucleotide excision-repair system results in an ultraviolet radiation-sensitive but viable cell, and loss of mismatch repair leads to a mutator phenotype, genetic experiments on microorganisms strongly indicate that loss of repair capacity for AP sites in DNA leads to rapid cell death. Because of the critical importance of the pathway, back-up activities occur at every catalytic step. Thus, a deaminated cytosine residue is not only recognized and cleaved by the abundant uracil-DNA glycosylase, but also is a substrate for a mismatch correction function in mammalian cells, the mismatch-specific thymine-DNA glycosylate (Neddermann & Jiricny, 1994). Similarly, minor AP endonuclease activities occur in addition to the major one in mammalian cells, and *E. coli* has two distinct AP endonuclease with very similar modes of action (Demple & Harrison 1994). The branched pathway shown in figure 2 may be similarly advantageous to cells in that the right-hand part of the scheme provides a back-up pathway for completion of

base excision-repair. This situation is in contrast to nucleotide excision-repair, where no back-up system has been detected when any of the components of the multi-subunit complex for damage recognition/DNA incision/damage excision is defective. Consequently, DNA repair-deficient inherited human diseases similar to xeroderma pigmentosum, but with defects in base excision-repair components, have not been detected except for a single patient (Prigent *et al.* 1994). They would be expected to be very rare, because defects in both a main pathway and a back-up pathway might be required. Nevertheless, further studies on base excision-repair is likely to reveal this pathway as a key strategy of cells for retaining genomic stability.

REFERENCES

Anderson, C.W. 1994 Protein kinases and the response to DNA damage. *Semin. Cell Biol.* **5**, 427–436.

Berger, N.A. 1985 Poly(ADP-ribose) in the cellular response to DNA damage. *Radiat. Res.* **101**, 4–15.

Caldecott, K.W., McKeown, C.K., Tucker, J.D., Ljungquist, S. & Thompson, L.H. 1994 An interaction between the mammalian DNA repair protein XRCC1 and DNA ligase III. *Molec. Cell Biol.* **14**, 68–76.

Cleaver, J.E. & Morgan, W.F. 1991 Poly(ADP-ribose) polymerase: A perplexing participant in cellular responses to DNA breakage. *Mutat. Res.* **257**, 1–18.

Demple, B. & Harrison, L. 1994 Repair of oxidative damage to DNA: Enzymology and Biology. *A. Rev. Biochem.* **63**, 915–948.

De Murcia, G. & de Murcia, J.M. 1994 Poly(ADP-ribose) polymerase: a molecular nick-sensor. *Trends Biol. Sci.* **19**, 172–176.

Dianov, G., Price, A. & Lindahl, T. 1992 Generation of single-nucleotide repair patches following excision of uracil residues from DNA. *Molec. Cell Biol.* **12**, 1605–1612.

Dianov, G., Sedgwick B., Daly, G., Olsson, M., Lovett, S. & Lindahl, T. 1994 Release of 5′-terminal deoxyribose-phosphate residues from incised abasic sites in DNA by the *Escherichia coli* RecJ protein. *Nucl. Acids Res.* **22**, 993–998.

DiGiuseppe, J. A. & Dresler, S.L. 1989 Bleomycin-induced DNA repair synthesis in permeable human fibroblasts: mediation of long-patch and short-patch repair by distinct DNA polymerases. *Biochemistry, Wash.* **28**, 9515–9520.

Eki, T. & Hurwitz, J. 1991 Influence of poly(ADP-ribose) polymerase on the enzymatic synthesis of SV40 DNA. *J. biol. Chem.* **266**, 3087–3100.

Ferro, A.M., McElwain, M.C. & Olivera, B.M. 1984 Poly(ADP-ribosylation) of DNA topoisomerase I: A nuclear response to DNA-strand interruptions. *Cold Spring Harb Symp. quant. Biol.* **49**, 683–690.

Friedberg, E.C. 1985 Excision Repair. DNA glycosylases and AP endonucleases. In *DNA Repair*, pp. 141–149. New York: Freeman & Co.

Gottlieb, T.M. & Jackson, S.P. 1993 The DNA-dependent protein kinase: requirement for DNA ends and association with Ku antigen. *Cell* **72**, 131–142.

Goulian, M., Richards, S.H., Heard, C.J. & Bigsby, B.M. 1990 Discontinuous DNA synthesis by purified mammalian proteins. *J. biol. Chem.* **265**, 18461–18471.

Graves, R.J., Felzenswalb, I., Laval, J. & O'Connor, T.R. 1992 Excision of 5′-terminal deoxyribose phosphate from damaged DNA is catalyzed by the Fpg protein of *Escherichia coli*. *J. biol. Chem.* **267**, 14429–14435.

Harrington, J.J. & Lieber, M.R. 1994 The characterization

of a mammalian DNA structure-specific endonuclease. *EMBO J.* **13**, 1235–1246.

Ishimi, Y., Claude, A., Bullock, P. & Hurwitz, J. 1988 Complete enzymatic synthesis of DNA containing the SV40 origin of replication. *J. biol. Chem.* **263**, 19723–19733.

Kawasaki, I., Bae, Y.S., Eki, T., Kim, Y. & Ikeda, H. 1994 Homologous recombination of monkey α-satellite repeats in an *in vitro* simian virus 40 replication system: Possible association of recombination with DNA replication. *Molec. Cell. Biol.* **14**, 4173–4182.

Kenny, M.K., Balogh, L.A. & Hurwitz, J. 1988 Mechanism of action of a host protein required for replication of adenovirus DNA templates devoid of the terminal protein. *J. biol. Chem.* **263**, 9801–9808.

Li, C., Goodchild, J. & Baril, E.F. 1994 DNA ligase I is associated with the 21 S complex of enzymes for DNA synthesis in HeLa cells. *Nucl. Acids Res.* **22**, 632–638.

Lindahl, T. 1971*a* An exonuclease specific for double-stranded DNA: deoxyribonuclease IV from rabbit tissues. *Methods Enzymol.* **210**, 148–153.

Lindahl, T. 1971*b* Excision of pyrimidine dimers from ultraviolet-irradiated DNA by exonucleases from mammalian cells. *Eur. J. Biochem.* **18**, 407–414.

Lindahl, T. 1993 Instability and decay of the primary structure of DNA. *Nature Lond.* **362**, 709–715.

Lindahl, T. & Barnes, D.E. 1992 Mammalian DNA ligases. *A. Rev. Biochem.* **61**, 251–281.

Ljungquist, S., Kenne, K., Olsson, L. & Sandström, M. 1994 Altered DNA ligase III activity in the CHO EM9 mutant. *Mutat. Res.* **314**, 177–186.

Lovett, S.T. & Kolodner, R.D. 1989 Identification and purification of a single-stranded-DNA-specific exonuclease encoded by the *recJ* gene of *Escherichia coli*. *Proc. natn. Acad. Sci. U.S.A.* **86**, 2627–2631.

Lu, X. & Lane, D.P. 1993 Differential induction of transcriptionally active p53 following UV or ionizing radiation: Defects in chromosome instability syndromes? *Cell* **75**, 765–778.

Manley, J.L., Fire, A., Samuels, M. & Sharp, P.A. 1983 *In vitro* transcription: Whole-cell extract. *Methods Enzymol.* **101**, 568–582.

Matsumoto, Y. & Bogenhagen, D.F. 1991 Repair of a synthetic abasic site involves concerted reactions of DNA synthesis followed by excision and ligation. *Molec. Cell. Biol.* **11**, 4441–4447.

Molinete, M., Vermeulen, W., Bürkle, A., Ménissier-de Murcia, J., Küpper, J.H., Hoeijmakers, J.H.J. & de Murcia, G. 1993 Overproduction of the poly(ADP-ribose) polymerase DNA-binding domain blocks alkylation-induced DNA repair synthesis in mammalian cells. *EMBO J.* **12**, 2109–2118.

Murante, R.S., Huang, L., Turchi, J.J. & Bambara, R.A. 1994 The calf 5′- to 3′-exonuclease is also an endonuclease with both activities dependent on primers annealed upstream of the point of cleavage. *J. biol. Chem.* **269**, 1191–1196.

Natarajan, A.T., Csukas, I. & van Zeeland, A.A. 1981 Contribution of incorporated 5-bromodeoxyuridine in DNA to the frequencies of sister-chromatid exchanges induced by inhibitors of poly-(ADP-ribose)-polymerase. *Mutat. Res.* **84**, 123–125.

Neddermann, P. & Jiricny, J. 1993 The purification of a mismatch-specific thymine-DNA glycosylase from HeLa cells. *J. biol. Chem.* **268**, 21218–21224.

Neddermann, P. & Jiricny, J. 1994 Efficient removal of uracil from G·U mispairs by the mismatch-specific thymine DNA glycosylase from HeLa cells. *Proc. Natn. Acad. Sci. U.S.A.* **91**, 1642–1646.

Nelson, W.G. & Kastan, M.B. 1994 DNA strand breaks: the DNA template alterations that trigger p53-dependent DNA damage response pathways. *Molec. Cell. Biol.* **14**, 1815–1823.

Oikawa, A., Tohda, H., Kanai, M., Miwa, M. & Sugimura, T. 1980 Inhibitors of poly(adenosine diphosphate ribose) polymerase induce sister chromatid exchanges. *Biochem. biophys. Res. Comm.* **97**, 1311–1316.

Panzeter, P.L., Zweifel, B., Malanga, M., Waser, S.H., Richard, M.-C. & Althaus, F.R. 1993 Targeting of histone tails by poly(ADP-ribose). *J. biol. Chem.* **268**, 17662–17664.

Price, A. 1992 Action of *Escherichia coli* and human 5′ → 3′ exonuclease functions at incised apurinic/apyrimidinic sites in DNA. *FEBS Lett.* **300**, 101–104.

Price, A. & Lindahl, T. 1991 Enzymatic release of 5′-terminal deoxyribose phosphate residues from damaged DNA in human cells. *Biochemistry Wash.* **30**, 8631–8637.

Prigent, C., Satoh, M.S., Daly, G., Barnes, D.E. & Lindahl, T. 1994 Aberrant DNA repair and DNA replication due to an inherited enzymatic defect in human DNA ligase I. *Molec. Cell. Biol.* **14**, 310–317.

Satoh, M.S. & Lindahl, T. 1992 Role of poly(ADP-ribose) formation in DNA repair. *Nature, Lond.* **356**, 356–358.

Satoh, M.S., Poirier, G.G. & Lindahl, T. 1993 NAD-dependent repair of damaged DNA by human cell extracts. *J. biol. Chem.* **268**, 5480–5487.

Satoh, M.S., Poirier, G.G. & Lindahl, T. 1994 Dual function for poly(ADP-ribose) synthesis in response to DNA strand breakage. *Biochemistry, Wash.* **33**, 7099–7106.

Smulson, M., Istock, N., Ding, R. & Cherney, B. 1994 Deletion mutants of poly(ADP-ribose) polymerase support a model of cyclic association and dissociation of enzyme from DNA ends during DNA repair. *Biochemistry, Wash.* **33**, 6186–6191.

Snyder, R.D. & Regan, J.D. 1982 DNA repair in normal human and xeroderma pigmentosum group A fibroblasts following treatment with various methanesulfonates and the demonstration of a long-patch (u.v.-like) repair component. *Carcinogenesis* **3**, 7–14.

Waga, S., Bauer, G. & Stillman, B. 1994 Reconstitution of complete SV40 DNA replication with purified replication factors. *J. biol. Chem.* **269**, 10923–10934.

Waldman, A.S. & Waldman, B.S. 1991 Stimulation of intrachromosomal homologous recombination in mammalian cells by an inhibitor of poly(ADP-ribosylation). *Nucl. Acids Res.* **19**, 5943–5947.

Withka, J.M., Wilde, J.A., Bolton, P.H., Mazumder, A. & Gerlt, J.A. 1991 Characterization of conformational features of DNA heteroduplexes containing aldehydic abasic sites. *Biochemistry, Wash.* **30**, 9931–9940.

Wood, R.D., Robins, P. & Lindahl, T. 1988 Complementation of the xeroderma pigmentosum DNA repair defect in cell-free extracts. *Cell* **53**, 97–106.

9

Nucleotide excision repair in the yeast *Saccharomyces cerevisiae*: its relationship to specialized mitotic recombination and RNA polymerase II basal transcription

ERROL C. FRIEDBERG[1], A. JANE BARDWELL[1]*, LEE BARDWELL[1]§,
WILLIAM J. FEAVER[2], ROGER D. KORNBERG[2], JESPER Q.
SVEJSTRUP[2], ALAN E. TOMKINSON[3] AND ZHIGANG WANG[1].

[1] *Laboratory of Molecular Pathology, Department of Pathology, The University of Texas Southwestern Medical Canter, Dallas, Texas 75235, U.S.A.*
[2] *Department of Cell Biology, Stanford University School of Medicine, Stanford, California 94305, U.S.A.*
[3] *Institute of Biotechnology, The University of Texas Health Science Center at San Antonio, San Antonio, Texas 78245, U.S.A.*

SUMMARY

Nucleotide excision repair (NER) in eukaryotes is a biochemically complex process involving multiple gene products. The budding yeast *Saccharomyces cerevisiae* is an informative model for this process. Multiple genes and in some cases gene products that are indispensable for NER have been isolated from this organism. Homologues of many of these yeast genes are structurally and functionally conserved in higher organisms, including humans. The yeast Rad1/Rad10 heterodimeric protein complex is an endonuclease that is believed to participate in damage-specific incision of DNA during NER. This endonuclease is also required for specialized types of recombination. The products of the *RAD3, SSL2(RAD25) SSL1* and *TFB1* genes have dual roles in NER and in RNA polymerase II-dependent basal transcription.

1. INTRODUCTION

The genetic versatility of the yeast *Saccharomyces cerevisiae* has facilitated the isolation and characteriz-ation of multiple mutants which are defective in nucleotide excision repair (NER) (Friedberg *et al.* 1991; Prakash *et al.* 1993). The genetic complexity of NER revealed by these mutants provided early clues that the biochemistry of this process involves a large number of gene products. Many of the yeast genes involved in NER have since been cloned and sequenced and shown to have functional homologues in humans (see later discussion) (Friedberg *et al.* 1991; Hoeijmakers 1993; Prakash *et al.* 1993). Hence, the biochemical com-plexity of this process is apparently general in eukaryotes. At present nine genes are known to be indispensable for NER in yeast (table 1) and there is indirect evidence for at least two other genes in this class. Additionally, at least three other genes are known to be involved in NER, but are not absolutely required for this process (table 1). This paper reviews the known functions of the polypeptides encoded by

several of these genes, with an emphasis on their participation in other aspects of DNA metabolism, notably mitotic recombination and transcription.

2. DAMAGE-SPECIFIC INCISION DURING NER

The specific recognition of base damage and the incision of the affected polynucleotide strand at such sites are unique and distinctive hallmarks of NER. Over a decade ago it was first demonstrated that damage-specific incision of DNA during NER in the prokaryote *E. coli* involves cutting of the affected DNA strand on each side of a damaged base, thereby generating an oligonucleotide fragment ~ 12 nucleotides in length that includes the base damage, which is ultimately excised (Grossman & Thiagalingam 1993; Sancar & Tang 1993; Van Houten & Snowden 1993). This bimodal incision paradigm appears to be universal, since studies have provided indirect evidence for such a mechanism in human cells (Svoboda *et al.* 1993), though the size of the oligonucleotide fragment generated in such cells is more than twice that in *E. coli*. Genetic and biochemical studies have identified two endonucleases that operate during NER in *S. cerevisiae*, consistent with a bimodal damage-specific mechanism in this organism as well.

* Present address: Genelabs Technologies Inc., Redwood City, California 94063, U.S.A.
§ Present address: Department of Molecular and Cell Biology, University of California at Berkeley, Berkeley, California 94720, U.S.A.

Table 1. *Nucleotide excision repair genes from* S. cerevisiae

cloned genes that are indispensable for NER

RAD1	non-essential for viability
RAD2	non-essential for viability
RAD4	non-essential for viability
RAD10	non-essential for viability
RAD14	non-essential for viability
RAD3	essential for viability
SSL2(RAD25)	essential for viability
SSL1	essential for viability
TFB1	essential for viability

suspected genes that are indispensable for NER

TFB2	probably essential for viability
TFB3	probably essential for viability

Genes that are not absolutely required for NER

RAD7	non-essential for viability
RAD16	non-essential for viability
RAD23	non-essential for viability

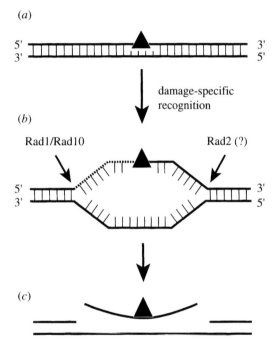

Figure 1. Possible roles of the Rad1/Rad10 and Rad2 endonucleases in bimodal incision during nucleotide excision repair in yeast. Biochemical events associated with damage-specific recognition are believed to result in a localized region of denaturation, incorporating the site of base damage. The (known) Rad3 and Ssl2 DNA helicases may well participate in this denaturation process. The properties of the purified Rad1/Rad10 endonuclease *in vitro* suggest that it could specifically recognize the duplex/3′ single strand junction on the damaged strand, thereby generating a nick 5′ to the site of base damage. The duplex/3′ single strand junction on the opposite DNA strand must be protected from such cleavage. If the Rad2 endonuclease is endowed with the ability to recognize duplex/5′-single strand junctions such specificity could account for cleavage of the damaged strand 3′ to the site of damage.

(a) *The Rad1/Rad10 endonuclease*

Complete mutational inactivation of the *RAD1* or *RAD10* genes results in extreme sensitivity to ultraviolet (UV) radiation and a total defect in NER in cell-free extracts (Wang *et al.* 1993). Such mutants are also defective in specialized forms of mitotic recombination (Friedberg *et al.* 1991; Prakash *et al.* 1993). The *RAD1* and *RAD10* genes encode polypeptides with apparent molecular masses of ~ 24 and ~ 130 kDa respectively (Friedberg *et al.* 1991; Prakash *et al.* 1993). Both polypeptides have been purified to physical homogeneity (Friedberg *et al.* 1991; Prakash *et al.* 1993) and form a stable and specific heterodimeric complex with 1:1 stoichiometry (Tomkinson *et al.* 1994). The Rad1/Rad10 complex, but not either protein alone catalyses the Mg^{2+}-dependent nicking of supercoiled DNA and the degradation of M13 circular single-stranded DNA, but does not cleave double-stranded linear DNA (Sung *et al.* 1993; Tomkinson *et al.* 1993). More refined analyses using polymer substrates of defined length and sequence have demonstrated that the Rad1/Rad10 endonuclease specifically recognizes the junction between double-stranded DNA and 3′ single stand tails (A. J. Bardwell *et al.* 1994*b*). Duplex polymers and partially duplex polymers with duplex/5′-single strand tails are not recognized by the enzyme. Single-stranded 49 mer polymers with no secondary structure are also not degraded by the Rad1/Rad10 endonuclease. Hence, it is likely that the degradation of M13 circular single-stranded DNA reflects the recognition of duplex-3′-single strand junctions in regions of DNA with secondary structure, rather than single-stranded DNA per se. Supercoiled DNA is a dynamic structure that contains transient single-stranded loops or bubbles. Presumably the Rad1/Rad10 endonuclease cleaves at the duplex/single strand junctions of these loops.

(b) *The role of the Rad1/Rad10 endonuclease in* NER *and recombination*

The specificity of the Rad1/Rad10 endonuclease for duplex/3′single strand junctions suggests a plausible model for its participation in DNA damage-specific incision during NER. The model requires the elaboration of Y-shaped duplex-single strand junctions flanking sites of base damage (figure 1). Such junctions would mark the limits of a region of localized unwinding of the DNA duplex conceptually similar to the denaturation 'bubbles' postulated during transcription and replication. We will return to a consideration of how such a NER 'bubble' may be generated in a later section of the paper. The specific recognition of the duplex/3′-single strand junction 5′ to a site of base damage (figure 1) is expected to constitute a substrate for the Rad1/Rad10 endonuclease. The polypeptide product of the *RAD2* gene is also a single-stranded endonuclease (Habraken *et al.* 1993) and is an attractive candidate for a second junction-specific endonuclease, possibly endowed with duplex/5′-single strand polarity. As such this enzyme might recognize the duplex/5′-single strand junction 3′ to a site of base damage (figure 1). To the extent that *rad1*, *rad10* and *rad2* mutants have been studied, there is no evidence that they manifest a residual capacity for incision of DNA. Hence, the mechanism of NER *in vivo* presumably provides for coordinated incisions at both

Y junctions in the model substrate shown in figure 1, such that Rad1/Rad10-mediated incisions do not occur in the absence of functional Rad2 protein and vice versa. Such coordinated catalysis is consistent with the evidence suggesting that the Rad1, Rad10 and Rad2 proteins are part of a multiprotein complex (repairosome) (see later discussion).

The junction-specific endonuclease activity of the Rad1/Rad10 protein complex also accommodates its known role in mitotic recombination between repeated sequences. Fishman-Lobell and Haber (1992) generated a model plasmid substrate containing two copies of the *E. coli lacZ* gene, one of which contains a 117 base pair (b.p.) cutting site for the HO mating-type endonuclease. Upon induction of the HO endo-nuclease a sequence-specific double-strand break is introduced in the copy of the *lacZ* gene containing the 117 b.p. cutting site. This cleavage introduces about 60 b.p. of 3′ terminal DNA in one of the *lacZ* sequences which is not present in the other. Mutants defective in the *RAD1* gene were not able to effect recombination between these repeated *lacZ* sequences. However, when both *lacZ* sequences contained HO endonuclease cutting sites, i.e., when complete homology between the repeated sequences was restored, recombination was effected in both wild-type and *rad1* mutants. Physical analysis of recombination intermediates suggests that *rad1* (and *rad10*) mutants are unable to remove the 3′ non-homologous 60 b.p. region, which is consequently trapped as a duplex/3′-single strand junction structure that stalls the completion of re-combination. In wild-type cells this junction is pre-sumably recognized by the Rad1/Rad10 endo-nuclease, resulting in the removal of non-homologous DNA. In contrast to the *RAD1* and *RAD10* genes, the *RAD2* gene is not required for mitotic recombination between repeated sequences (Friedberg *et al.* 1991; Prakash *et al.* 1993).

3. THE COUPLING OF NER AND TRANSCRIPTION

RNA polymerase II transcription in yeast requires the participation of multiple proteins designated factors a, b, d, e and g, corresponding to the mammalian transcription factors TFIIE, TFIIH, TFIID, TFIIB and TFIIF respectively (Conaway & Conaway 1993; Feaver *et al.* 1994). All of these proteins combine with RNA polymerase II to form a large transcription complex at the promoter prior to the initiation of transcription. The fate of this complex during tran-script elongation is unclear, aside from evidence that factor d (TFIID) remains at the promoter and factor g (TFIIF) plays a role in elongation.

Factor b (TFIIH) holoenzyme is comprised of multiple subunits, some of which are required for a protein kinase that phosphorylates the C-terminal domain of the β subunit of RNA polymerase II (Svejstrup *et al.* 1994*a*). Four polypeptides of 95, 89, 70, and 50 kDa are encoded by genes designated *SSL2(RAD25) RAD3, TFB1* and *SSL1* respectively. All four of these genes have been shown to be essential for

viability in haploid yeast cells (Friedberg *et al.* 1991; Gileadi *et al.* 1992; Gulyas & Donahue 1992; Yoon *et al.* 1992; Prakash *et al.* 1993), and conditional–lethal *rad3* and *ssl2* mutants have been shown to be defective in RNA polymerase II-dependent transcription under restrictive conditions (Qiu *et al.* 1993; Guzder *et al.* 1994). Two other genes designated *TFB2* and *TFB3* encode polypeptides of ~ 55 and ~ 38 kDa that are tightly associated with the Rad3, Tfb1 and Ssl1 polypeptides, resulting in a stable core factor b complex of five polypeptides *in vitro* (Feaver *et al.* 1993). Studies on the interactions between these five polypeptides have demonstrated that Rad3 protein specifically interacts with Ssl1 (L. Bardwell *et al.* 1994) and Ssl1 protein also interacts with Tfb1 protein (Feaver *et al.* 1993; L. Bardwell *et al.* 1994). Rad3 protein has also been shown to interact with Ssl2 protein (L. Bardwell *et al.* 1994).

In addition to their requirement for RNA polymerase II basal transcription, the Ssl2, Rad3, Tfb1 and Ssl1 polypeptides are required for NER. This conclusion stems from the demonstration that purified core factor b complex corrects defective NER in cell-free extracts of *rad3, tfb1* and *ssl1* mutants (Wang *et al.* 1994; Z. Wang *et al.*, unpublished observations). Similarly, core factor b with bound Ssl2 protein corrects defective NER in extracts of an *ssl2* mutant (Wang *et al.* 1994). It has been independently demonstrated that an *ssl2* mutant is defective in the removal of pyrimidine dimers from DNA *in vivo* (Sweder & Hanawalt 1994). Purified Rad3 protein alone does not complement defective NER in extracts of *rad3* mutants, and purified Ssl2 protein only partially corrects the defect in *ssl2* extracts (Wang *et al.* 1994). Hence, Rad3 and Ssl2 proteins (and presumably Ssl1, Tfb1 and the 55 and 38 kDa polypeptides) participate in NER as components of a multiprotein complex.

(a) *The role of factor b polypeptides in* NER

The specific biochemical role(s) of the factor b subunits in NER is unknown. A biochemical function has been identified for Rad3 protein, which is a DNA–DNA and DNA–RNA helicase with strict 5′→3′ polarity with respect to the strand to which it is bound (Friedberg *et al.* 1991; Prakash *et al.* 1993). The Rad3 DNA–DNA helicase activity is retained in factor b (Z. Wang *et al.* unpublished observations). A mutant *rad3* allele that encodes a helicase-defective form of Rad3 protein supports the viability of cells, but confers a NER-defective phenotype (Friedberg *et al.* 1991; Prakash *et al.* 1993). Similarly, factor b purified from a different strain carrying a similar mutation (which also renders defective NER) supports normal transcription *in vitro* (Feaver *et al.* 1993). Hence, it appears that the helicase function of Rad3 protein is required for NER but not for its role in transcription.

The translated sequence of the yeast *SSL2* gene suggests that it also encodes a DNA helicase (Gulyas & Donahue 1992). The highly conserved human hom-ologue of *SSL2* designated *XPB* (*ERCC3*) has in fact been shown to encode a protein with 3′→5′ DNA helicase activity (Schaeffer *et al.* 1994). While it remains to be directly demonstrated that purified yeast Ssl2 protein is also a $3' \to 5'$ DNA helicase, such is likely to be the case. A mutation in a conserved helicase motif of *SSL2* is lethal (Prakash *et al.* 1993), suggesting that the (presumed) Ssl2 yeast helicase is required for transcription. At present the possibility that this catalytic activity is additionally required for NER cannot be excluded.

It is not obvious precisely what role(s) the helicase activity of the Rad3 (and possibly Ssl2) protein plays in NER. Earlier we discussed a hypothetical substrate generated during NER with 3' and 5' duplex-single strand junctions, as an appropriate substrate for endonucleolytic cleavage by the Rad1/Rad10 (and Rad2) endonuclease. Conceivably such a NER 'bubble' is produced through the action of one or other (or both) of these helicases.

4. A MULTIPROTEIN NER COMPLEX (REPAIROSOME) IN YEAST

Core factor b interacts with Rad2 and Rad4 proteins (A.J. Bardwell *et al.* 1994*a*). Furthermore, *in vitro*-translated Rad2 protein co-immunoprecipitates with *in vitro*-translated Tfb1 and Ssl2 proteins (A.J. Bardwell *et al.* 1994*a*). Neither Rad1, Rad10 or Rad14 proteins have been shown to interact with factor b or its individual subunits. Nonetheless, extensive purification of yeast extracts for RNA polymerase II-dependent transcription activity *in vitro* has yielded a fraction that corrects defective NER in *rad1, rad10, rad2, rad3, rad14, ssl2* and to a lesser extent *rad4* mutants (Svejstrup *et al.*, 1994*b*). These results provide evidence for a multiprotein complex in yeast cells comprising at least the five core subunits of factor b plus Ssl2, Rad2, Rad14, Rad1/Rad10 complex and Rad4 proteins.

The structural and functional relationships between this complex, which we designate the NER *repairosome*, and the factor b holoenzyme required for transcription initiation remain to be elucidated. Conceivably core factor b is incorporated into two multiprotein complexes, one of which participates in transcription initiation and the other in NER. It also remains to be determined whether the repairosome alluded to here participates exclusively in NER that is coupled to transcription, repair in transcriptionally silent regions of DNA, or both. Recent studies suggest that TFIIH (yeast factor b) and TFIIE (yeast factor a) are required for the initiation of transcription but not for transcript elongation in a mammalian cell-free system (Goodrich & Tjian 1994). Hence, the transcription apparatus may be devoid of NER proteins during the latter process. Following arrest at sites of base damage the stalled transcription complex may require the presence of factor b for transcription to 'reinitiate' after repair of base damage is completed. Under these conditions factor b may be provided in a preassembled repairosome that facilitates both the repair of the template strand and continued transcription. The human equivalent of the *E. coli* transcription repair coupling factor(s) (TRCF) (Hanawalt 1992) may play a crucial role in this recoupling of transcription and

repair proteins. A similar model has been suggested for human cells (Drabkin *et al.* 1994). As an alternative to its dissociation and reassociation with the transcription machinery, factor b(TFIIH) (though not specifically required for transcript elongation), may remain physically associated with the elongation complex and repairosome assembly at sites of arrested transcription may be completed by exchanging CTD kinase subunits for those of the repairosome and TRCF.

A preassembled repairosome may also participate in NER that is not coupled to transcription. If so, among the many interesting questions that remain to be answered are how such a complex loads onto DNA and searches and finds base damage.

5. WHY IS NER COUPLED TO TRANSCRIPTION?

The finding that components of the RNA polymerase II basal transcription machinery also participate in a highly specialized and occasional (following DNA damage) metabolic transaction of DNA provides a rational biochemical basis for the long-standing observation that NER occurs more rapidly in transcriptionally active regions of the genome than in transcriptionally silent regions (Hanawalt 1993; Bohr 1993). Such coupling might have provided several selective advantages during eukaryotic evolution. The direct coupling of NER to transcription possibly provides a mechanism for solving the problem of the accessibility of a large repairosome to sites of base damage in chromatin in extensive regions of the genome. Additionally, if the specific recognition of base damage in the template strand during transcription is indeed effected by arrested transcription as suggested (Hanawalt 1993), the rapid positioning of NER proteins at such sites provides for efficient repair of the informationally relevant strand of transcriptionally active genes, which by dint of their expression are presumably important for cellular metabolism. The observation that the template strand is indeed typically repaired more rapidly than the coding strand during transcription (Hanawalt 1993; Bohr 1993) is consistent with this prediction. Finally, the participation of core factor b complex in different multiprotein complexes required for the initiation of basal transcription and for NER provides a potential mechanism for limiting the rate of basal transcription in the presence of NER; a useful response of cells that have sustained DNA damage.

6. IMPLICATIONS OF NER IN YEAST FOR HUMAN HEREDITARY DISEASE

The *RAD1, RAD10, RAD2, RAD4, RAD14, RAD3, SSL2, SSL1* and *TFB1* genes are conserved in the human genome (Hoeijmakers & Bootsma 1990; Hoeijmakers 1993; Prakash *et al.* 1993; Weeda 1993; Humbert *et al.* 1994). With the current exception of the human *RAD10* homologue, mutational inactivation of any of these human genes is associated with the cancer-prone hereditary disease xeroderma pigmentosum (XP). Additionally, mutations in the human *XPD*, *XPB* and *XPG* genes (the homologues of the yeast *RAD3*, *SSL2* and *RAD2* genes) can confer the phenotype of XP together with features of a second hereditary disease called Cockayne syndrome, and some mutations in the *XPD* gene can confer a disease called trichothiodystrophy (TTD) (Hoeijmakers & Bootsma 1990; Hoeijmakers 1993; Weeda 1993). The molecular basis of the relationship between these multiple diverse syndromes is a challenging conundrum. The genetic and molecular versatility of *S. cerevisiae* offers the promise of important insights into these and other complexities of NER in eukaryotes.

Studies from the laboratories of ECF and RDK were supported by research grants from the United States Public Health Service. Studies from AET's laboratory were supported by a grant from the Council for Tobacco Research, U.S.A. We thank our laboratory colleagues for review of the manuscript.

REFERENCES

Bardwell, A.J., Bardwell, L., Iyer, N. *et al.* 1994*a* Yeast nucleotide excision repair proteins Rad2 and Rad4 interact with RNA polymerase II transcription factor b(TFIIH). *Molec. Cell. Biol.* **14**, 3565–3576.

Bardwell, A.J., Bardwell, L., Tomkinson, A.E. & Friedberg, E.C. 1994*b* Specific cleavage of model recombination and repair intermediates by the yeast Rad1/Rad10 DNA endonuclease. *Science, Wash.* **265**, 2082–2085.

Bardwell, L., Bardwell, A.J., Feaver, W.J., Svejstrup, J.Q., Kornberg, R.D. & Friedberg, E.C. 1994 Yeast RAD3 protein binds directly to both SSL2 and SSL1 proteins: implications for the structure and function of transcription/repair factor b. *Proc. natn. Acad. Sci. U.S.A.* **91**, 3926–3930.

Bohr, V.A. 1993 Gene-specific DNA repair: characteristics and relations to genomic instability. In *DNA repair mechanisms* (ed. V. A. Bohr, K. Wassermann & K. H. Kraemer). pp. 217–230. Copenhagen: Munksgaard.

Conaway, R.C. & Conaway, J.W. 1993 General initiation factors for RNA polymerase II. *A. Rev. Biochem.* **62**, 161–190.

Drabkin, R., Sancar, A. & Reinberg, D. 1994 Where transcription meets repair. *Cell* **77**, 9–12.

Feaver, W.J., Svejstrup, J.Q., Bardwell, L. *et al.* Dual roles of a multiprotein complex from *S. cerevisiae* in transcription and DNA repair. *Cell* **75**, 1379–1387.

Fishman-Lobell, J. & Haber, J.E. 1992 Removal of nonhomologous DNA ends in double-strand break recombination: the role of the yeast ultraviolet repair gene *RAD1*. *Science, Wash.* **258**, 480–484.

Friedberg, E.C., Siede, W. & Cooper, A.J. 1991 Cellular responses to DNA damage in yeasts. In *The molecular and cellular biology of the yeast Saccharomyces*, vol. I (*Genome dynamics, protein synthesis, and energetics*) (ed. J. Broach, E. Jones & J. Pringle), pp. 147–192. Cold Spring Harbor, New York: Cold Spring Harbor Laboratory.

Gileadi, O., Feaver, W.J. & Kornberg, R.D. 1992 Cloning of a subunit of yeast RNA polymerase II transcription factor b and CTD kinase. *Science, Wash.* **257**, 1389–1392.

Goodrich, J.A. & Tjian, R. 1994 Transcription factors IIE and IIH and ATP hydrolysis direct promoter clearance by RNA polymerase II. *Cell* **77**, 145–156.

Grossman, L. & Thiagalingam, S. 1993 Nucleotide excision repair, a tracking mechanism in search of damage. *J. biol. Chem.* **268**, 16871–16874.

Gulyas, K.D. & Donahue, T.F. 1992 *SSL2*, a suppressor of a stem-loop mutation in the *HIS4* leader encodes the yeast homolog of human *ERCC-3*. *Cell* **69**, 1031–1042.

Guzder, S.N., Qiu, H., Sommers, C.H., Sung, P., Prakash, L. & Prakash, S. 1994 DNA repair gene *RAD3* of *S. cerevisiae* is essential for transcription by RNA polymerase II. *Nature, Lond.* **369**, 578–581.

Habraken, Y., Sung, P., Prakash, L. & Prakash, S. 1993 Yeast excision repair gene RAD2 encodes a single-stranded DNA endonuclease. *Nature, Lond.* **366**, 365–368.

Hanawalt, P.C. 1992 Transcription-dependent and transcription-coupled DNA repair responses. In *DNA repair mechanisms* (ed. V. A. Bohr, K. Wassermann & K. H. Kraemer), pp. 231–246. Copenhagen: Munksgaard.

Hoeijmakers, J.H.J. 1993 Nucleotide excision repair II: from yeast to mammals. *Trends Genet.* **9**, 211–217.

Hoeijmakers, J.H.J. & Bootsma, D. 1990 Molecular genetics of eukaryotic DNA excision repair. *Cancer Cells* **2**, 311–320.

Humbert, S., van Vuuren, H., Lutz, Y., Hoeijmakers, J.H.J., Egly, J.-M. & Moncollin, V. 1994 Characterization of p44/SSl1 and p34 subunits of the BTF2/TFIIH transcription/repair factor. *EMBO J.* **13**, 2393–2398.

Prakash, S., Sung, P. & Prakash, L. 1993 DNA repair genes and proteins of *Saccharomyces cerevisiae*. *A. Rev. Genet.* **27**, 33–70.

Qiu, H., Park, E., Prakash, L. & Prakash, S. 1993 The *Saccharomyces cerevisiae* DNA repair gene *RAD25* is required for transcription by RNA polymerase II. *Genes Dev.* **7** 2161–2171.

Sancar, A. & Tang, M.-S. 1993 Nucleotide excision repair. *Photochem. Photobiol.* **57**, 905–921.

Schaeffer, L., Moncollin, V., Roy, R. *et al.* 1994 The ERCC2/DNA repair protein is associated with the class II BTF2/TFIIH transcription factor. *EMBO J.* **13**, 2388–2392.

Sung, P., Reynolds, P., Prakash, L. & Prakash, S. 1993 Purification and characterization of the *Saccharomyces cerevisiae* RAD1/RAD10 endonuclease. *J. biol. Chem.* **268**, 26391–26399.

Svejstrup, J.Q., Feaver, W.J., LaPointe, J., Gulyas, K.D., Donahue, T.F. & Kornberg, R.D. 1994*a* Multiple forms of RNA polymerase 2 transcription factor 2H and dissociation of the C-terminal repeat domain kinase, TF2K. *Cell.* (In the press.)

Svejstrup, J.Q., Wang, Z., Feaver, W.J., Donahue, T.F., Friedberg, E.C. & Kornberg, R.D. 1994*b* Different forms of RNA polymerase transcription factor 2H (TF2H) for transcription and DNA repair: holo TF2H and a nucleotide excision repairosome. (Submitted.)

Svoboda, D.L., Taylor, J.-S., Hearst, J.E. & Sancar, A. DNA repair by eukaryotic nucleotide excision nuclease. Removal of thymine dimer and psoralen monoadduct by HeLa cell-free extract and of thymine dimer by *Xenopus laevis* oocytes. *J. biol. Chem.* **268**, 1931–1936.

Sweder, K.S. & Hanawalt, P.C. 1994 The COOH terminus of suppressor of stem loop (SSL2/RAD25) in yeast is essential for overall genomic excision repair and transcription-coupled repair. *J. biol. Chem.* **269**, 1852–1857.

Tomkinson, A.E., Cooper, A.J., Bardwell, L., Tappe, N.J. & Friedberg, E.C. 1993 Rad1 and Rad10 proteins from yeast are subunits of a single-stranded DNA endonuclease. *Nature, Lond.* **362**, 860–862.

Tomkinson, A.E., Bardwell, A.J., Tappe, N., Ramos, W. & Friedberg, E.C. 1994 Purification of Rad1 protein from *Saccharomyces cerevisiae* and further characterization of the Rad1/Rad10 endonuclease complex. *Biochemistry* **17**, 5305–5311.

Van Houten, B. & Snowden, A. 1993 Mechanism of action of the *Escherichia coli* UvrABC nuclease: clues to the damage recognition problem. *BioEssays* **15**, 51–58.

Wang, Z., Wu, X. & Friedberg, E.C. 1993 Nucleotide excision repair of DNA in cell-free extracts of the yeast *Saccharomyces cerevisiae*. *Proc. natn. Acad. Sci. U.S.A.* **90**, 4907–4911.

Wang, Z., Svejstrup, J.Q., Feaver, W.J., Wu, X., Kornberg, R.D. & Friedberg, E.C. 1994 Transcription factor b(TFIIH) is required during nucleotide excision repair in yeast. *Nature, Lond.* **368**, 74–76.

Weeda, G., Hoeijmakers, J.H.J. & Bootsma, D. 1993 Genes controlling nucleotide excision repair in eukaryotic cells. *BioEssays* **15**, 249–258.

Yoon, H., Miller, S.P., Pabich, E.K. and Donahue, T.F. 1992 *SSL*1, a suppressor of a *HIS*4 5-UTR stem-loop mutation, is essential for translation initiation and affects UV resistance in yeast. *Genes Dev.* **6**, 2463à2477.

10

Proteins that participate in nucleotide excision repair of DNA in mammalian cells

RICHARD D. WOOD

Imperial Cancer Research Fund, Clare Hall Laboratories, South Mimms, Herts EN6 3LD, U.K.

SUMMARY

The most versatile strategy for repair of damage to DNA, and the main process for repair of uv-induced damage, is nucleotide excision repair. In mammalian cells, the complete mechanism involves more than 20 polypeptides, and defects in many of these are associated with various forms of inherited disorders in humans. The syndrome xeroderma pigmentosum (XP) is associated with mutagen hypersensitivity and increased cancer frequency, and studies of the nucleotide excision repair defect in this disease have been particularly informative. Many of the XP proteins are now being characterized. XPA binds to DNA, with a preference for damaged base pairs. XPC activity is part of a protein complex with single-stranded DNA binding activity. The XPG protein is a nuclease.

1. INTRODUCTION

The main process used by cells to remove damage caused to DNA by ultraviolet light (uv) is called 'nucleotide excision repair'. It is a widely applicable repair mechanism, because in addition to removing the common uv-induced cyclobutane pyrimidine dimers and (6–4) photoproducts from irradiated DNA, a wide range of other kinds of DNA lesions can be eliminated, including many types of chemical adducts. Examples of chemical alterations acted upon by the process are adducts of purine residues with polycyclic aromatic hydrocarbons like benzpyrene diolepoxide, acetyl-aminofluorene linkages to guanine nucleotides, some products of reaction of cisplatin with DNA, and monoadducts and crosslinks of psoralen derivatives with pyrimidine bases. Adducts that are not removed include base pair mismatches and loopouts; these are acted upon by the separate enzymes of mismatch excision repair. Base residues modified by deamination or reaction with oxygen radicals are thought to be poor substrates for the nucleotide excision repair pathway, and these seem generally to be removed by an alternate pathway involving DNA glycosylases and apurinic endonucleases of the base excision repair pathway (see Lindahl *et al.*, this volume).

Considerable progress is now being made by many laboratories in understanding the process of nucleotide excision repair in eukaryotes, and its relationship to a fascinating group of human inherited syndromes. The importance of nucleotide excision repair is most dramatically illustrated by the existence of several human inherited syndromes in humans that are caused by mutations in repair genes. These disorders include xeroderma pigmentosum (XP), Cockayne's syndrome (CS), and trichothiodystrophy (Bootsma *et al.*, this volume). Most afflicted individuals are hypersensitive to uv light from the sun, and neurological and developmental abnormalities of various types are often

found. XP patients have a greatly elevated risk of developing skin cancer in sun-exposed portions of the body.

In outline, the nucleotide excision repair mechanism in eukaryotes is reasonably simple. DNA lesions are recognized, and then two incisions occur flanking the damage to remove an oligonucleotide containing the modified residue. The oligonucleotide is excised and repair DNA synthesis takes place to form a patch. Both *in vivo* and *in vitro* measurements in human cell systems show that the repair patch formed is about 30 nucleotides long (see Shivji *et al.* 1992; Szymkowski *et al.* 1993). For uv-induced cyclobutane pyrimidine dimers and for psoralen-DNA monoadducts, an oligo-nucleotide of 27–32 nucleotide residues is removed, corresponding to incision ∼ 5 phosphodiester bonds to the 3′ side of the lesion, and ∼ 22–24 phosphodiester bonds to the 5′ side of the lesion (Svoboda *et al.* 1993).

From the biochemical and genetic viewpoints however, the eukaryotic mechanism is complex and more than 20 polypeptides are known to participate in the complete process (Bootsma *et al.* and Friedberg *et al.*, this volume). In mammalian cells, these proteins and their corresponding genes have been recognized in several different ways. A major class is composed of the genes and proteins that can correct the defect in XP and CS. Cell fusion studies have identified seven nucleotide excision repair-deficient complementation groups in XP (groups A to G). The XP correcting factors are required for the first steps of nucleotide excision repair, and genes or proteins for most groups have been identified within the last four years (table 1). Some XP patients are also affected with CS; these include all known XP-B patients and some in groups D and G. There are also two CS groups (CS-A and CS-B) where CS occurs independently of XP. Genes defective in these latter CS groups appear to be involved in the special situation of preferential or transcribed genes. A second category of excision repair

Table 1. *Some proteins involved in nucleotide excision repair in human cells*

protein	MM, from open reading frame (kDa)	apparent MM, SDS-page	characteristics	other functions
XPA	31	40–42 (doublet)	Zn metalloprotein; DNA damage-binding	
XPB (ERCC3)	89	89	ATP-dependent 3′–5′ DNA helicase	component of TFIIH in human cells
XPC	106	125	binds single-stranded DNA	
HHR23B	43	58	associated with XPC	N-terminal domain has homology to ubiquitin
XPD (ERCC2)	87	80	ATP-dependent 5′–3′ DNA helicase	component of TFIIH in human cells
XPE (2 subunits)	127, ?	125, 41	binds damaged DNA	
ERCC1	33	40	part of endonuclease[a]	a pathway of mitotic recombination
XPF (ERCC4?)	?	?	part of endonuclease[a]	as above
XPG (ERCC5)	133	180–200	DNA endonuclease	
RPA (3 subunits)	68, 29, 13, 6	70, 32–34, 11–	single-stranded DNA binding	DNA replication; recombination
PCNA	29	36	formation of primer-template binding complex	DNA replication

[a] Deduced from properties of the yeast homologue; see text.

proteins is composed of the ERCC (excision repair cross-complementing) factors. These have their origin in the study of uv-sensitive mutants of rodent cell lines isolated in the laboratory. There are eleven known complementation groups of such rodent mutants, and human *ERCC* genes that can complement the repair defect in many of the groups have been isolated. There is some overlap of the ERCC, XP, and CS factors (table 1). The third category of nucleotide excision repair proteins includes those known to participate in DNA replication: RPA, PCNA, DNA polymerase ε or δ, DNA ligase, and probably other components of the DNA replication machinery.

2. SOME PROTEINS INVOLVED IN NUCLEOTIDE EXCISION REPAIR IN HUMAN CELLS

(a) The XPA protein

XPA is a 31 kDa polypeptide containing a zinc-finger motif (Miyamoto *et al.* 1992). The protein binds DNA, with a preference for damaged over undamaged duplex DNA. Preferential binding to both uv-damaged and cisplatin-damaged DNA has been demonstrated (Jones & Wood 1993). Non-damaged single-stranded DNA is also bound. In uv-irradiated DNA, (6–4) photo-products appear to be much better substrates for binding than cyclobutane dimers, as pyrimidine dimer photolyase has little efffect on the binding of XPA to uv-irradiated DNA (Jones & Wood 1993). This preference may provide an explanation for the much higher efficiency of nucleotide excision repair in removing (6–4) photoproducts from DNA than cyclo-butane pyrimidine dimers. The large difference in the rate of repair of the two lesions, known for some time

in vivo, has been recently shown in *in vitro* systems. Normal human cell extracts repair a single (6–4) photoproduct with tenfold or greater efficiency than a cyclobutane pyrimidine dimer (Szymkowski *et al.* 1993).

The high uv-sensitivity of XP-A cell lines, the affinity of XPA for damaged DNA, and the re-quirement of the protein for the introduction of incisions in uv-irradiated DNA *in vivo* (Miura *et al.* 1992) and *in vitro* (Shivji *et al.* 1992) all provide strong evidence that the XPA protein is a major factor in the recognition/incision stages of DNA damage in mam-malian cells. The relative affinity of XPA for a damaged versus an undamaged nucleotide pair is only several hundred to a 1000-fold (Robins *et al.* 1991; Jones & Wood 1993), and so other factors must contribute to the specificity of nucleotide excision repair in recognizing DNA damage.

(b) The XPE protein

Many research groups have found an activity in mammalian cell extracts that can bind to uv-damaged oligonucleotides in gel retardation assays. The major activity includes a polypeptide of ∼ 125 kDa, distinct from XPA, that is identical with the DNA damage-binding protein first purified from human tissue by Feldberg and Grossman (1976). The binding activity has recently been co-purified with an associated 41 kDa protein by Keeney *et al.* (Keeney *et al.* 1993). Significantly, binding activity is absent in extracts from some (but not all) cell lines derived from XP-E patients (Chu & Chang 1988; Hirschfeld *et al.* 1990; Kataoka & Fujiwara 1991; Keeney *et al.* 1992). Microinjection of the two-protein complex into those XP-E fibroblasts that are defective in the binding factor restores full repair synthesis to the cells (Keeney *et al.* 1994). This is a strong argument that defects in one or both of the proteins are indeed responsible for XP-E. The human gene that encodes the 125 kDa protein has been cloned (Takao *et al.* 1993). The discrimination of the XPE protein for uv photoproducts over non-damaged nucleotides is high (Hwang & Chu 1993; Reardon *et al.* 1993), being similar to the *E. coli* UvrA protein, and considerably greater than the relative affinity of XPA protein. Like XPA, the XPE protein shows a much greater affinity (on the order of tenfold) for uv-induced (6–4) photoproducts than for cyclobutane pyrimidine dimers (Abramic *et al.* 1991; Treiber *et al.* 1992; Hwang & Chu 1993; Keeney *et al.* 1993). At present, the actual role of XPE protein in repair is somewhat puzzling. XP-E cell lines are only moderately hypersensitive to uv light, and show about 50% of normal repair capability even in those cases where the DNA-damage binding activity is completely missing.

(c) *The ERCC1/ERCC4/XPF protein complex*

In yeast, the RAD1 and RAD10 proteins form a stable and specific complex that has endonuclease activity on single stranded DNA and can nick negatively supercoiled double stranded DNA (Sung *et al.* 1993*b*; Tomkinson *et al.* 1993, 1994). This activity is thought to be responsible for one of the specific incisions in the damaged DNA strand during nucleotide excision repair. Interestingly, the *RAD1* and *RAD10* gene products are also involved in a pathway of recombination between direct repeats in yeast, probably by removing non-homologous single-strand ends during the process (Fishman-Lobell & Haber 1992).

The human homologue of yeast RAD10 is the ERCC1 protein. *In vitro* analysis using cell-free DNA repair systems has recently revealed the existence of a complex of about 100 kDa or slightly larger that contains ERCC1, ERCC4, and XPF correcting activities (Biggerstaff *et al.* 1993; van Vuuren *et al.* 1993). By analogy with yeast, ERCC4 and XPF may be equivalent to one another and homologous to RAD1. The complex also contains an activity that corrects the repair deficiency in extracts from the sole mutant representing complementation group 11 of rodent cells (van Vuuren *et al.* 1993); the relationship of this activity to ERCC4/XPF is under investigation in several laboratories. ERCC1 and ERCC4 mutants are generally much more sensitive to chemical cross-linking agents such as mitomycin C and cisplatin than are mutants of other ERCC or XP groups (Hoy *et al.* 1985). This suggests a probable role of the complex as a nuclease in a form of DNA recombination similar to that of the RAD1–RAD10 complex in yeast.

(d) *The XPG protein*

During excision of a 12–13 mer oligonucleotide containing DNA damage in *E. coli*, both of the repair incisions flanking a lesion are made by the UvrB and UvrC protein complex, but two different active sites in the complex are used, one mainly involving UvrB for the 3′ incision and one involving UvrC for the 5′

incision (Lin *et al.* 1992; Lin & Sancar 1992). In eukaryotic cells the incisions are ∼ 27–29 nucleotides apart and it appears likely that an even further division of labour is employed, with two different nuclease complexes used to mediate the dual incisions.

Indeed, the human XPG protein has been shown to be a further endonuclease, active on MI3 bacteriophage DNA (O'Donovan *et al.* 1994). The *S. cerevisiae* homologue of XPG is the RAD2 protein, with an overall 39% similarity confined to two domains (Scherly *et al.* 1993). Like XPG, yeast RAD2 is a nuclease (Habraken *et al.* 1993). A simplification in the list of XP and ERCC genes was made when *in vitro* analysis placed ERCC5 and XPG in the same complementation group (O'Donovan & Wood 1993). The identity of ERCC5 and XPG is confirmed by the DNA sequences of the genes (MacInnes *et al.* 1993; Scherly *et al.* 1993; Shiomi *et al.* 1994). It thus appears that two endonucleases are required during eukaryotic nucleotide excision repair, and it is likely that the incisions on the two sides of the lesion are catalysed sequentially or simultaneously by the two activities. Selective cleavage of damaged DNA must result from the interaction of these DNA endonucleases with other components of the repair complex.

(e) *The XPC protein complex*

Group C is one of the most common forms of XP (Kraemer *et al.* 1987). Measurements of cellular repair synthesis show that XP-C cells have 10–20% of the repair synthesis displayed by normal cells. This residual repair synthesis arises because XP-C cells repair uv-induced pyrimidine dimers in limited domains (Mansbridge & Hanawalt 1983), even though the cells are unable to remove pyrimidine dimers from most of the genome. The residual repair is strongly associated with transcriptionally active DNA (Venema *et al.* 1990), and repair of the transcribed strand of expressed genes can still take place in XP-C cells (Venema *et al.* 1991). Thus, the XPC protein appears to be involved in repair of the (non-transcribed) bulk of the genome, and may be dispensable for the repair of the transcribed strand of some or all active genes.

Recently nucleotide excision repair synthesis was reconstituted *in vitro* by combining a PCNA-depleted XP-C cell extract, PCNA and a 160 kDa XPC factor purified about 2000-fold from HeLa cells (Shivji *et al.* 1994). The XPC factor is involved in an early stage of repair, as its presence is required during the first stage of repair, before initiation of gap-filling by PCNA. However, some incisions in uv-irradiated DNA are formed by XP-C cell extracts in the absence of XPC protein. These are 'unproductive' nicks that are unstable in cell extracts and give rise to only a limited amount of synthesis in damaged DNA, most of it in open circular DNA and thus representing incomplete repair events. The XPC factor restores the ability of XP-C cell extracts to introduce incisions in damaged DNA that are stable and lead to full repair (Shivji *et al.* 1994).

Legerski and co-workers isolated a cDNA designated XPCC that corrects the DNA repair defect and uv-

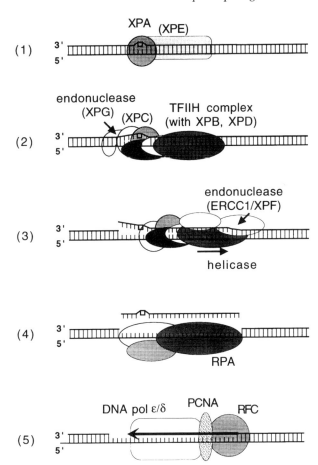

Figure 1. A speculative model for nucleotide excision repair in mammalian cells. Double-stranded DNA is indicated schematically, with the 3′ end at the left of the top strand, and damage is illustrated as a square box causing distortion of the duplex. The steps indicated from top to bottom are: (1) Recognition of a lesion in duplex DNA by XPA protein. Other proteins such as XPE may also participate in this step. (2) Incision of the damaged strand on one side of the lesion by an endonuclease. The nuclease may be correctly positioned for incision by interaction with other proteins forming a 'repairosome' that binds to DNA and promotes local denaturation around the lesion. (3) Unwinding of the damaged region by DNA helicase activities associated with TFIIH, and incision on the other side of the lesion. (4) Displacement of the damaged oligonucleotide by DNA helicase activity and single-stranded DNA binding protein. (5) Synthesis of a repair patch by a holoenzyme system consisting of DNA polymerase ε or δ, RFC, and PCNA.

The model is based on known and predicted properties of the various proteins indicated, and on the observed position of dual incisions produced by nucleotide excision repair in eukaryotes. Many features are uncertain. For instance, it is not known which nuclease complex makes the 5′ incision, and which the 3′, and in what order. Similarly, duplex unwinding near the lesion might occur before, during, or after incision.

hypersensitivity of XPC cells (Legerski & Peterson 1992). The cDNA encodes a hydrophilic polypeptide with a predicted molecular mass of 92 kDa. The cDNA shares some homology with the *S. cerevisiae* gene RAD4, but the sequence provided few clues to the function of the protein. Changes were found in this sequence in DNA from several XP-C cell lines (Li *et al.* 1993). To reconcile the 160 kDa XP-C factor that we found in

HeLa cells to that encoded by the XPCC cDNA, we speculated that the XP-C factor was a protein dimer in solution, or a complex of two or more proteins. Recently, Masutani *et al.* (1994) have isolated homogeneous XP-C factor from HeLa cells as a heterodimeric complex of two proteins (XPC and HHR23B) encoded by open reading frames of 106 and 43 kDa. From their data it is apparent that the 92 kDa product identified by Legerski & Peterson (Legerski & Peterson 1992) can be formed by initiation at an ATG codon present in the 106 kDa protein, and that the true N-terminus is part of a previously undetected segment. Our hydrodynamic estimate of 160 kDa for the size of XP-C correcting activity is in reasonably good agreement with the findings of Masutani *et al.*, being intermediate between the sum of molecular masses predicted by the two open reading frames (149 kDa) and the sum of masses predicted by migration of the polypeptides on SDS-PAGE ($125+58 = 183$ kDa).

(f) XPB, XPD and the TFIIH complex of proteins

Activities that can unwind double-stranded DNA participate in many DNA metabolic processes. At least two DNA helicases are involved in the core nucleotide excision repair process in eukaryotic cells: XPD(ERCC2) and XPB(ERCC3) in human cells and their homologues RAD3 and SSL2 in yeast (see Friedberg *et al.*, this volume). These genes are of special interest because both RAD3 and SSL2 are essential for viability in yeast, a property different from the other RAD proteins. Both XPB and XPD proteins have been shown to be DNA helicases (Schaeffer *et al.* 1993; Sung *et al.* 1993 a; Schaeffer *et al.* 1994). The DNA helicase activities of XPD and XPB may be involved in recognition of DNA damage, and/or in the displacement of the damaged oligonucleotide after incision and before repair synthesis.

Remarkably, XPB and XPD have both been found to be components of TFIIH/BTF2 (Schaeffer *et al.* 1993; Drapkin *et al.* 1994; Schaeffer *et al.* 1994; van Vuuren *et al.* 1994), a part of the RNA polymerase II basal transcription initiation complex. Functional XPB and XPD are needed for repair of non-transcribed, as well as transcribed DNA. The best interpretation of the results at present is that XPB has a dual function, serving in a DNA unwinding step during nucleotide excision repair, as well as during transcription initiation. The involvement of XPB and XPD in basal transcription may explain the clinical presentation of XP-B and XP-D patients, which includes neurological dysfunction and developmental problems in addition to the repair deficiency. For a discussion of this point the reader is referred to the article by Bootsma *et al.* in this volume.

(g) DNA repair synthesis and ligation

Nucleotide excision repair also uses proteins that function in the DNA replication machinery. RPA and PCNA proteins, previously isolated as cellular factors required for SV40 DNA replication *in vitro*, are needed for DNA repair. RPA is a trimeric single-stranded

DNA binding protein complex that seems to be essential for the formation and/or the stabilization of the incised intermediate structures. It may function in both early and late stages of repair (Coverley *et al.* 1991, 1992). PCNA is required for the gap-filling DNA synthesis step (Nichols & Sancar 1992; Shivji *et al.* 1992), indicating that the synthesis involves DNA polymerase δ or ε. DNA polymerase ε was purified by Nishida *et al.* (1988) as the polymerase that functioned in nucleotide excision repair in a permeabilized cell system. Recently it has been argued by M. Lee's group that DNA polymerase δ is required for nucleotide excision repair (Zeng *et al.* 1994). This conclusion is tentative, because a new method using nuclear extract protein was used to stimulate damage-dependent DNA synthesis *in vitro*, and it was not demonstrated that the synthesis was a result of nucleotide excision repair. Further study would be required to rule out the real possibility that the synthesis observed was caused by base excision repair, or even nick translation. By analogy with DNA replication, it is probable that a complex forms comprising RPA, PCNA, RFC and polymerase. To seal the nick remaining after DNA repair synthesis, three ligases are available in human cells. DNA Ligase I is a good candidate for the rejoining in nucleotide excision repair, as mutations in the corresponding gene cause a hypersensitivity to damaging agents including alkylating agents and uv (Barnes *et al.* 1992).

A speculative and schematic model of nucleotide excision repair in mammalian cells is given in figure 1, showing some possible roles for the proteins discussed here.

REFERENCES

Abramic, M., Levine, A.S. & Protić, M. 1991 Purification of an ultraviolet-inducible, damage-specific DNA-binding protein from primate cells. *J. biol. Chem.* **266**, 22493–22500.

Barnes, D.E., Tomkinson, A.E., Lehmann, A.R., Webster, A.D.B. & Lindahl, T. 1992 Mutations in the DNA ligase I gene of an individual with immunodeficiencies and cellular hypersensitivity to DNA damaging agents. *Cell* **69**, 495–503.

Biggerstaff, M., Szymkowski, D.E. & Wood, R.D. 1993 Co-correction of the ERCC1, ERCC4 and xeroderma pigmentosum group F DNA repair defects *in vitro*. *EMBO J.* **12**, 3685–3692.

Chu, G. & Chang, E. 1988 Xeroderma pigmentosum group E cells lack a nuclear factor that binds to damaged DNA. *Science, Wash.* **242**, 564–567.

Coverley, D., Kenny, M.K., Lane, D.P. & Wood, R.D. 1992 A role for the human single-stranded DNA binding protein HSSB/RPA in an early stage of nucleotide excision repair. *Nucl. Acids Res.* **20**, 3873–3880.

Coverley, D., Kenny, M.K., Munn, M., Rupp, W.D., Lane, D.P. & Wood, R.D. 1991 Requirement for the replication protein SSB in human DNA excision repair. *Nature, Lond.* **349**, 538–541.

Drapkin, R., Reardon, J.T., Ansari, A. *et al.* 1994 Dual role of TFIIH in DNA excision-repair and in transcription by RNA-polymerase-II. *Nature, Lond.* **368**, 769–772.

Feldberg, R.S. & Grossman, L. 1976 A DNA binding protein from human placenta specific for ultraviolet damaged DNA. *Biochemistry* **15**, 2402–2408.

Fishman-Lobell, J. & Haber, J.E. 1992 Removal of non-

homologous DNA ends in double-strand break recombination: the role of the yeast ultraviolet repair gene *RAD1*. *Science, Wash.* **258**, 480–484.

Habraken, Y., Sung, P., Prakash, L. & Prakash, S. 1993 Yeast excision repair gene RAD2 encodes a single-stranded DNA endonuclease. *Nature, Lond.* **366**, 365–368.

Hirschfeld, S., Levine, A.S., Ozato, K. & Protić, M. 1990 A constitutive damage-specific DNA-binding protein is synthesized at higher levels in UV-irradiated primate cells. *Molec. Cell. Biol.* **10**, 2041–2048.

Hoy, C., Thompson, L., Mooney, C. & Salazar, E. 1985 Defective DNA cross-link removal in Chinese hamster cell mutants hypersensitive to bifunctional alkylating agents. *Cancer Res.* **45**, 1737–1743.

Hwang, B.J. & Chu, G. 1993 Purification and characterization of a human protein that binds to damaged DNA. *Biochemistry* **32**, 1657–1666.

Jones, C.J. & Wood, R.D. 1993 Preferential binding of the xeroderma pigmentosum group A complementing protein to damaged DNA. *Biochemistry* **32**, 12096–12104.

Kataoka, H. & Fujiwara, Y. 1991 UV damage-specific DNA-binding protein in xeroderma-pigmentosum complementation group E. *Biochem. biophys. Res. Commun.* **175**, 1139–1143.

Keeney, S., Chang, G.J. & Linn, S. 1993 Characterization of a human DNA-damage binding protein implicated in xeroderma pigmentosum E. *J. biol. Chem.* **268**, 21293–21300.

Keeney, S., Eker, A.P.M., Brody, T. *et al.* 1994 Correction of the DNA-repair defect in xeroderma-pigmentosum group-E by injection of a DNA damage-binding protein. *Proc. natn. Acad. Sci. U.S.A.* **91**, 4053–4056.

Keeney, S., Wein, H. & Linn, S. 1992 Biochemical heterogeneity in xeroderma-pigmentosum complementation group-E. *Mutat. Res.* **273**, 49–56.

Kraemer, K.H., Lee, M.M. & Scotto, J. 1987 Xeroderma pigmentosum: cutaneous, ocular, and neurologic abnormalities in 830 published cases. *Arch. Dermatol.* **123**, 241.

Legerski, R. & Peterson, C. 1992 Expression cloning of a human DNA-repair gene involved in xeroderma pigmentosum group C. *Nature, Lond.* **359**, 70–73.

Li, L., Bales, E.S., Peterson, C. & Legerski, R. 1993 Characterization of molecular defects in xeroderma pigmentosum group C. *Nature Genet.* **5**, 413–417.

Lin, J.J., Phillips, A.M., Hearst, J.E. & Sancar, A. 1992 Active-site of (A)BC excinuclease 2. Binding, bending, and catalysis mutants of UvrB reveal a direct role in 3′ and an indirect role in 5′ incision. *J. biol. Chem.* **267**, 17693–17700.

Lin, J.J. & Sancar, A. 1992 Active site of (A)BC excinuclease 1. Evidence for 5′ incision by UvrC through a catalytic site involving Asp399, Asp438, Asp466, and His538 residues. *J. biol. Chem.* **267**, 17688–17692.

MacInnes, M.A., Dickson, J.A., Hernandez, R.R. *et al.* 1993 Human ERCC5 cDNA-cosmid complementation for excision repair and bipartite amino acid domains conserved with RAD proteins of *Saccharomyces cerevisiae* and *Schizosaccharomyces pombe*. *Molec. Cell Biol.* **13**, 6393–6402.

Mansbridge, J. & Hanawalt, P. 1983 Domain-limited repair of DNA in ultraviolet irradiated fibroblasts from xeroderma pigmentosum complementation group C. In *Cellular responses to DNA damage* (ed. E. Friedberg and B. Bridges), pp. 195–207. New York: Alan R. Liss.

Masutani, C., Sugasawa, K., Yanagisawa, J. *et al.* 1994 Purification and cloning of a nucleotide excision repair complex involving the xeroderma pigmentosum group C protein and a human homologue of yeast RAD23. *EMBO J.* **13**, 1831–1843.

Miura, M., Domon, M., Sasaki, T., Kondo, S. & Takasaki, Y. 1992 Restoration of proliferating cell nuclear antigen

(PCNA) complex-formation in xeroderma-pigmentosum group-A cells following cis-diammine-dichloro-platinum(II)-treatment by cell-fusion with normal-cells. *J. cell. Physiol.* **152**, 639–645.

Miyamoto, I., Miura, N., Niwa, H., Miyazaki, J. & Tanaka, K. 1992 Mutational analysis of the structure and function of the xeroderma-pigmentosum group-A complementing protein – identification of essential domains for nuclear-localization and DNA excision repair. *J. biol. Chem.* **267**, 12182–12187.

Nichols, A.F. & Sancar, A. 1992 Purification of PCNA as a nucleotide excision repair protein. *Nucl. Acids Res.* **20**, 3559–3564.

Nishida, C., Reinhard, P. & Linn, S. 1988 DNA repair synthesis in human fibroblasts requires DNA polymerase δ. *J. biol. Chem.* **263**, 501–510.

O'Donovan, A., Scherly, D., Clarkson, S.G. & Wood, R.D. 1994 Isolation of active recombinant XPG protein, a human DNA repair endonuclease. *J. biol. Chem.* **269**, 15961–15964.

O'Donovan, A. & Wood, R.D. 1993 Identical defects in DNA repair in xeroderma pigmentosum group G and rodent ERCC group 5. *Nature, Lond.* **363**, 185–188.

Reardon, J.T., Nichols, A.F., Keeney, S. *et al.* 1993 Comparative analysis of binding of human damaged DNA-binding protein (XPE) and *Escherichia coli* damage recognition protein (UvrA) to the major ultraviolet photoproducts – t[c,s]t, t[t,s]t, t[6–4]t, and t[dewar]t. *J. biol. Chem.* **268**, 21301–21308.

Robins, P., Jones, C.J., Biggerstaff, M., Lindahl, T. & Wood, R.D. 1991 Complementation of DNA repair in xeroderma pigmentosum group A cell extracts by a protein with affinity for damaged DNA. *EMBO J.* **10**, 3913–3921.

Schaeffer, L., Moncollin, V., Roy, R. *et al.* 1994 The ERCC2/DNA repair protein is associated with the class-II BTF2/TFIIH transcription factor. *EMBO J.* **13**, 2388–2392.

Schaeffer, L., Roy, R., Humbert, S. *et al.* 1993 DNA repair helicase: A component of BTF2 (TFIIH) basic transcription factor. *Science, Wash.* **260**, 58–63.

Scherly, D., Nouspikel, T., Corlet, J., Ucla, C., Bairoch, A. & Clarkson, S.G. 1993 Complementation of the DNA repair defect in xeroderma pigmentosum group G cells by a human cDNA related to yeast *RAD2*. *Nature, Lond.* **363**, 182–185.

Shiomi, T., Harada, Y.-n., Saito, T., Shiomi, N., Okuno, Y. & Yamaizumi, M. 1994 An ERCC5 gene with homology to yeast RAD2 is involved in group G xeroderma pigmentosum. *Mutat. Res.* **314**, 167–175.

Shivji, M.K.K., Eker, A.P.M. & Wood, R.D. 1994 The DNA repair defect in xeroderma pigmentosum group C and a complementing factor from HeLa cells. *J. biol. Chem.* 269, 22749–22757.

Shivji, M.K.K., Kenny, M.K. & Wood, R.D. 1992 Proliferating cell nuclear antigen is required for DNA excision repair. *Cell* **69**, 367–374.

Sung, P., Bailly, V., Weber, C., Thompson, L.H., Prakash,

L. & Prakash, S. 1993*a* Human xeroderma pigmentosum group D gene encodes a DNA helicase. *Nature, Lond.* **365**, 852–855.

Sung, P., Reynolds, P., Prakash, L. & Prakash, S. 1993*b* Purification and characterization of the Saccharomyces cerevisiae RAD1–RAD10 endonuclease. *J. biol. Chem.* **268**, 26391–26399.

Svoboda, D.L., Taylor, J.S., Hearst, J.E. & Sancar, A. 1993 DNA repair by eukaryotic nucleotide excision nuclease: removal of thymine dimer and psoralen monoadduct by HeLa cell-free extract and of thymine dimer by *Xenopus laevis* oocytes. *J. biol. Chem.* **268**, 1931–1936.

Szymkowski, D.E., Lawrence, C.W. & Wood, R.D. 1993 Repair by human cell extracts of single (6–4) and cyclobutane thymine–thymine photoproducts in DNA. *Proc. natn. Acad. Sci. U.S.A.* **90**, 9823–9827.

Takao, M., Abramic, M., Moos, M. *et al.* 1993 A 127 kDa component of a uv-damaged DNA-binding complex, which is defective in some xeroderma pigmentosum group E patients, is homologous to a slime-mold protein. *Nucl. Acids Res.* **21**, 4111–4118.

Tomkinson, A.E., Bardwell, A.J., Bardwell, L., Tappe, N.J. & Friedberg, E.C. 1993 Yeast DNA repair and recombination proteins Rad1 and Rad10 constitute a single-stranded-DNA endonuclease. *Nature, Lond.* **362**, 860–862.

Tomkinson, A.E., Bardwell, A.J., Tappe, N., Ramos, W. & Friedberg, E.C. 1994 Purification of Rad1 protein from *Saccharomyces cerevisiae* and further characterization of the Rad1/Rad10 endonuclease complex. *Biochemistry* **33**, 5305–5311.

Treiber, D.K., Chen, Z.H. & Essigmann, J.M. 1992 An ultraviolet light-damaged DNA recognition protein absent in xeroderma pigmentosum group E cells binds selectively to pyrimidine (6–4) pyrimidone photoproducts. *Nucl. Acids Res.* **20**, 5805–5810.

van Vuuren, A.J., Appeldoorn, E., Odijk, H., Yasui, A., Jaspers, N.G.J. & Hoeijmakers, J.H.J. 1993 Evidence for a repair enzyme complex involving ERCC1, ERCC4, ERCC11 and the xeroderma pigmentosum group F proteins. *EMBO J.* **12**, 3693–3701.

van Vuuren, A.J., Vermeulen, W., Weeda, G. *et al.* 1994 Correction of xeroderma pigmentosum repair defect by basal transcription factor BTF2 (TFIIH). *EMBO J.* **13**, 1645–1653.

Venema, J., van Hoffen, A., Karcagi, V., Natarajan, A.T., van Zeeland, A.A. & Mullenders, L.H.F. 1991 Xeroderma pigmentosum complementation group-C cells remove pyrimidine dimers selectively from the transcribed strand of active genes. *Molec. Cell Biol.* **11**, 4128–4134.

Venema, J., van Hoffen, A., Natarajan, A.T., Van Zeeland, A.A. & Mullenders, L.H.F. 1990 The residual repair capacity of xeroderma pigmentosum complementation group C fibroblasts is highly specific for transcriptionally active DNA. *Nucl. Acids Res.* **18**, 443–448.

Zeng, X.R., Jiang, Y.Q., Zhang, S.J., Hao, H.L. & Lee, M.Y.W.T. 1994 DNA-polymerase-delta is involved in the cellular-response to UV damage in human-cells. *J. biol. Chem.* **269**, 13748–13751.

11

Nucleotide excision repair syndromes: molecular basis and clinical symptoms

DIRK BOOTSMA, GEERT WEEDA, WIM VERMEULEN,
HANNEKE VAN VUUREN, CHRISTINE TROELSTRA,
PETER VAN DER SPEK AND JAN HOEIJMAKERS

Medical Genetics Centre, Department of Cell Biology and Genetics, Erasmus University Rotterdam, P.O. Box 1738, 3000 DR Rotterdam, The Netherlands

SUMMARY

The phenotypic consequences of a nucleotide excision repair (NER) defect in man are apparent from three distinct inborn diseases characterized by hypersensitivity of the skin to ultraviolet light and a remarkable clinical and genetic heterogeneity. These are the prototype repair syndrome, xeroderma pigmentosum (XP) (seven genetic complementation groups, designated XP-A to XP-G), Cockayne's syndrome (two groups: CS-A and CS-B) and PIBIDS, a peculiar photosensitive form of the brittle hair disease trichothiodystrophy (TTD, at least two groups of which one equivalent to XP-D).

To investigate the mechanism of NER and to resolve the molecular defect in these NER deficiency diseases we have focused on the cloning and characterization of human DNA repair genes. One of the genes that we cloned is *ERCC3*. It specifies a chromatin binding helicase. Transfection and microinjection experiments demonstrated that mutations in *ERCC3* are responsible for XP complementation group B, a very rare form of XP that is simultaneously associated with Cockayne's syndrome (CS). The ERCC3 protein was found to be part of a multiprotein complex (TFIIH) required for transcription initiation of most structural genes and for NER. This defines the additional, hitherto unknown vital function of the gene. This ERCC3 gene and several other NER genes involved in transcription initiation will be discussed.

1. NUCLEOTIDE EXCISION REPAIR

Nucleotide excision repair (NER) is one of the repair systems which are operational in the cell to ensure proper functioning and faithful transmission of genetic information. NER recognizes and eliminates a wide spectrum of structurally unrelated lesions such as ultraviolet light (UV) induced photoproducts, bulky chemical adducts and certain types of crosslinks. In most organisms, if not all, two NER subpathways operate. One deals with the rapid and efficient removal of lesions in the transcribed strand of active genes, that block ongoing transcription (transcription-coupled repair, Bohr *et al.* 1985). The second deals with the (more slow) removal of lesions in the bulk DNA, including the non-transcribed strand of active genes (genome overall repair). The generally accepted scheme for this process in eukaryotic cells is mainly based on our knowledge of NER in *E. coli* (Lin & Sancar 1992). This scheme (outlined in figure 1) includes the initial detection of DNA lesions and dual incision of the damaged strand at both sites of the lesion. Both steps most likely involve chromatin remodelling and include the cooperative action of a large number of proteins. Similarly a set of proteins is engaged in the excision of the DNA fragment containing the lesion. Finally the gap is filled in by DNA synthesis (unscheduled DNA synthesis, UDS, figure 2), using the opposite strand as template, and is closed by ligation. It is likely that the two NER subpathways have a number of steps in common using the same proteins or protein complexes. On the other side, convincing evidence exists for the presence of proteins which act specifically in one of the two subpathways. Examples of each of these categories of proteins or protein complexes will be discussed in this presentation.

2. NER MUTANTS AND DISEASES

Following the isolation of NER deficiency mutants in *E. coli*, a large number of eukaryotic mutants have been discovered. They were isolated in many species including yeast, Drosophila, rodent cell lines and man. They display sensitivity to UV light and numerous DNA damaging agents. The collection of yeast (*Saccharomyces cerevisiae*) NER mutants includes at least 11 different complementation groups, comprising the RAD3 epistasis group (see table 1). These complementation groups most likely represent 11 different genes playing a role in NER. Most of these genes have been cloned (for an overview see Hoeijmakers 1993*a*). Similarly, a large number of mammalian NER mutants have been generated in the laboratory using rodent cell

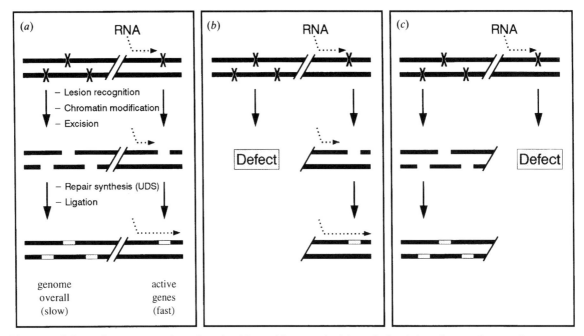

Figure 1. Schematic representation of nucleotide excision repair (*a*), and the defects in xeroderma pigmentosum complementation group C, XP-C (*b*) and Cockayne's syndrome (*c*). Two subpathways can be distinguished. One deals with the rapid and efficient removal of lesions in the transcribed strand of active genes (transcription coupled repair). The other is the more slow and less efficient repair of the bulk DNA, including the non-transcribed strand of active genes (genome overall repair). In XP-C the defect is limited to genome overall repair (*b*), in Cockayne's syndrome only transcription-coupled repair is defective (*c*).

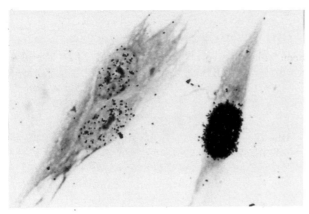

Figure 2. Unscheduled DNA synthesis (UDS) in normal human primary fibroblasts. Cells were exposed to ultraviolet light and grown in the presence of tritiated-thymidine for two hours, fixed and autoradiographed. The heavily labelled cell is in S-phase, the other two cells are in the G1- or G2-phase of the cell cycle and are weakly labelled as a result of UDS.

lines (Hoeijmakers 1993*b*). Cell fusion has identified a minimum of 11 complementation groups (table 1). By introducing human DNA into these rodent mutant cells the NER defect could be completed. These experiments resulted in the cloning of at least five different human DNA repair genes. These genes were designated *ERCC* (for <u>e</u>xcision <u>r</u>epair <u>c</u>ross <u>c</u>omplementing) followed by the number of the rodent complementation group corrected by the human gene.

In man the source of NER mutants is an interesting and still extending group of rare genetic diseases characterized by hypersensitivity of the skin of patients to sunlight (UV) (table 1). The prototype DNA repair syndrome is xeroderma pigmentosum (XP). In 1968 Cleaver discovered that the UV sensitivity of XP cells was the result of deficient repair of UV-induced DNA lesions (Cleaver 1968). By fusion of cells from different XP patients de Weerd-Kastelein *et al.* (1972) demonstrated genetic heterogeneity in this disease. At present seven distinct NER-deficient complementation groups can be distinguished (XP-A–G) representing seven different human genes involved in NER. Several of them have shown to be similar to ERCC genes cloned by transfection of rodent cells. A NER defect was also found in two other rare inborn disorders: Cockayne syndrome (CS) and PIBIDS, the photosensitive form of the brittle hair disease trichothiodystrophy (TTD). CS is represented by two complementation groups (CS-A and CS-B), whereas the NER defect of PIBIDS patients has been assigned to three complementation groups. Very interestingly two of the PIBIDS groups overlap with XP complementation groups: XP-B (Vermeulen *et al.* 1994) and XP-D (Stefanini *et al.* 1992). The third group (TTD-A) is represented by one patient only (TTD1BR, Stefanini *et al.* 1993). XP shows, in addition to sun sensitivity, other cutaneous manifestations, including pigmentation abnormalities and – in many but not all cases – an elevated frequency of skin cancer. In some individuals skin abnormalities are accompanied by progressive neurological degeneration and retarded growth. A different type of neurologic dysfunction is seen in CS, which is associated with dysmyelination of neurons. Other characteristic symptoms of CS in addition to photosensitivity are short stature, skeletal deformation, immature sexual development and a wizened facial appearance. The photosensitivity is not accompanied by pigmentation abnormalities and increased cancer incidence. PIBIDS patients manifest the CS symptoms and in addition the

Table 1. *Eukaryotic* NER *deficiency mutants*

origin	mutant	genes
human genetic diseases	xeroderma pigmentosum (XP)	*XPA, B,C,D,E,F,G*
	Cockayne's syndrome (CS)	*CSA, B*
	combined XP/CS	*XPB, D, G*
	trichothiodystrophy (TTD)	*XPB, D; TTDA*
rodent cell lines	UV-sensitive mutants	*ERCC1–11*
Saccharomyces cerevisiae	RAD3 epistasis group	*RAD1–4,7,10,14,16,23,25*, a.o.

hallmarks of TTD: brittle hair and nails and ichthyosis. Like CS patients PIBIDS individuals do not appear to be cancer-prone.

A few patients have been described having combined symptoms of XP and CS. A typical example is patient XP11BE (Robbins *et al.* 1974) who has been for a long time the only representative of XP complementation group B. The NER defect in these combined XP/CS patients has been assigned to XP-B, XP-D and XP-G (Vermeulen *et al.* 1993).

Thus a remarkable clinical heterogeneity is found to be associated with NER impairment. It has been shown that defects in one gene can give rise to classical XP, XP/CS or PIBIDS symptoms. This holds for XP-B and XP-D and to a lesser extent for XP-G. This clinical and genetical heterogeneity suggests that the syndromes involved represent different manifestations of a much broader clinical entity (Hoeijmakers 1993*b*; Bootsma & Hoeijmakers 1993). Obviously, it is difficult to adequately explain the entire spectrum and unusual combination of clinical features on the basis of a NER defect.

3. NATURE OF DEFICIENCY IN NER SYNDROMES

At the cellular level NER deficiency is reflected by hypersensitivity to UV and to agents that mimic the effect of UV. In most XP (including XP/CS) and PIBIDS patients UV-induced UDS is reduced or absent. The repair deficiency is most severe in XP groups A, B and G. In these groups and in XP-D, E and F the deficiency affects both overall genome repair and preferential repair of active genes. Apparently the defects are located in common steps of both subpathways. In XP-C the NER defect is limited to the repair of the overall genome (Venema *et al.* 1990*a*) (figure 1). In PIBIDS both subpathways are affected whereas in CS the NER defect is limited to preferential repair of the transcribed strand of active genes (Venema *et al.* 1990*b*) (figure 1). The overall genome repair system in CS is still functional. The nearly normal levels of UDS found in CS cells after UV exposure are in agreement with the small contribution of preferential repair to the total repair synthesis. The preferential repair defect prevents a rapid recovery of RNA synthesis after UV treatment. This may cause the increased UV sensitivity of CS patients.

Available evidence suggests that all seven XP groups are deficient in early steps of NER which occur at or

before the incision step (Tanaka *et al.* 1975; de Jonge *et al.* 1985). The gene products could be involved in modification of the DNA structure for the incision step, in altering the chromatin structure such that the damaged DNA is rendered accessible to the repair enzymes or in the incision step itself.

4. CLONED HUMAN NER GENES

Cloning and functional characterization of the genes involved in the different complementation groups of XP, CS and PIBIDS contributed considerably to our understanding of the molecular basis of the NER defects and their relationships with the clinical symptoms. In the last few years rapid progress has been made in this direction. Table 2 summarizes the genes that have been cloned so far and shown to be involved in NER deficiency syndromes. Five of the seven XP genes have been isolated, two of them (*XPB* and *XPD*) are also involved in PIBIDS and, with *XPG*, in combined XP/CS. One CS gene, *CSB* (*ERCC6*) has been cloned. This is the first human gene isolated that functions specifically in the preferential repair of the transcribed strand of active genes. Similarly *XPC* is the first gene cloned that is specifically involved in the genome–overall repair subpathway, whereas *XPA, XPB, XPD* and *XPG* are involved in common steps of both subpathways.

Some aspects of *CSB, XPC* and *XPB* will be discussed below.

(a) CSB (ERCC6)

ERCC6 was cloned by transfection-correction of rodent UV-sensitive cells of complementation group 6 with human DNA (Troelstra *et al.* 1992). This large gene (more than 85 kb) encodes a protein with putative chromatin and nucleotide-binding domains and the gene motifs conserved between two superfamilies of established and presumed DNA and RNA helicases (Troelstra *et al.* 1992) (figure 3). The gene is located on chromosome region 10q11–21. From cytogenetic and Southern blot analysis of cells from a CS patient it became evident that one of the *ERCC6* alleles was deleted suggesting a possible role of *ERCC6* in CS. UV-sensitivity and inhibition of recovery of RNA synthesis after UV-exposure of CS-B cells was complemented by transfection of functional *ERCC6* cDNA. Isolation of the two *ERCC6* alleles of a CS-B patient revealed the presence of mutations which result in severely trunc-

Table 2. *Cloned human* NER *genes involved in* NER *syndromes*

gene	homology to	reference
XPA	*RAD14*	Tanaka *et al.* (1990)
		Bankmann *et al.* (1992)
XPB (*ERCC3*)	RAD25 (SSL2)	Weeda *et al.* (1990)
	Drosophila 'haywire'	Gulyas & Donahue (1992)
		Park *et al.* (1992)
		Mounkes *et al.* (1992)
XPC	RAD4 (?)	Legerski & Peterson (1992)
		Masutani *et al.* (1994)
XPD (*ERCC2*)	RAD3	Weber *et al.* (1990)
		Flejter *et al.* (1992)
XPG (*ERCC5*)	RAD2	Mudgett & MacInnes (1990)
		Scherly *et al.* (1993)
		O'Donovan & Wood (1993)
CSB (*ERCC6*)	RAD26	Troelstra *et al.* (1992)
		van Gool *et al.* (1994)
		Huang *et al.* (1994)

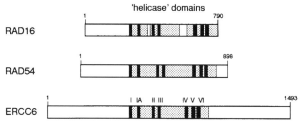

Figure 3. ERCC6 and two other repair proteins RAD16 and RAD54 sharing a region containing putative helicase domains. The seven consensus helicase motifs (I, IA etc.) are indicated. The entire helicase region (stippled) of the ERCC6 protein appears to be highly homologous to a similar region in proteins from a rapidly expanding family of (postulated) helicases. RAD16 is involved in nucleotide excision repair and RAD54 in recombination repair in yeast.

ated ERCC6 gene-products not expected to be functional (Troelstra *et al.* 1992). These observations prove the involvement of *ERCC6* in CS complementation group B. Following the new rules for nomenclature of NER genes the gene is now designated *CSB*. The presumed helicase activity of *CSB* should fit into the mechanism of transcribed strand-specific repair of active genes that is deficient in CS-B. Several possibilities can be envisaged. The protein may be involved in scanning the transcribed strand for a stalled RNA polymerase-transcription complex at the site of a lesion, thereby guiding the NER machinery to lesions that block transcription. It may be involved in unwinding the RNA–DNA duplex closely behind the blocked transcription complex, thus dissociating it from the template and removing steric hindrance to the lesion. It may also function in moving the RNA polymerase backwards to facilitate repair of the lesion and to save the messenger. These are still speculative models which have to be tested in biochemical experiments using purified proteins and *in vitro* repair assay systems.

(b) XPC *(complex with* HHR23B*)*

XP complementation group C is one of the most common forms of this disease. XP-C is not associated with accelerated neurodegeneration. This is consistent with the idea that transcription-coupled repair, which is still functional in XP-C, is crucial for prevention of this type of neurodysfunction. As already mentioned the NER defect is located in the repair of non-transcribing regions of the DNA (genome overall repair)(figure 1c). The gene has been cloned by transfection of human cDNA directly into XP-C cells (Legerski and Peterson 1992). The predicted (and as later appeared incomplete (Masutani *et al.* 1994)) amino acid sequence of XPC shows limited homology to yeast RAD4 but does not give a clue to its function.

Recently, Hanaoka and his colleagues purified the XPC protein using an *in vitro* cell-free repair system containing uv-damaged SV40 minichromosomes as a substrate (Masutani *et al.* 1994). A protein of 58 kDa copurified with the 125 kDa XPC protein. Subsequent cDNA cloning revealed that the 58 kDa protein was encoded by one of the two human homologues of the *S.cerevisiae* repair gene *RAD23* (*HHR23B*) cloned independently by van der Spek in our laboratory (figure 4).

The co-purification results suggest that XP-C and HHR23B form a complex that, based on the nature of the XP-C mutation, is expected to operate specifically in the genome-overall repair pathway. Interestingly the other human homologue of yeast RAD23, HHR23A, has not been detected in the purified complex. No human NER syndrome with a defect in HHR23A or B has been identified so far (P. J. van der Spek, unpublished observations), indicating possible functional redundancy.

The HHR23A and B proteins are ubiquitin-fusion proteins harbouring an ubiquitin-like domain at the N-terminus (figure 4). The function of this domain is unknown. In the case of RAD23 it has been demonstrated that the ubiquitin-like part is required for the repair function of the yeast protein (Watkins *et al.* 1993). A number of ubiquitin fusion proteins has been identified. In the case of a ribosomal ubiquitin-fusion protein it was indicated that the ubiquitin domain functions as a chaperon, facilitating ribosome assembly (Finley *et al.* 1989). Similarly, this domain in HHR23B may be involved in assembly of the

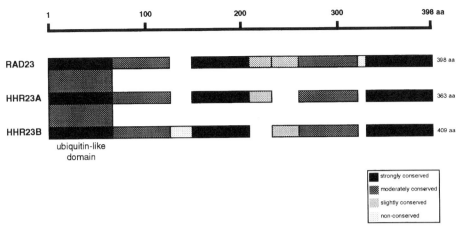

Figure 4. Homology between yeast and human RAD23 proteins. The two human proteins HHR23A and HHR23B have been isolated by using the sequence of the yeast NER protein RAD23. All three contain a ubiquitin-like domain at the N-terminus. As indicated other domains of these proteins also show (different levels of) homology.

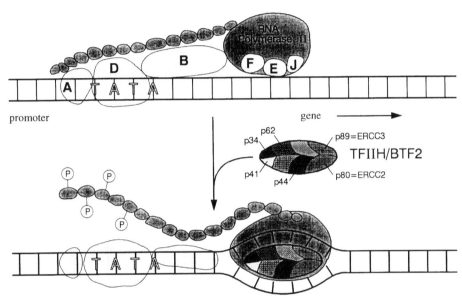

Figure 5. A simplified representation of the role of the transcription factor TFIIH/BTF2 in basal gene transcription. RNA polymerase II and a number of basal transcription factors are assembled in a closed complex on the promoter (upper part). TFIIH/BTF2 is involved in melting the DNA duplex and possibly in phosphorylation of the C-terminal part of the RNA polymerase. The result is an elongation-competent complex (lower part). ERCC3 (p89) and ERCC2 (p80) are part of the TFIIH/BTF2 factor. Several other NER proteins have shown to be components of this factor as well (see text).

XPC/HHR23B complex. Alternatively or in addition, the ubiquitin moiety may stabilize the protein (complex). The specific function of this complex in genome-overall repair still remains to be elucidated.

(c) XPB (ERCC3)

The human gene correcting the NER defect in rodent cells of complementation group 3 (*ERCC3*) was cloned by Weeda *et al.* (1990). Its role in XP complementation group B was established by microinjection of *ERCC3* cDNA into cells of patient XP11BE. This resulted in correction of the NER defect in cells of this patient who had combined symptoms of XP and CS. Recently we found that the NER defect in PIBIDS patient TTD6VI is the result of a mutation in *ERCC3* as well (Vermeulen *et al.* 1994). Both NER subpathways are defective in XP-

B cells, indicating that ERCC3 is involved in a common step. The protein contains the seven conserved domains characteristic for a helicase.

A dual role of *ERCC3* in NER and in basal transcription of all structural genes was demonstrated by van Vuuren *et al.* (1994) following the discovery of Egly and coworkers at Strasbourg that the ERCC3 protein is one of the essential components of the human basal transcription factor BTF2/TFIIH (Schaeffer *et al.* 1993) (figure 5). Subsequently we found that microinjection of the purified BTF2/TFIIH complex in cells of all other XP and TTD complementation groups resulted in selective correction of the NER defect of XP-D patients and of a PIBIDS patient representing TTD complementation group B (Vermeulen *et al.* 1994; for a recent review see Bootsma and Hoeijmakers 1994). With some slight variations, probably due to differences in purification strategies, a similar overlap between NER and transcription is found in yeast (*see* Friedberg *et al.*, this meeting).

5. DNA REPAIR AND TRANSCRIPTION, TWO ASPECTS OF THE SAME DISEASE

These exciting findings shed a new light onto the clinical features of XP, XP/CS and PIBIDS that were difficult to rationalize on the basis of a NER defect (Bootsma and Hoeijmakers, 1993). It is plausible that at least some of the unusual symptoms of these diseases are due to the impairment of the transcription function of the corresponding proteins. Most mutations in these genes will be incompatible with life because of the vital nature of the basal transcription mechanism. This explains the rarity of these disorders. Only a subtle defect in general transcription might be tolerated. This may afflict the expression of genes in a specific manner. It is known that the requirement for transcription factors varies from promoter to promoter. This requirement depends on the sequence surrounding the transcription initiation site, the topological state of the DNA, the local chromatin structure and other factors (see Stanway 1993). It is likely that the effect on expression of a particular gene will also be influenced by the site of the mutation responsible for the transcription defect. These are all factors that may determine the clinical heterogeneity found in these diseases.

We speculate that the neurological abnormalities associated with dysmyelination in CS are due to poor expression of one of the myelin genes (see mouse models described by Popko *et al.* 1987). Similarly, the brittle hair symptoms of TTD might be related to a decreased expression of cysteine-rich matrix proteins, the severe growth defect to suboptimal expression of growth determining genes and immature sexual development to reduced expression of β-tubulin in the testis, required for spindle formation during meiosis (observed in ERCC3-deficient Drosophila mutants, Mounkes *et al.* 1992). Hence, we consider the specific features of CS and PIBIDS being the consequence of the transcription defect, whereas the photosensitivity observed in these diseases, and (albeit clinically different) also in XP, as a consequence of the DNA repair defect of these disorders. A crucial question in this respect is whether the defect in classical CS (CS-A and CS-B) also affects the basal transcription mechanism. The predicted severely truncated ERCC6 geneproducts in cells of a CS-B patient (Troelstra *et al.* 1992) suggest that *ERCC6* is not a vital gene. This is in contrast with *ERCC2* and *ERCC3* involved in the XP/CS and PIBIDS phenotype. Further studies on the function of *ERCC6* (and the still unknown *CSA* gene) are required to solve this problem.

The dual function of *ERCC3* and several other DNA repair genes in repair and in transcription implies that a mutation in these genes, depending on its location, may influence only one of the two functions. A sole effect on transcription would explain the forms of trichothiodystrophy and Cockayne Syndrome without photosensitivity.

It is still very difficult to explain the pattern of cancer predisposition in these NER syndromes. Cancer predisposition is observed in many, but not all, patients having a defect in the genome-overall repair pathway. Exceptions are photosensitive TTD patients and several XP patients representing most of the XP complementation groups. Cancer predisposition is absent in patients with a defect in active gene repair and with normal genome-overall repair (classical Cockayne Syndrome). This suggests that the genome-overall repair pathway is associated with cancer formation. However, the exceptions indicate that other factors may also be involved. The nature of these factors is unknown. They may be independent from the NER and transcription function of the genes involved. However, the interplay of defective DNA repair and impairment of transcription in cancer predisposition remains a possibility. The generation of mouse models by mimicking mutations found in patients in *ERCC3* and other repair genes may be helpful in elucidating these important questions.

The authors thank their colleagues in the Medical Genetics Centre (MGC) who contributed to this work. In particular we are indebted to Jean-Marc Egly and coworkers at Strasbourg. The work of our group is supported by the Dutch Cancer Society, the Netherlands Organization of Advancement of Pure Science and the Commission of the European Community.

REFERENCES

Bankmann, M., Prakash, L. & Prakash, S. 1992 Yeast RAD14 and human xeroderma pigmentosum group A DNA repair genes encode homologous proteins. *Nature, Lond.* **355**, 555–558.

Bohr V.A., Smith, C.A., Okumoto, D.S. & Hanawalt, P.C. 1985 DNA repair in an active gene: removal of pyrimidine dimers from the DHFR gene of CHO cells is much more efficient than in the genome overall. *Cell* **40**, 359–369.

Bootsma, D. & Hoeijmakers, J.H.J. 1993 DNA repair engagement with transcription. *Nature, Lond.* **363**, 114–115.

Bootsma, D. & Hoeijmakers, J.H.J. 1994 The molecular basis of nucleotide excision repair syndromes. *Mutat. Res.* **307**, 15–23.

Cleaver, J.E. 1968 Defective repair replication of DNA in xeroderma pigmentosum. *Nature, Lond.* **218**, 652–656.

de Jonge, A.J.R., Vermeulen, W., Keijzer, W., Hoeijmakers, J.H.J. & Bootsma, D. 1985 Microinjection of *Micrococcus luteus* uv-endonuclease restores uv-induced unscheduled DNA synthesis in cells of 9 xeroderma pigmentosum complementation groups. *Mutat. Res.* **150**, 99–105.

de Weerd-Kastelein, E.A., Keijzer, W. & Bootsma, D. 1972 Genetic heterogeneity of xeroderma pigmentosum demonstrated by somatic cell hybridization. *Nature new Biol.* **238**, 80–83.

Finley, D., Bartel, B. & Varshavsky, A. 1989 The tails of ubiquitin precursors are ribosomal proteins whose fusion to ubiquitin facilitates ribosome biogenesis. *Nature, Lond.* **338**, 394–401.

Flejter W.L., McDaniel, L.D., Johns, D., Friedberg E.C. & Schultz, R.A. 1992 Correction of xeroderma pigmentosum complementation group D mutant cell phenotypes by chromosome and gene transfer: involvement of the human *ERCC2* DNA repair gene. *Proc. natn. Acad. Sci. U.S.A.* **89**, 261–265.

Gulyas K.D. & Donahue, T.F. 1992 *SSL2*, a suppressor of a stem-loop mutation in the HIS leader encodes the yeast homolog of human *ERCC3*. *Cell* **69**, 1031–1042.

Hoeijmakers, J.H.J. 1993*a* Nucleotide excision repair I: from *E. coli* to yeast. *TIG* **9**, 173–177.

Hoeijmakers, J.H.J. 1993*b* Nucleotide excision repair II: from yeast to mammals. *TIG* **9**, 211–217.

Huang, M.-E., Chuat, J.-C. & Galibert, F. 1994 A possible yeast homolog of human active-gene-repairing helicase ERCC6. *Biochem. biophys. Res. Commun.* **201**, 310–317.

Legerski, R. & Peterson, C. 1992 Expression cloning of a human DNA repair gene involved in xeroderma pigmentosum group C. *Nature, Lond.* **359**, 70–73.

Lin, J.J. & Sancar, A. 1992 (A)BC excinuclease: The *Escherichia coli* nucleotide excision repair enzyme. *Molec. Microbiol.* **6**, 2219–2224.

Masutani, C., Sugasawa, K., Yanagisawa, J. *et al.* 1994 Purification and cloning of a nucleotide excision repair complex involving the xeroderma pigmentosum group C protein and a human homolog of yeast RAD23. *EMBO J.* **13**, 1831–1843.

Mounkes L.C., Jones, R.C., Liang, B.-C., Gelbart, W. & Fuller, M.T. 1992 A *Drosophila* model for xeroderma pigmentosum and Cockayne's syndrome: *haywire* encodes the fly homolog of *ERCC3*, a human excision repair gene. *Cell* **71**, 925–937.

Mudgett, J.S. & MacInnes, M.A. 1990 Isolation of the functional human excision repair gene *ERCC5* by intercosmid recombination. *Genomics* **8**, 623–633.

O'Donovan, A. & Wood, R.D. 1993 Identical defects in DNA repair in xeroderma pigmentosum group G and rodent ERCC group 5. *Nature, Lond.* **363**, 185–188.

Park, E., Guzder, S.M., Koken M.H.M. *et al.* 1992 *RAD52* (*SSL2*), the yeast homolog of the human xeroderma pigmentosum group B DNA repair gene, is essential for viability. *Proc. natn. Acad. Sci. U.S.A.* **89**, 11416–11420.

Popko, B., Puckett, C., Lai, E. *et al.* 1987 Myelin deficient mice: Expression of myelin basic protein and generation of mice with varying levels of myelin. *Cell* **48**, 713–721.

Robbins, J.H., Kraemer, K.H., Lutzner, M.A., Festoff, B.W. & Coon, H.G. 1974 Xeroderma pigmentosum. An inherited disease with sun sensitivity, multiple cutaneous neoplasms and abnormal repair. *Ann. int. Med.* **80**, 221–248.

Schaeffer L, Roy, R., Humbert, S. *et al.* 1993 The basic transcription factor BTF2/TFIIH contains a DNA helicase involved in both transcription and DNA repair. *Science, Wash.* **260**, 58–63.

Scherly, D., Nouspikel, T., Corlet, J., Ucla, C., Bairoch, A. & Clarkson, S.G. 1993 Complementation of the DNA repair defect in xeroderma pigmentosum group G cells by a human cDNA related to yeast *RAD2*. *Nature, Lond.* **363**, 182–185.

Stanway, C.A. 1993 Simplicity amidst complexity in transcription initiation. *BioEssays* **15**, 559–560.

Stefanini, M., Giliani, S., Nardo, T. *et al.* 1992 DNA repair investigations in nine Italian patients affected by trichothiodystrophy. *Mutat. Res.* **273**, 199–125.

Stefanini, M., Vermeulen, W., Weeda, G. *et al.* 1993 A new nucleotide-excision-repair gene associated with the disorder trichothiodystrophy. *Am. J. hum. Genet.* **53**, 817–821.

Tanaka, K., Sekiguchi, M. & Okada, Y. 1975 Restoration of ultraviolet-induced unscheduled DNA synthesis of xeroderma pigmentosum cells by the concomitant treatment with bacteriophage T4 endonuclease V and HVJ (Sendai virus). *Proc. natn. Acad. Sci. U.S.A.* **72**, 4071–4075.

Tanaka, K., Miura, N., Satokata, I. *et al.* 1990 Analysis of a human DNA excision repair gene involved in group A xeroderma pigmentosum and containing a zinc-finger domain. *Nature, Lond.* **348**, 73–76.

Troelstra C., van Gool, A., de Wit, J., Vermeulen, W., Bootsma, D. & Hoeijmakers, J.H.J. 1992 *ERCC6*, a member of a subfamily of putative helicases is involved in Cockayne's syndrome and preferential repair of active genes. *Cell* **71**, 939–953.

van Gool, A.J., Verhage, R., Swagemakers, S.M.A., *et al.* RAD26, the functional *S. cerevisiae* homolog of the Cockayne Syndrome B gene *ERCC6*. *EMBO J.* **13**, 5361–5369.

van Vuuren, A.J., Vermeulen, W., Ma, L. *et al.* 1994 Correction of xeroderma pigmentosum repair defect by basal transcription factor BTF2(TFIIH). *EMBO J.* **13**, 1645–1653.

Venema, J., van Hoffen, A., Natarajan, A.T., van Zeeland, A.A. & Mullenders, L.H.F. 1990*a* The residual repair capacity of xeroderma pigmentosum complementation group C fibroblasts is highly specific for transcriptionally active DNA. *Nucl. Acids Res.* **18**, 443–448.

Venema, J., Mullenders, L.H.F., Natarajan, A.T., van Zeeland, A.A. & Mayne, L.V. 1990*b* The genetic defect in Cockayne's syndrome is associated with a defect in repair of UV-induced DNA damage in transcriptionally active DNA. *Proc. natn. Acad. Sci. U.S.A.* **87**, 4707–4711.

Vermeulen, W., van Vuuren, A.J., Chipoulet, M. *et al.* 1994 Three unusual repair deficiencies associated with transcription factor BTF2(TFIIH). Evidence for the existence of a transcription syndrome. *Cold Spring Harb. Symp. quant. Biol.* (In the press.)

Vermeulen, W., Jaeken, J., Jaspers, N.G.J., Bootsma, D. & Hoeijmakers, J.H.H. 1993 Xeroderma pigmentosum complementation group G associated with Cockayne's syndrome. *Am. J. hum. Genet.* **53**, 185–192.

Watkins, J.F., Sung, P., Prakash, L. & Prakash, S. 1993 The *Saccharomyces cerevisiae* DNA repair gene *RAD23* encodes a nuclear protein containing a ubiquitin-like domain required for biological function. *Molec. Cell Biol.* **13**, 7757–7765.

Weber C.A., Salazar, E.P., Stewart, S.A. & Thompson, L.H. 1990 *ERCC2*: cDNA cloning and molecular characterization of a human nucleotide excision repair gene with high homology to yeast RAD3. *EMBO J.* **9**, 1437–1448.

Weeda, G., van Ham, R.C.A., Vermeulen, W., Bootsma, D., van der Eb, A.J. & Hoeijmakers, J.H.J. 1990 A presumed DNA helicase, encoded by the excision repair gene *ERCC-3* is involved in the human repair disorders xeroderma pigmentosum and Cockayne's syndrome. *Cell* **62**, 777–791.

12

On the regulation of the p53 tumour suppressor, and its role in the cellular response to DNA damage

DAVID P. LANE[1], CAROL A. MIDGLEY[1], TED R. HUPP[1], XIN LU[2], BORIVOJ VOJTESEK[3] AND STEVEN M. PICKSLEY[1]

[1] *CRC Cell Transformation Group, Department of Biochemistry, University of Dundee, Dundee DD1 4HN, U.K.*
[2] *Ludwig Institute for Cancer Research, St. Mary's Hospital Medical School, Norfolk Place, London W2 1PG, U.K.*
[3] *Masaryk Memorial Cancer Institute, Zluty Kopec, 656 53 Brno, Czech Republic*

SUMMARY

The p53 gene is required for the normal apoptotic response of mammalian cells to DNA damage caused by ionizing radiation and DNA damaging drugs. DNA damage results in the accumulation of biologically active p53. This response is potentially lethal and is therefore highly regulated. By using both biochemical and cell biological approaches a number of discrete control pathways have been identified. These include analysis of cellular and viral proteins that bind to p53 to inactivate its function, the discovery of cells with defects in the p53 activation pathway and the analysis of an allosteric regulation of p53 function controlled by phosphorylation.

1. INTRODUCTION

The genetic material of all living organisms is continuously being damaged both by natural chemical processes and by exogenous agents such as chemicals and ionizing radiations present in the environment. Organisms are protected from the mutagenic affects of this barrage by efficient DNA-repair processes. Inherited defects in these repair processes result in a predisposition to the development of cancer. Recently it has become clear that, in addition to the genes involved in the mechanics of repair itself, other genes may also play a crucial role in protecting the organism from the effects of DNA damage. These genes seem to act by preventing the division of cells that have sustained DNA damage. One of this latter group of genes is that encoding the p53 protein. Experiments with mice that lack functional p53 genes has shown that they are extraordinarily predisposed to the development of cancer and that their cells are resistant to radiation-induced programmed cell death (Donehower *et al.* 1992; Clarke *et al.* 1993; Lowe *et al.* 1993). The p53 protein acts to induce cell death after its activation in response to DNA damage.

Loss of p53 function is a key step in the development of most human cancers. In most cases these tumours have lost one p53 allele completely but continue to express the other parental allele. Closer analysis shows that this remaining expressed allele contains an inactivating point mutation. The response that p53 induces after DNA damage must be highly regulated to ensure that it is selective and efficient. Three mechanisms of regulation have so far been discovered. Firstly, both cellular and viral gene products have been discovered that will bind to p53 and inactivate its

function in the induction of a DNA damage-induced growth arrest. Of particular interest is the *mdm2* gene, because overexpression of the MDM2 protein is frequently found in some human sarcomas. Secondly, p53 is regulated by the control of protein stability. The protein normally has a very short half-life and is present in minute quantities. However, it accumulates rapidly in cells subjected to DNA damage (Maltzman & Czyzyk 1984; Lu & Lane 1993). This response appears to be highly regulated so that on whole-body irradiation, only certain populations of cells accumulate detectable levels of p53. In the small intestine this population of cells exactly coincides with the stem cells in that zone where most apoptosis is seen (Merritt *et al.* 1994). Finally, biochemical evidence suggests that p53 is subject to a very exact allosteric regulation, controlled by phosphorylation of multiple sites within a novel C-terminal regulatory domain. All these control processes are involved in a critical cellular decision process, principally whether to permit survival, or programme cell death, after DNA damage. Understanding this decision process and its regulation in normal and tumour cells will allow a deeper understanding of cancer therapies based on the use of ionising radiation and DNA damaging drugs. It may also shed some light on the mechanisms by which the cell monitors the success of its DNA repair processes.

2. MATERIALS AND METHODS

(a) *Pepscan analysis of the MDM2 binding site on p53*

Human and murine p53 was synthesized as a set of overlapping peptides composed of 15 amino acids. Each peptide overlapped the previous one in the series by five amino acids and each peptide was synthesized with an N-terminal tail of four spacer amino acids, the last of which was biotinylated. The panel of peptides was arrayed on 96-well microtitre plates coated with streptavidin and then incubated with extracts containing MDM2 protein. The bound MDM2 was then detected by an enzyme-linked immunosorbent assay (ELISA) method by using a mouse monoclonal anti-MDM2 antibody and a peroxidase conjugated anti-immunoglobulin as previously described (Picksley *et al.* 1994).

(b) *Defects in the accumulation of p53 after DNA damage*

Primary fibroblasts where obtained from the Human Genetic Mutant Cell Repository (Cornell Cell Reposiformes, New Jersey, U.S.A.) Their ability to accumulate p53 protein after exposure to DNA damaging agents and SV40 virus infection was measured by quantitative p53 ELISA and by indirect immunohistochemistry using a panel of anti-p53 monoclonal antibodies as previously described (Lu & Lane 1993).

(c) *Allosteric regulation of p53 function*

The p53 protein was purified by chromatography on heparin agarose, ion exchange and molecular sieve columns as recently described from both baculovirus and *E. coli* expression systems. Its activity as a sequence-specific DNA binding protein was measured in a gel retardation assay (Hupp *et al.* 1992, 1993).

3. RESULTS AND DISCUSSION
(a) *Identification of the MDM2 binding site on p53 by using synthetic peptides*

The MDM2 protein can form a tight protein–protein complex with p53 (Barak & Oren 1992; Momand *et al.* 1992). When the MDM2 protein binds p53 it acts to neutralize the activity of p53 as a sequence-specific transcription factor (Momand *et al.* 1992; Oliner *et al.* 1993; Wu *et al.* 1993; Zauberman *et al.* 1993). This is thought to be the mechanism by which MDM2 can act

as a dominant transforming oncogene. This is because, in tumours where the gene encoding MDM2 is amplified, p53's tumour suppressor function is neutralized (Oliner *et al.* 1992). Consistent with this, high levels of MDM2 can block the p53-dependant G1 growth arrest induced by ionizing radiation. It is possible that MDM2 may have a natural physiological role in down-modulating the p53 response as it was recently found that the MDM2 gene is positively regulated by p53 (Barak *et al.* 1993; Wu *et al.* 1993). This then sets up a feedback loop between p53 and MDM2 (figure 1), and may also represent a paradigm for the regulation of growth control by p53 (reviewed in Picksley & Lane 1993).

A small molecule that could disrupt the p53–MDM2 interaction would have therapeutic potential. It might be used to liberate active wild-type p53 from those tumours that have amplified the MDM2 gene and thus contain no free active p53. It might also be used to affect the duration of the p53 response, for example in response to radiation therapy, perhaps increasing the degree of apoptosis induced at a given dose of radiation. To identify such a small molecule it is important to localize and characterize as precisely as possible the site of interaction between p53 and MDM2. Early work using yeast two hybrid screens and fragments of p53 produced by using recombinant DNA methods had localized the MDM2 binding site to the N-terminal 42 amino acids of p53 (Oliner *et al.* 1993). This corresponds to the region of p53 known to be able to act as a transcriptional transactivation domain (Unger *et al.* 1992). Although these recombinant DNA-based approaches are very powerful they become labour intensive when high resolution is required. As an alternative we have begun to explore the use of monoclonal antibodies, synthetic peptide libraries and phage peptide display libraries to study protein–protein interactions.

By using a panel of monoclonal antibodies raised to p53 to immunoprecipitate p53 in the free form, or p53 complexed to MDM2, it was found that, although antibodies to the C-terminus of p53 could recognize both the free form and the MDM2 complex, an antibody Bp53-19 directed to the N-terminus of the protein could not immunoprecipitate p53 when it was bound to MDM2 but could immunoprecipitate the free protein (Picksley *et al.* 1994).

To localize precisely the binding site for this antibody on p53 it was tested for its ability to interact with a set of overlapping synthetic peptides that each contained 15 amino acids of the human p53 open reading frame. These peptides contain a four amino acid spacer group, the terminal amino acid being biotinylated. Each peptide in the series overlaps the previous one by ten amino acids so that the series progresses in steps of five amino acids. The peptides were displayed using streptavidin coated microtitre wells. A strong and specific signal was obtained with peptides four, five and six when the antibody was used to probe the peptide array. This mapped the binding site of the antibody to the region of overlap between these three peptides: namely the sequence DLWKL which is amino acids 21–25 of human p53 (figure 2).

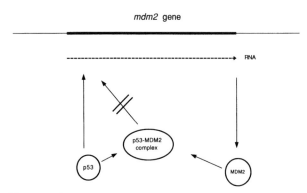

Figure 1. The p53-MDM2 feedback loop (adapted from Wu *et al.* 1993).

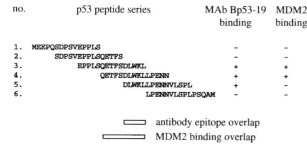

no.	p53 peptide series	MAb Bp53-19 binding	MDM2 binding
1.	MEEPQSDPSVEPPLS	−	−
2.	SDPSVEPPLSQETFS	−	−
3.	EPPLSQETFSDLWKL	+	+
4.	QETFSDLWKLLPENN	+	+
5.	DLWKLLPENNVLSPL	+	−
6.	LPENNVLSPLPSQAM	−	−

▭ antibody epitope overlap

▭ MDM2 binding overlap

Figure 2. Peptides that are recognized by monoclonal antibody Bp53-19 or that are bound by MDM2 protein.

Because the peptide array had worked so well for the mapping of the antibody binding site it seemed reasonable to try and see if MDM2 protein itself would bind to any of the peptides. The MDM2 protein was produced by using a baculovirus-based expression vector and the insect cell extract incubated with the peptide coated wells. To detect any MDM2 protein remaining bound after extensive washing, the wells were then treated with an anti-MDM2 antibody. This antibody was finally detected using a peroxidase conjugated rabbit anti-mouse IgG. Two peptides, numbers three and four in the series, gave a strong signal. On this basis we were able to localize the MDM2 binding site on p53 to the ten amino acids QETFS-DLWKL (figure 2). This represents amino acids 16–25 of human p53 (the same region of mouse p53 also bound MDM2). This site is coincident with, but extends beyond, the binding site for the antibody lending strong support to the conclusion that this is a key area of the molecule for the MDM2 interaction.

To examine the specificity of the interaction in more detail we had peptides synthesized in which each residue of the motif was in turn replaced with alanine. The results obtained with this alanine scan series identified the six amino acids TFSDLW (amino acids 18–23) as being completely intolerant to substitution by alanine if MDM2 binding activity was to remain detectable. The identification of the MDM2 binding site has proved to be of particular interest in the light of recent point-mutational studies carried out by other groups. Dr Vousden's laboratory has found that deletion of residues 13–19 of p53 inactivates p53's ability to bind MDM2 consistent with the above peptide data, but leaves the p53 protein still competent to act as a transcription factor (Marston *et al.* 1993). However, Dr levine's laboratory has found that the double point mutation of residues 22 and 23 (22L to 22Q and 23W to 23S) completely inactivates the transcriptional activity of p53 (Lin *et al.* 1994). These two residues of p53 have been completely conserved in all vertebrate species whose p53 sequence is known. Because our binding data show that these residues are required for MDM2 binding it becomes apparent that the MDM2 binding site physically overlaps the putative binding site for an essential transcription factor that p53 will interact with. It is interesting that this same region of p53 is also recognized by the Adenovirus E1b 55 kDa protein that is also known to block p53 function in transcription assays. A model for these interactions is shown in figure 3.

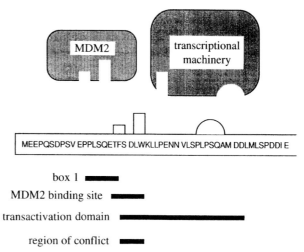

MEEPQSDPSV EPPLSQETFS DLWKLLPENN VLSPLPSQAM DDLMLSPDDI E

box 1 ▬

MDM2 binding site ▬▬

transactivation domain ▬▬▬▬▬▬

region of conflict ▬

Figure 3. A diagram representing the MDM2 binding domain and the transactivation domain at the N-terminus of p53, and the shared region of interaction/region of conflict.

Using these results it may be possible to devise small molecules that could disrupt specifically the interaction of p53 with MDM2 leaving its ability to interact with transcription factors intact. On a broader front the use of biotinylated peptide sets seems to offer special advantages for probing protein–protein interactions.

(b) Defects in the accumulation of p53 after DNA damage

The accumulation of p53 protein in cells exposed to DNA damaging agents has been seen using both qualitative immunostaining techniques and quantitative ELISA and immunoblotting assays (Lu & Lane 1993). The principal mechanism responsible for the accumulation seems to be post transcriptional as the response is not inhibited by agents that block transcription (Maltzman & Czyzyk 1984). The accumulated p53 in cells exposed to DNA damage has a longer half life than p53 produced in untreated cells so that regulation of p53 degradation is likely to be a major mechanism involved in the response. It is also possible that the p53 mRNA is preferentially translated in DNA damaged cells as it is known that selective translational control can be an important regulatory mechanism in other stress responses such as heat shock. The induction of p53 accumulation can be seen in whole animals (Hall *et al.* 1993) as well as in tissue culture systems. The response seems to be regulated by cellular factors, as well as by dose, because for example p53 accumulation in the cells of the small intestine is not uniform following exposure to ionizing radiation (Merrit *et al.* 1994). The accumulation of p53 can be directly induced by double strand breaks since introduction of a restriction enzyme into mammalian cells will cause p53 to accumulate (Lu & Lane 1993). The response is blocked by exposure of cells to caffeine which also suggests that it can be modulated by the cellular environment. To begin to identify the pathway and mechanism by which p53 accumulates after DNA damage we screened primary fibroblasts from individuals with a genetic predisposition to genetic instability. Although in contrast to the reports of others (Kastan *et al.* 1992) we found no exceptional defect in fibroblasts from patients with ataxia telangiectasia (AT) we did discover that fibroblasts derived from two out of eleven Blooms syndrome patients had a profoundly defective response (Lu & Lane 1993). These cells failed to accumulate p53 normally in response to ionizing radiation, UV radiation or SV40 infection. However, when fused to normal mouse cells they were able to accumulate human p53 after UV radiation and both northern blotting experiments and more recently polymerase chain reaction (PCR)-based methods suggest that they contain normal amounts of p53 mRNA. The defect in these cells is therefore probably not in the p53 gene itself as it can be complemented in trans. If that is the case then it would imply that all three signals for p53 accumulation have a common mechanistic step that is defective in these cells. We are attempting to identify the defect in these cells using cDNA expression libraries. Inactivation of such a gene function would be expected to produce a cancer susceptibility and so we are currently looking for variation in the p53 response among the normal human population and in inbred strains of mice.

(c) *Allosteric regulation of p53 function*

The sequence-specific DNA binding function of p53 is important for its tumour suppressor function (Kern *et al.* 1992). p53 binds to DNA elements in gene products which are synthesized after DNA damage linking the biochemical activity of p53 to the DNA damage response. Of particular interest is the discovery that the cell-cycle kinase inhibitor p21/WAF-1 is transcriptionally regulated by p53 (El-Deiry *et al.* 1993). The recently solved crystal structure of the conserved core DNA-binding domain of p53 consists of a novel β-sandwich that functions as a scaffold for two large loops and a loop-sheet-helix motif that constitute the DNA binding interface (Cho *et al.* 1994). A single point mutation within this protease-resistant core DNA binding domain inactivates p53 sequence-specific DNA binding function and results in a global de-stabilization in the proper folding of the core domain (Vojtesek *et al.* 1994).

The biochemical studies aimed at understanding how this sequence-specific DNA binding function of wild-type p53 is regulated have revealed two important control processes. The first involves a form of auto-regulation dependent upon a C-terminal regulatory motif which functions to lock p53 tetramers in a biochemically latent state (Hupp *et al.* 1992). Removal of this motif results in the constitutive activation of the protein. This modification can occur in a cell cycle regulated manner as a result of alternate splicing, at least in rodent cell systems (Kulesz-Martin *et al.* 1994). The inhibitory activity of the C-terminal motif can, however, be neutralized *in vitro* by post-translational modification, specifically by phosphorylation. The second point of regulation involves the function of two distinct protein kinases (casein kinase II and protein kinase C) which can activate allosterically the latent sequence-specific DNA binding function of p53 *in vitro*

(Hupp & Lane 1994). These latter results suggest that p53 may be regulated by distinct signalling pathways, which is consistent with the central role played by p53 in growth control. What is the physiological significance of the activation of latent p53? Work in our laboratory has demonstrated that the latent form of p53 is synthesized in a variety of eukaryotic cell lines, as its phosphorylation and subsequent activation *in vivo* appears to be rate-limiting. The inability of cells to catalyse complete activation of p53 may relate to the tight regulation of the activity of this protein. Because expression of active p53 is not compatible with cell survival, the cell may have evolved a mechanism to ensure that large levels of active protein are not switched on unless required as part of the response to DNA damage. Experiments with antibodies directed to the negative regulatory motif at the C-terminus of p53 have shown that some mutant p53 proteins retain a latent DNA binding function which could in theory be reactivated to therapeutic effect, restoring the function of wild-type p53 to tumour cells (Hupp *et al.* 1993). These biochemical studies on the regulation of p53 function offer another route by which to discover the pathways that link the growth arrest and apoptotic responses to the DNA damage detection and repair pathways.

This work was supported by the Cancer Research Campaign, the Joseph Steiner Foundation and the Howard Hughes Medical Institute. DPL is a Gibb Fellow of the Cancer Research Campaign and an International Scholar of the Howard Hughes Medical Institute.

REFERENCES

Barak, Y. & Oren, M. 1992 Enhanced binding of a 95 kDa protein to p53 in cells undergoing p53-mediated growth arrest. *EMBO J.* **11**, 2115–2121.

Barak, Y., Juven, T., Haffner, R. & Oren, M. 1993 *mdm2* expression is induced by wild type p53 activity. *EMBO J.* **12**, 461–468.

Chen, C.-Y., Oliner, J.D., Zhan, Q., Fornace, A.J., Vogelstein, B. & Kastan, M.B. 1994 Interactions between p53 and MDM2 in a mammalian cell cycle checkpoint pathway. *Proc. natn. Acad. Sci. U.S.A.* **91**, 2684–2688.

Cho, Y., Gorina, S., Jeffrey, P.D. & Pavletich, N.P. 1994 Crystal structure of p53 tumour suppressor-DNA complex: detailed view of the mutation hotspots. *Science, Wash.* **265**, 346–355.

Clarke, A.R., Purdie, C.A., Harrison, D.J., Morris, R.G., Bird, C.C., Hooper, M.L. & Wyllie, A.H. 1993 Thymocyte apoptosis is induced by p53-dependent and independent pathways. *Nature, Lond.* **362**, 849–852.

Donehower, L.A., Harvey, M., Slagle, B.L., McArthur, M.J., Montgomery, C.A., Butel, J.S. & Bradley, A. 1992 Mice deficient for p53 are developmentally normal but susceptible to spontaneous tumours. *Nature, Lond.* **356**, 215–221.

El-Diery, W.S., Tokino, T., Velculescu, V.E., Levy, D.B., Parsons, R., Trent, J.M., Lin, D., Mercer, W.E., Kinzler, K.W. & Vogelstein, B. 1993 WAF1, a potential mediator of p53 tumour suppression. *Cell* **75**, 817–825.

Hall, P.A., McKee, P.H., Menage, H.du.P., Dover, R. & Lane, D.P. 1993 High levels of p53 proteins in UV-irradiated normal human skin. *Oncogene* **8**, 203–207.

Hupp, T.R., Meek, D.W., Midgley, C.A. & Lane, D.P. 1992

Regulation of the specific DNA binding function of p53. *Cell* **71**, 875–886.

Hupp, T.R., Meek, D.M., Midgley, C.A. & Lane, D.P. 1993 Activation of the cryptic DNA binding function of mutant forms of p53. *Nucl. Acids Res.* **21**, 3167–2174.

Hupp, T.R. & Lane, D.P. 1994 Regulation of the cryptic sequence-specific DNA binding function of p53 by protein kinases. *Cold Spring Harb. Symp. quant. Biol.* (In the press.)

Kastan, M.B., Zhan, Q., El-Deiry W.S., Carrier, F., Jacks, T., Walsh, W.V., Plunkett, B.S., Vogelstein, B. & Fornace, A.J. 1992 A mammalian cell cycle checkpoint pathway utilizing p53 and GADD45 is defective in ataxia-telangiectasia. *Cell* **71**, 587–597.

Kern, S.E., Pietenpol, J.A., Thioagalingam, S., Seymour, A., Kinzler, K., & Vogelstein, B. 1992 Oncogenic forms of p53 inhibit p53 regulated gene expression. *Science, Wash.* **256**, 827–830.

Kulesz-Martin, M.F., Lisafield, B., Huang, H., Kisiel, N.D. & Lee, L. 1994 Endogenous p53 protein generated from alternatively spliced p53 RNA in mouse epidermal cells. *Molec. Cell Biol.* **14**, 1698–1708.

Lin, J., Chen, J., Elenbaas, B. & Levine, A.J. 1994 Several hydrophobic residues in the p53 amino-terminal domain are required for transcriptional activation, binding to mdm-2 and the adenovirus E1B 55-kD protein. *Genes Dev.* **8**, 1235–1246.

Lowe, S., Schmidt, E.M., Smith, S.W., Osborne, B.A. & Jacks, T. 1993 p53 is required for radiation-induced apoptosis in mouse thymocytes. *Nature, Lond.* **362**, 847–849.

Lu, X. & Lane, D.P. 1993 Differential induction of transcriptionally active p53 following UV or ionising radiation: defects in chromosome instability syndromes. *Cell* **75**, 765–778.

Maltzman, W. & Czyzyk, K.L. 1984 UV irradiation stimulates levels of p53 cellular tumour antigen in nontransformed mouse cells. *Molec. Cell Biol.* **4**, 1689–1694.

Marston, N.J., Crook, T. & Vousden. 1994 Interaction of p53 with MDM2 is independent of E6 and does not mediate wild type transformation suppressor function. *Oncogene* **9**, 2707–2716.

Merritt, A.J., Potten, C.S., Kemp, C.J., Hickman, J.A., Balmain, A., Lane, D.P. & Hall, P.A. 1994 The role of p53 in spontaneous and radiation-induced apoptosis in the gastrointestinal tract of normal and p53 deficient mice. *Cancer Res.* **54**, 614–617.

Momand, J., Zambetti, G.P., Olson, D.C., George, D.L. & Levine, A.J. 1992 The mdm-2 oncogene product forms a complex with the p53 protein and inhibits p53-mediated transactivation. *Cell* **69**, 1237–1245.

Oliner, J.D., Kinzler, K.W., Meltzer, P.S., George, D.L. & Vogelstein, B. 1992 Amplification of a gene encoding a p53-associated protein in human sarcomas. *Nature, Lond.* **358**, 80–83.

Oliner, J.D., Pietenpol, J.A., Thiagalingam, S., Gyuris, J., Kinzler, K.W. & Vogelstein, B. 1993 Oncoprotein MDM2 conceals the activation domain of tumour suppressor p53. *Nature, Lond.* **362**, 857–860.

Picksley, S.M. & Lane, D.P. 1993 The p53-MDM2 autoregulatory feedback loop: a paradigm for the regulation of growth control by p53? *Bioessays* **15**, 689–690.

Picksley, S.M., Vojtesek, B., Sparks, A. & Lane, D.P. 1994 Immunochemical analysis of the interaction of p53 with MDM2; – fine mapping o the MDM2 binding site on p53 using synthetic peptides. *Oncogene* **9**, 2523–2529.

Vojtesek, B., Dolezalova, H., Lauerova, L., Svitakova, M., Havlis, P., Kovarik, J., Midgley, C.A. & Lane, D.P. 1994 Conformational changes in p53 analysed using new antibodies to the core DNA binding domain of the protein. Oncogene. (In the press.)

Wu, X., Bayle, J.H., Olson, D. & Levine, A.J. 1993 The p53-mdm-2 autoregulatory feedback loop. *Genes Dev.* **7**, 1126–1132.

Zauberman, A., Barak, Y., Ragimov, N., Levy, N. & Oren, M. 1993 Sequence-specific DNA binding by p53: identification of target sites and lack of binding to p53-MDM2 complexes. *EMBO J.* **12**, 2799–2808.

13

Mismatch repair, genetic stability and tumour avoidance

PAUL MODRICH

Department of Biochemistry and Howard Hughes Medical Institute, Duke University Medical Center, Durham, North Carolina, U.S.A.

SUMMARY

Escherischia coli methyl-directed mismatch repair eliminates premutagenic lesions that arise via DNA biosynthetic errors; components of the repair system also block ectopic recombination between diverged DNA sequences. A mismatch-dependent, methyl-directed excision reaction that accounts for function of the system in replication fidelity has been reconstituted in a purified system dependent on ten activities. The reaction displays a broad specificity for mismatched base pairs and is characterized by an unusual bidirectional excision capability. Human cell nuclear extracts support strand-specific mismatch correction in a reaction that is similar to bacterial repair, with respect to both mismatch specificity and unusual features of mechanism. Like the bacterial system, the human pathway also functions in mutation avoidance because several classes of mutator human cells are deficient in the reaction. These include an alkylation-tolerance cell line that is resistant to the cytotoxic action of N-methyl-N'-nitro-nitrosoguanidine, as well as hypermutable RER$^+$ tumour cells such as those associated with hereditary non-polyposis colon cancer. *In vitro* experiments indicate that the human repair reaction is dependent on at least six activities, excluding DNA ligase, and that distinct defects in the system can lead to the RER$^+$ phenotype.

1. INTRODUCTION

Current appreciation of the mechanisms of mismatch repair and the significance of this process in mutation avoidance has resulted largely from work in bacterial systems (Claverys & Lacks 1986; Meselson 1988; Modrich 1991). The genetic stabilization provided by the prototypic *Escherichia coli* methyl-directed mismatch repair pathway has been attributed to its roles in ensuring the fidelity of both chromosome replication and homologous genetic recombination (Meselson 1988; Radman 1988; Modrich 1991). The discussion that follows will highlight the molecular mechanisms that underly the fidelity functions of the *E. coli* pathway and will summarize evidence indicating that human cells possess a functional homologue of the bacterial system. As in the case of the methyl-directed pathway, genetic inactivation of the human system confers a large increase in spontaneous mutability, as well as resistance to the cytotoxic action of simple DNA alkylators. Moreover, defects in the human system are also associated with a strong predisposition to tumour development in certain tissues.

2. MECHANISM OF METHYL-DIRECTED MISMATCH EXCISION REPAIR

Because mismatches are comprised of normal Watson–Crick bases, postreplication correction of DNA biosynthetic errors relies on secondary signals within the helix that are used to identify the newly synthesized strand. As anticipated by Wagner & Meselson (1976), the requisite strand-specificity for mismatch repair in *E. coli* is based on patterns of adenine methylation at d(GATC) sites (Meselson 1988; Modrich 1991). Owing to the postsynthetic nature of this modification, GATC sequences in newly synthesized DNA are unmethylated and it is this transient existence in unmodified form that permits the repair system to identify the daughter DNA strand.

A mismatch-provoked, methyl-directed excision reaction, which can account for function of mismatch repair in *E. coli* replication fidelity, has been reconstituted in a purified system that depends on ten activities (Lahue *et al.* 1989; Cooper *et al.* 1993). Availability of this system has led to identification of key intermediates in the reaction. As illustrated in figure 1, repair is initiated by the mismatch-provoked incision of the unmodified strand at a hemimethylated GATC site. This reaction, which depends on the products of the *mutH*, *mutL*, and *mutS* mutator genes as well as ATP hydrolysis, displays an exquisite sensitivity for mismatched base pairs (Au *et al.* 1992; Nelson *et al.* 1993). Analysis of interaction of the three Mut proteins with heteroduplex DNA has indicated that initiation involves binding of MutS to a mismatch (Su & Modrich 1986; Su *et al.* 1988) followed by ATP-dependent addition of MutL (Grilley *et al.* 1989). Assembly of this complex leads to activation of a latent, MutH-associated GATC endonuclease in a reaction that depends on ATP hydrolysis by MutS (Au *et al.* 1992).

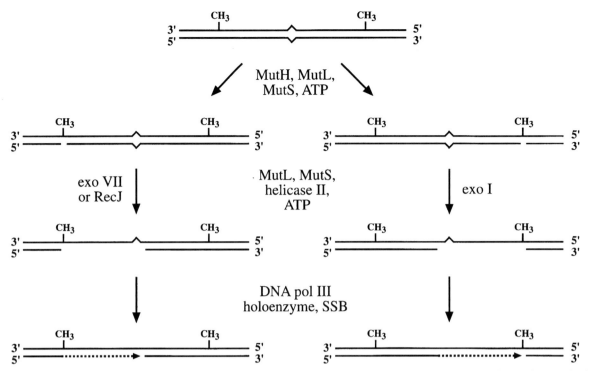

Figure 1. A mismatch-provoked, methyl-directed excision reaction. Repair is initiated by the mismatch-provoked incision of the unmodified strand at a hemimethylated GATC site. Reproduced with permission from Grilley *et al.* (1993).

Interaction of the mismatch and the GATC sequence that determines strand-specificity is thought to involve formation of a DNA loop (Grilley 1992).

Inasmuch as a pre-existing strand-break bypasses the requirement for both MutH and a hemimethylated GATC site (Längle-Rouault *et al.* 1987; Lahue *et al.* 1989), it is clear that the function of these two elements in methyl-directed repair is provision of a single-strand break which serves as the primary signal for targeting correction to the unmodified DNA strand. Surprisingly, GATC incision by MutH during the initiation of repair can occur either 3′ or 5′ to the mismatch on the unmodified strand (Au *et al.* 1992), an observation that reflects the novel bidirectional capability of the methyl-directed system (see figure 1). The excision stage of repair depends on MutS, MutL, DNA helicase II (the *mutU* gene product) and one of several exonucleases (Lahue *et al.* 1989; Cooper *et al.* 1993). This step is strictly exonucleolytic in nature, with hydrolysis initiating at the incised GATC site and proceeding toward the mismatch to terminate a set of discrete sites within a 100 nucleotide region beyond the mispair (Grilley *et al.* 1993). When the incised GATC sequence resides 3′ to the mismatch, excision requires exonuclease I, a 3′→5′ hydrolytic activity, while excision from a 5′ GATC site depends on the 5′→3′ hydrolytic activity of RecJ or exonuclease VII (Cooper *et al.* 1993). Each of these three exonucleases is specific for single-stranded DNA (Lehman & Nussbaum 1964; Chase & Richardson 1974; Lovett & Kolodner 1989). Excision from either side of the mismatch depends on the cooperative action of DNA helicase II and an appropriate hydrolytic activity (Grilley *et al.* 1993). It has, therefore, been inferred that helicase II displacement renders the incised strand sensitive to the

appropriate single-strand exonuclease. The gap produced by this complex excision reaction is repaired by DNA polymerase III holoenzyme in the presence of single-strand binding protein ssb, with DNA ligase restoring covalent integrity to the helix (Lahue *et al.* 1989).

3. MutS AND MutL MODULATE RECOMBINATION BETWEEN DIVERGED DNAs

In addition to their fidelity role in chromosome replication, components of the methyl-directed system also act to reduce the yield of recombinants when crossovers are selected in regions of imperfect homology. Analysis of recombination in *E. coli* and *Salmonella typhimurium* has demonstrated that the frequency of crossovers is reduced by one to several orders of magnitude when homology in the region of interest differs by 1% to 20% at the nucleotide level (Rayssiguier *et al.* 1989; Shen & Huang 1989; Petit *et al.* 1991). This effect is clearly dependent on MutS and MutL proteins because recombinant yield in crosses involving such quasi-homologous (i.e. homeologous) sequences is increased dramatically in *mutS* and *mutL* mutants (Rayssiguier *et al.* 1989; Petit *et al.* 1991). Radman and colleagues (Rayssiguier *et al.* 1989) proposed that the antirecombination activity of MutS and MutL is indicative of their function as a barrier to illegitimate exchanges between divergent sequences. This idea was confirmed by the demonstration that *mutS* and *mutL* products control the frequency of *E. coli* chromosomal rearrangements that result from recombination between divergent *rhs* repeats (Petit *et al.* 1991).

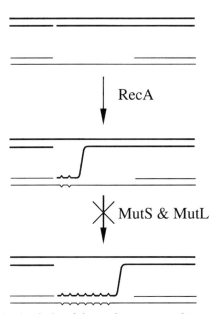

Figure 2. Analysis of homeologous strand-transfer intermediates that accumulate in the presence of MutS and MutL demonstrated that the Mut proteins block the branch migration step of the reaction. This is, presumably, in response to occurrence of mismatches within the recombination heteroduplex.

In contrast to the large increase in homeologous exchange observed in *mutS* and *mutL* mutants, *mutH* and helicase II mutations have little effect on recombinant yield in crosses involving sequences that are divergent by 1% or more (Rayssiguier *et al.* 1989; Petit *et al.* 1991). This suggests that the antirecombination activity of MutS and MutL may involve features of mechanism that are either distinct from, or in addition to, that of the mismatch-provoked excision reaction outlined above. Whereas the molecular basis of this phenomenon remains unclear, a dramatic effect of MutS and MutL on RecA-catalysed strand transfer between divergent sequences has been demonstrated *in vitro*. Worth *et al.* (1994) have demonstrated that although MutS and MutL are without effect on RecA-mediated M13-M13 or fd-fd strand transfer, these proteins abolish heteroduplex formation between M13 and fd DNAs – which are 3% divergent at the nucleotide level. Inhibition of strand transfer between these homeologous DNAs can be observed in the presence of MutS alone but this effect is dramatically potentiated by MutL, an observation consistent with the known order of addition of the two proteins to a mispair (Grilley *et al.* 1989). Analysis of homeologous strand-transfer intermediates that accumulate in the presence of MutS and MutL demonstrated that the Mut proteins block the branch migration step of the reaction, presumably in response to occurrence of mismatches within the recombination heteroduplex (see figure 2). Although MutS and MutL block branch migration through regions of diverged sequence, the proteins do not destabilize previously formed homeologous heteroduplex (Worth *et al.* 1994). Thus it is postulated that branch migration intermediates trapped by the proteins are subject to disassembly by an, as yet, unidentified mechanism.

4. STRAND-SPECIFIC MISMATCH REPAIR IN HUMAN CELLS

Study of strand-specific mismatch repair in eukaryotic organisms has been hampered by the lack of definitive information on the nature of strand signals that might operate in these organisms. For this reason we (Holmes *et al.* 1990), and Kunkel and colleagues (Thomas *et al.* 1991) have used heteroduplexes containing a site-specific, strand-specific incision to explore the potential existence of such reactions in higher cells. The rationale for use of such substates was based on previous observations in bacterial systems. As mentioned above, a preexisting strand break bypasses the requirements for MutH and a hemimethylated GATC site in the *E. coli* methyl-directed reaction (Längle-Rouault *et al.* 1987; Lahue *et al.* 1989); it has been postulated that DNA termini are the natural signal governing mismatch repair in *Streptococcus pneumoniae* (Claverys & Lacks 1986). Use of such substrates has led to identification of mismatch-provoked, nick-directed excision repair systems in extracts derived from both *Drosophila melanogaster* (Holmes *et al.* 1990) and human (Holmes *et al.* 1990; Thomas *et al.* 1991) cells.

Analysis of the human nick-directed reaction has revealed striking similarities to the bacterial methyl-directed pathway with respect to both specificity and mechanism. Both systems are characterized by a similar broad specificity for base–base (Holmes *et al.* 1990; Modrich 1991; Thomas *et al.* 1991; Fang *et al.* 1993; Fang & Modrich 1993) and insertion–deletion mispairs (Thomas *et al.* 1991; Parker & Marinus 1992; Parsons *et al.* 1993). Furthermore, repair efficiencies for different mispairs are similar in the two systems with C–C being the weakest substrate in both cases (Holmes *et al.* 1990; Modrich 1991; Thomas *et al.* 1991). In addition to differential rates of correction of different heteroduplexes, which is indicative of mismatch recognition, nick-directed repair events observed in human cell-free extracts are mismatch-provoked as judged by two additional criteria. Repair, which is inhibited by aphidicolin, is accompanied by mismatch-dependent, aphidicolin-sensitive DNA synthesis that is localized to the region between the mispair and the nick that directs the reaction (Holmes *et al.* 1990; Thomas *et al.* 1991). Furthermore, inhibition of extract DNA synthesis by aphidicolin or by omission of exogenous dNTPs leads to the mismatch-dependent formation of single-strand gaps that span the mispair and the single-strand break that directs the reaction (Fang *et al.* 1993; Fang & Modrich 1993). With circular heteroduplexes, in which the nick is asymmetrically disposed relative to the mismatch, these excision tracts are localized to the shorter path joining the two sites – irrespective of whether the strand break is located 3′ or 5′ to the mispair as viewed along this path (see figure 3). With either kind of heteroduplex, single strand gaps were found to extend from the site of the strand break to terminate at a number of discrete sites in the region 90 to 170 nucleotides beyond the location of the mismatch. This is reminiscent of excision tracts observed in the bacterial pathway (Grilley *et al.* 1993) and it, therefore, appears the human nick-

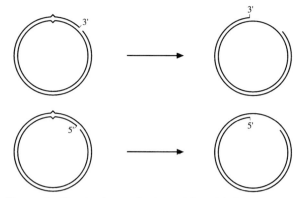

Figure 3. Circular heteroduplexes. The nick is asymmetrically disposed relative to the mismatch; these excision tracts are localized to the shorter path joining the two sites irrespective of whether the strand break is located 3′ or 5′ to the mispair, as viewed along this path.

directed reaction displays a bidirectional excision capability similar to that documented for *E. coli* methyl-directed repair.

This high degree of conservation with respect to specificity and mechanism, led to the suggestion that the human strand-specific pathway is a functional homologue of the bacterial methyl-directed system (Holmes *et al.* 1990; Thomas *et al.* 1991; Fang & Modrich 1993). This idea has been confirmed dramatically during the past year, with the demonstration that strand-specific mismatch repair plays a critical role in maintenance of genetic stability in human cells.

5. A METHYLATION-TOLERANT CELL LINE IS DEFECTIVE IN MISMATCH REPAIR

The initial demonstration of a human mismatch-repair deficiency was in the MT1 cell line. This cell line was derived from TK6 lymphoblastoid cells after frameshift mutagenesis and selection for mutants resistant to the cytotoxic effects of *N*-methyl-*N*′-nitro-nitrosoguanidine (MNNG) (Goldmacher *et al.* 1986). Although several hundred times more resistant to killing by MNNG than the TK6 parental line, MT1 cells do not display an elevated capacity for repair of alkylated DNA. Rather, alkylated bases simply persist in chromosomes of MT1 cells and, in fact, this line is somewhat more sensitive to mutagenesis by MNNG than the parental line is (Goldmacher *et al.* 1986). Therefore, the MT1 line tolerates DNA adducts that lead to death in wild-type cells.

In addition to this alkylation-tolerant phenotype, MT1 cells are also hypermutable in the *absence* of alkylating agent (Goldmacher *et al.* 1986). The rate of generation of spontaneous *HPRT* mutations is elevated about 60-fold, with exon mutations including transitions, transversions and single nucleotide insertions (Kat *et al.* 1993). MT1 and TK6 cells are also distinguished by poor clone-forming ability at low cell densities, in the case of the former line, and by differences in cell-cycle progression phenotype after exposure to MNNG doses that lead to 90% killing (Goldmacher *et al.* 1986). Because the mutagenesis

procedure used to isolate MT1 yields a very small *HPRT* mutant fraction, the several phenotypes of MT1 cells have been attributed to a single genetic alteration (Goldmacher *et al.* 1986).

Our interest in the MT1 line was prompted by its hypermutable phenotype and by the observation of Karran and Marinus (1982) that *E. coli* mismatch repair mutants are more resistant than wild-type cells to killing by MNNG. Indeed, these observations led Thilly and coworkers (Goldmacher *et al.* 1986) and Karran & Bignami (1992) to propose that tolerance of mammalian cells to the cytotoxic action of DNA methylating agents might be associated with a mismatch-repair deficiency. This proposal was confirmed with the demonstration that MT1 cells are defective in strand-specific mismatch correction (Kat *et al.* 1993). As judged by *in vitro* assay, the mutator line is defective in repair of each of the eight base–base mismatches, with repair blocked prior to the excision stage of the reaction. In addition to demonstrating that mismatch repair contributes to genetic stability of human cells, these findings also imply that the human repair system recognizes mispairs involving certain kinds of damaged bases. In particular, they indicate that recognition and processing of such lesions by the mismatch-repair system is involved in targeting for death those cells that have suffered unacceptable levels of alkylation damage. Although the affected gene responsible for the MT1 phenotype has not been identified, the nature of the MT1 mutation provides further support for the contention that the human strand-specific mismatch-repair pathway is a functional homologue of the bacterial methyl-directed system.

In experiments based on a similar premise, Karran and colleagues (Branch *et al.* 1993) have found that extracts of alkylation-resistant variants of CHO and RajiF12 Burkitt's lymphoma cells are deficient in a G–T binding activity. However, in contrast to MT1, these variant cell lines are only slightly hypermutable. This difference may, at least, partly reflect the distinct methods used to isolate the two classes of alkylation-resistant cell lines. While MT1 was isolated after frameshift mutagenesis and single-step selection for high level MNNG resistance (Goldmacher *et al.* 1986), the CHO and RajiF12 variants were isolated after multistep selection for cells able to survive exposure to continuously increasing doses of alkylating agent (Aquilina *et al.* 1988; Branch *et al.* 1993). It is evident that such differing selection protocols may yield distinct genetic outcomes. It is also evident that rationalization of results obtained with the two kinds of alkylation-resistant cell lines must await identification of the genetic defect in MT1 cells and clarification of the DNA metabolic role of the G–T binding protein that is defective in the CHO and RajiF12 variant lines.

6. MISMATCH REPAIR DEFICIENCY AND CANCER PREDISPOSITION

Nowell (1976) suggested a model for cancer development based on genetic destabilization (giving rise to mitotic errors and simpler mutations), progressive genetic change and clonal selection. The demonstration that progressive genetic alterations can be associated with development of several human cancers (Weinberg 1989; Fearon & Vogelstein 1990; Stanbridge 1990) confirmed a key element of this proposal but the origins of the mutations involved in tumourigenesis have been uncertain. For example, Loeb (1991) has argued that although a one or two mutation mechanism for tumour development can be reconciled with the mutation rate of a healthy human cell (estimated to be approximately 10^{-10} per nucleotide per generation), it is difficult to rationalize cancer incidence with normal spontaneous mutability if three or more mutations are necessary for disease development. Although such arguments neglect the impact of exposure to exogenous mutagens, the finding that cancer cells can harbour a substantial number of mutations (Callahan & Campbell 1989; Fearon & Vogelstein 1990) has resulted in reiteration of the argument that acquisition of a genetically unstable phenotype may play a role in tumourigenesis (Harwood *et al.* 1991; Loeb 1991).

Dramatic evidence indicative of a role for hypermutability in development of certain cancers has appeared during the past year with the demonstration that certain sporadic tumours and most tumours developing in patients afflicted with hereditary nonpolyposis colorectal cancer (HNPCC) harbour frequent mutations within $(CA)_n$ and other simple microsatellite repeat sequences (Aaltonen *et al.* 1993; Han *et al.* 1993; Ionov *et al.* 1993; Peltomäki *et al.* 1993*b*; Risinger *et al.* 1993; Thibodeau *et al.* 1993; Merlo *et al.* 1994; Mironov *et al.* 1994; Shridhar *et al.* 1994). HNPCC is one of the most common familial cancer syndromes, and in addition to colorectal carcinoma, a subset of affected individuals is also predisposed to endometrial, hematologic, gastric, pancreatic, ovarian, skin, and urinary tract cancer (Lynch *et al.* 1993). With the apparent exception of some small cell and non-small cell lung cancers (Merlo *et al.* 1994; Shridhar *et al.* 1994), the tissue distribution of sporadic cancers in which microsatellite variability has been observed is similar to that observed in HNPCC patients (Han *et al.* 1993; Peltomäki *et al.* 1993*b*).

$(CA)_n$ and other simple repeat sequences are prone to slipped-strand mispairing and are thought to be particularly susceptible to insertion–deletion mutagenesis during replication (Levinson & Gutman 1987*b*; Kunkel 1993). Thus tumours displaying microsatellite mutations have been designated RER$^+$ (as opposed to RER$^-$) based on the supposition that observed sequence variations result from Replication ERrors (Aaltonen *et al.* 1993; Ionov *et al.* 1993). That hypermutability does indeed contribute to incidence of $(CA)_n$ mutations in RER$^+$ tumour cells has been confirmed by clonal analysis of $(CA)_n$ repeats in colorectal tumour cells (Parsons *et al.* 1993). In contrast to stability of the microsatellite sequence in RER$^-$ colorectal tumour cells, cell lines derived from two independent RER$^+$ tumours displayed a 100-fold elevation in mutability of $(CA)_n$ repeats (Parsons *et al.* 1993).

Because mismatch-repair mutations dramatically destabilize $(CA)_n$ repeats in both *E. coli* and *S. cerevisiae*

(Levinson & Gutman 1987*a*; Strand *et al.* 1993), we have begun to screen extracts derived from RER$^-$ and RER$^+$ tumour cell lines for mismatch-repair defects. Although normal mismatch-correction activity was observed with four RER$^-$ colorectal tumour lines, six independent RER$^+$ colorectal lines were found to be defective in nick-directed correction of base–base, as well as insertion–deletion mispairs of the 2-, 3-, or 4-nucleotide slipped-strand class (Parsons *et al.* 1993; M. Longley, G.-M. Li, S. Markowitz, B. Vogelstein and P. Modrich, unpublished results). Similar results have been obtained by Kunkel and colleagues with four colorectal and two endometrial RER$^+$ tumour lines (Umar *et al.* 1994). These repair-defective lines fall into several classes based on *in vitro* complementation data (Parsons *et al.* 1993; Umar *et al.* 1994). Furthermore, although the observed defect in repair of slipped-strand mismatches accounts for microsatellite instability in these RER$^+$ cell lines, their inability to correct base–base mismatches led to the suggestion that they would also prove to be unstable with respect to base substitution mutagenesis (Parsons *et al.* 1993). The finding that *HPRT* mutability is increased 100-fold in several mismatch repair-deficient RER$^+$ lines supports this view (J. R. Eshleman, E. Z. Lang, G. K. Bowerfind, R. Parsons, B. Vogelstein, J. K. V. Wilson, M. L. Veigl, W. D. Sedwick and S. D. Markowitz, unpublished results).

HNPCC is inherited in an autosomal dominant fashion and is genetically heterogeneous. The responsible loci map to chromosomes 2p16, 3p21 and elsewhere in the human genome (Leach *et al.* 1993; Lindblom *et al.* 1993; Peltomäki *et al.* 1993*a*). The affected locus in 2p16 kindreds encodes a homologue of bacterial MutS that has been designated hMSH2 (Fishel *et al.* 1993; Leach *et al.* 1993), whereas that at 3p21 specifies the MutL homologue hMLH1 (Bronner *et al.* 1994; Papadopoulos *et al.* 1994). Affected individuals examined to date are heterozygous for germline *hMSH2* (Leach *et al.* 1993) or *hMLH1* mutations (Bronner *et al.* 1994; Papadopoulos *et al.* 1994). In the single instance in which an HNPCC colorectal cancer has been examined in detail, tumour cells retained the germline mutation and acquired a distinct somatic mutation in the other *hMSH2* copy (Leach *et al.* 1993). A similar situation has been observed with RER$^+$H6 cells that were derived from a sporadic colorectal tumour. This mismatch-repair-deficient line (Parsons *et al.* 1993) harbours defects in both *hMLH1* genes (Papadopoulos *et al.* 1994). Since somatic cells from an HNPCC patient have been found to be proficient in mismatch repair (Parsons *et al.* 1993), these genetic and biochemical findings strongly suggest that the initial event in development of most HNPCC and other RER$^+$ tumours is genetic destabilization due to loss of function of critical mismatch-repair activities.

7. FRACTIONATION OF THE HUMAN MISMATCH REPAIR SYSTEM

Using traditional biochemical methods and complementation of repair defective extracts derived from alkylation-tolerant and RER$^+$ tumour cells, we have identified six activities required for nick-directed mismatch repair in human cells. This set excludes the DNA ligase that we presume to be involved in the last stage of the reaction. One of the six activities, which complements the *hMLH1* mutant H6 line, has been obtained in homogeneous form (Guo-Min Li & Paul Modrich, unpublished results). The characterization of this activity will be described elsewhere, but it is interesting to note that this result implies involvement of the *hMLH1* MutL homologue in mismatch repair. Similarly, Hughes & Jiricny (1992) have isolated several mismatch-binding activities from human cells and peptide analysis of one of these indicates it to be the *hMSH2* product. The evolutionary conservation of general features of specificity and mechanism of mismatch repair outlined above therefore appears to reflect participation of related activities. Further evaluation of the degree to which details of mechanism have been preserved must await isolation and characterization of the other components of the system.

Work in the author's laboratory was supported by grants GM23719 and GM45190 from the National Institute of General Medical Sciences.

REFERENCES

Aaltonen, L.A., Peltomäki, P., Leach, F.S. *et al.* 1993 Clues to the pathogenesis of familial colorectal cancer. *Science, Wash.* **260**, 812–816.

Aquilina, G., Frosina, G., Zijno, A. *et al.* 1988 Isolation of clones displaying enhanced resistance to methylating agents in O^6-methylguanine-DNA methyltransferase-proficient CHO cells. *Carcinogenesis* **9**, 1217–1222.

Au, K.G., Welsh, K. & Modrich, P. 1992 Initiation of methyl-directed mismatch repair. *J. biol. Chem.* **267**, 12142–12148.

Branch, P., Aquilina, G., Bignami, M. & Karran, P. 1993 Defective mismatch binding and a mutator phenotype in cells tolerant to DNA damage. *Nature, Lond.* **362**, 652–654.

Bronner, C.E., Baker, S., Morrison, P.T. *et al.* 1994 Mutation in the DNA mismatch repair gene homologue *hMLH1* is associated with hereditary non-polyposis colon cancer. *Nature, Lond.* **368**, 258–261.

Callahan, R. & Campbell, G. 1989 Mutations in human breast cancer: an overview. *J. natn. Cancer Inst.* **81**, 1780–1786.

Chase, J.W. & Richardson, C.C. 1974 Exonuclease VII of *Escherichia coli*: mechanism of action. *J. biol. Chem.* **249**, 4553–4561.

Claverys, J.-P. & Lacks, S.A. 1986 Heteroduplex deoxyribonucleic acid base mismatch repair in bacteria. *Microbiol. Rev.* **50**, 133–165.

Cooper, D.L., Lahue, R.S. & Modrich, P. 1993 Methyl-directed mismatch repair is bidirectional. *J. biol. Chem.* **268**, 11823–11829.

Fang, W.-h., Li, G.-m., Longley, M., Holmes, J., Thilly, W. & Modrich, P. 1993 Mismatch repair and genetic stability in human cells. *Cold Spring Harbor Symp. quant. Biol.* **58**, 597–603.

Fang, W.-h. & Modrich, P. 1993 Human strand-specific mismatch repair occurs by a bidirectional mechanism similar to that of the bacterial reaction. *J. biol. Chem.* **268**, 11838–11844.

Fearon, E.R. & Vogelstein, B. 1990 A genetic model for colorectal tumorigenesis. *Cell* **61**, 759–767.

Fishel, R., Lescoe, M.K., Rao, M.R.S. *et al.* 1993 The human mutator gene homolog *MSH2* and its association with hereditary nonpolyposis cancer. *Cell* **75**, 1027–1038.

Goldmacher, V.S., Cuzick, R.A. & Thilly, W.G. 1986 Isolation and partial characterization of human cell mutants differing in sensitivity to killing and mutation by methylnitrosourea and *N*-methyl-*N'*-nitro-nitrosoguanidine. *J. biol. Chem.* **261**, 12462–12471.

Grilley, M., Griffith, J. & Modrich, P. 1993 Bidirectional excision in methyl-directed mismatch repair. *J. biol. Chem.* **268**, 11830–11837.

Grilley, M., Welsh, K.M., Su, S.-S. & Modrich, P. 1989 Isolation and characterization of the *Escherichia coli mutL* gene product. *J. biol. Chem.* **264**, 1000–1004.

Grilley, M.M. 1992 DNA and DNA-protein intermediates of methyl-directed mismatch correction in *Escherichia coli*. Ph.D. Thesis. Duke University.

Han, H.-J., Yanagisawa, A., Kato, Y., Park, J.-G. & Nakamura, Y. 1993 Genetic instability in pancreatic cancer and a poorly differentiated type of gastric cancer. *Cancer Res.* **53**, 5087–5089.

Harwood, J., Tachibana, A. & Meuth, M. 1991 Multiple dispersed spontaneous mutations: a novel pathway of mutagenesis in a malignant human cell line. *Molec. Cell. Biol.* **11**, 3163–3170.

Holmes, J., Clark, S. & Modrich, P. 1990 Strand-specific mismatch correction in nuclear extracts of human and *Drosophila melanogaster* cell lines. *Proc. natn. Acad. Sci. U.S.A.* **87**, 5837–5841.

Hughes, M.J. & Jiricny, J. 1992 The purification of a human mismatch-binding protein and identification of its associated ATPase and helicase activities. *J. biol. Chem.* **267**, 23876–23882.

Ionov, Y., Peinado, M.A., Malkhosyan, S., Shibata, D. & Perucho, M. 1993 Ubiquitous somatic mutations in simple repeated sequences reveal a new mechanism for colonic carcinogenesis. *Nature, Lond.* **363**, 558–561.

Karran, P. & Bignami, M. 1992 Self-destruction and tolerance in resistance of mammalian cells to alkylation damage. *Nucl. Acids Res.* **20**, 2933–2940.

Karran, P. & Marinus, M. 1982 Mismatch correction at O^6-methylguanine residues in *E. coli* DNA. *Nature, Lond.* **296**, 868–869.

Kat, A., Thilly, W.G., Fang, W.-h., Longley, M.J., Li, G.-M. & Modrich, P. 1993 An alkylation-tolerant, mutator human cell line is deficient in strand-specific mismatch repair. *Proc. natn. Acad. Sci. U.S.A.* **90**, 6424–6428.

Kunkel, T.A. 1993 Slippery DNA and diseases. *Nature, Lond.* **365**, 207–208.

Lahue, R.S., Au, K.G. & Modrich, P. 1989 DNA mismatch correction in a defined system. *Science, Wash.* **245**, 160–164.

Längle-Rouault, F., Maenhaut, M.G. & Radman, M. 1987 GATC sequences, DNA nicks and the MutH function in *Escherichia coli* mismatch repair. *EMBO J.* **6**, 1121–1127.

Leach, F.S., Nicolaides, N.C., Papadopoulos, N. *et al.* 1993 Mutations of a *mutS* homolog in hereditary nonpolyposis colorectal cancer. *Cell* **75**, 1215–1225.

Lehman, I.R. & Nussbaum, A.L. 1964 The deoxyribonucleases of *Escherichia coli* V. On the specificity of exonuclease I (phosphodiesterase). *J. biol. Chem.* **239**, 2628–2636.

Levinson, G. & Gutman, G.A. 1987a High frequencies of short frameshifts in poly-CA/TG tandem repeats borne by bacteriophage M13 in *Escherichia coli* K-12. *Nucl. Acids Res.* **15**, 5323–5338.

Levinson, G. & Gutman, G.A. 1987b Slipped-strand mispairing: A major mechanism for DNA sequence evolution. *Molec. Biol. Evol.* **4**, 203–221.

Lindblom, A., Tannergard, P., Werelius, B. & Nordenskjold,

M. 1993 Genetic mapping of a second locus predisposing to hereditary non-polyposis colon cancer. *Nature Genet.* **5**, 279–282.

Loeb, L.A. 1991 Mutator phenotype may be required for multistage carcinogenesis. *Cancer Res.* **51**, 3075–3079.

Lovett, S.T. & Kolodner, R.D. 1989 Identification and purification of a single-stranded-DNA-specific exonuclease encoded by the *recJ* gene of *Escherichia coli. Proc. natn. Acad. Sci. U.S.A.* **86**, 2627–2631.

Lynch, H.T., Smyrk, T.C., Watson, P. *et al.* 1993 Genetics, natural history, tumor spectrum, and pathology of hereditary nonpolyposis colorectal cancer: an updated review. *Gastroenterology* **104**, 1535–1549.

Merlo, A., Mabry, M., Gabrielson, E., Vollmer, R., Baylin, S.B. & Sidransky, D. 1994 Frequent microsatellite instability in primary small cell lung cancer. *Cancer Res.* **54**, 2098–2101.

Meselson, M. 1988 Methyl-directed repair of DNA mismatches. In *Recombination of the Genetic Material* (ed. K. B. Low), pp. 91–113. San Diego: Academic Press.

Mironov, N.M., Aguelon, A.-M., Potapova, G.I. *et al.* 1994 Alterations of $(CA)_n$ DNA repeats and tumor suppressor genes in human gastric cancer. *Cancer Res.* **54**, 41–44.

Modrich, P. 1991 Mechanisms and biological effects of mismatch repair. *A. Rev. Genet.* **25**, 229–253.

Nelson, S.F., McCusker, J.H., Sander, M.A., Kee, Y., Modrich, P. & Brown, P.O. 1993 Genomic mismatch scanning: a new approach to genetic linkage mapping. *Nature Genet.* **4**, 11–18.

Nowell, P.C. 1976 The clonal evolution of tumor cell populations. *Science, Wash.* **194**, 23–28.

Papadopoulos, N., Nicolaides, N.C., Wei, Y.-F. *et al.* 1994 Mutation of a *mutL* homolog in hereditary colon cancer. *Science, Wash.* **263**, 1625–1629.

Parker, B.O. & Marinus, M.G. 1992 Repair of DNA heteroduplexes containing small heterologous sequences in *Escherichia coli. Proc. natn. Acad. Sci. U.S.A.* **89**, 1730–1734.

Parsons, R., Li, G.-M., Longley, M.J. *et al.* 1993 Hypermutability and mismatch repair deficiency in RER$^+$ tumor cells. *Cell* **75**, 1227–1236.

Peltomäki, P., Aaltonen, L.A., Sistonen, P. *et al.* 1993*a* Genetic mapping of a locus predisposing to human colorectal cancer. *Science, Wash.* **260**, 810–812.

Peltomäki, P., Lothe, R.A., Aaltonen, L.A. *et al.* 1993*b* Microsatellite instability is associated with tumors that characterize the hereditary non-polyposis colorectal carcinoma syndrome. *Cancer Res.* **53**, 5853–5855.

Petit, M.-A., Dimpfl, J., Radman, M. & Echols, H. 1991 Control of large chromosomal duplications in *Escherichia coli* by the mismatch repair system. *Genetics* **129**, 327–332.

Radman, M. 1988 Mismatch repair and genetic recombination. In *Genetic recombination* (ed. R. Kucherlapati & G. R. Smith), pp. 169–192. Washington, D.C.: American Society for Microbiology.

Rayssiguier, C., Thaler, D.S. & Radman, M. 1989 The barrier to recombination between *Escherichia coli* and *Salmonella typhimurium* is disrupted in mismatch-repair mutants. *Nature, Lond.* **342**, 396–401.

Risinger, J.I., Berchuck, A., Kohler, M.F., Watson, P., Lynch, H.T. & Boyd, J. 1993 Genetic instability of microsatellites in endometrial carcinoma. *Cancer Res.* **53**, 5100–5103.

Shen, P. & Huang, H.V. 1989 Effect of base pair mismatches on recombination via the RecBCD pathway. *Molec. gen. Genet.* **218**, 358–360.

Shridhar, V., Siegfried, J., Hunt, J., del Mar Alonso, M. & Smith, D.I. 1994 Genetic instability of microsatellite sequences in many non-small cell lung carcinomas. *Cancer Res.* **54**, 2084–2087.

Stanbridge, E.J. 1990 Human tumor suppressor genes. *A. Rev. Genet.* **24**, 615–657.

Strand, M., Prolla, T.A., Liskay, R.M. & Petes, T.D. 1993 Destabilization of tracts of simple repetitive DNA in yeast by mutations affecting DNA mismatch repair. *Nature, Lond.* **365**, 274–276.

Su, S.-S., Lahue, R.S., Au, K.G. & Modrich, P. 1988 Mispair specificity of methyl-directed DNA mismatch correction in vitro. *J. biol. Chem.* **263**, 6829–6835.

Su, S.-S. & Modrich, P. 1986 *Escherichia coli mutS*-encoded protein binds to mismatched DNA base pairs. *Proc. natn. Acad. Sci. U.S.A.* **83**, 5057–5061.

Thibodeau, S.N., Bren, G. & Schaid, D. 1993 Microsatellite instability in cancer of the proximal colon. *Science, Wash.* **260**, 816–819.

Thomas, D.C., Roberts, J.D. & Kunkel, T.A. 1991 Heteroduplex repair in extracts of human HeLa cells. *J. biol. Chem.* **266**, 3744–3751.

Umar, A., Boyer, J.C., Thomas, D.C. *et al.* 1994 Defective mismatch repair in extracts of colorectal and endometrial cancer cell lines exhibiting microsatellite instability. *J. biol. Chem.* **269**, 14367–14370.

Wagner, R. & Meselson, M. 1976 Repair tracts in mismatched DNA heteroduplexes. *Proc. natn. Acad. Sci. U.S.A.* **73**, 4135–4139.

Weinberg, R.A. 1989 Oncogenes, anti-oncogenes, and the molecular basis of multistep carcinogenesis. *Cancer Res.* **49**, 3713–3721.

Worth, L., Clark, S., Radman, M. & Modrich, P. 1994 Mismatch repair proteins MutS and MutL inhibit RecA-catalyzed strand transfer between diverged DNAs. *Proc. natn. Acad. Sci. U.S.A.* **91**, 3238–3241.

14

Editing DNA replication and recombination by mismatch repair: from bacterial genetics to mechanisms of predisposition to cancer in humans

M. RADMAN[1], I. MATIC[1,3], J. A. HALLIDAY[1] AND F. TADDEI[1,2]

[1] *Laboratoire de Mutagénèse, Institut J. Monod, 2 Place Jussieu, 75251 Paris, France*
[2] *Ecole Nationale du Génie Rural des Eaux et des Forêts, 19 Avenue du Maine, 75015 Paris, France*
[3] *Laboratory of Biology and Microbial Genetics, Faculty of Food Technology and Biotechnology, University of Zagreb, 41000 Zagreb, Croatia*

SUMMARY

A hereditary form of colon cancer, hereditary non-polyposis colon cancer (HNPCC), is characterized by high instability of short repeated sequences known as microsatellites. Because the genes controlling microsatellite stability were known in bacteria and yeast, as was their evolutionary conservation, the search for human genes responsible for HNPCC became a 'targeted' search for known sequences. Mismatch-repair deficiency in bacteria and yeast produces multiple phenotypes as a result of its dual involvement in the editing of both replication errors and recombination intermediates. In addition, mismatch-repair functions are specialized in eukaryotes, characterized by specific mitotic (versus meiotic) functions, and nuclear (versus mitochondrial) localization. Given the number of phenotypes observed so far, we predict other links between mismatch-repair deficiency and human genetic disorders. For example, a similar type of sequence instability has been found in HNPCC tumours and in a number of neuro-muscular genetic disorders. Several human mitochondrial disorders display genomic instabilities reminiscent of yeast mitochondrial mismatch-repair mutants.

In general, the process of mismatch repair is responsible for the constant maintenance of genome stability and its faithful transmission from one generation to the next. However, without genetic alteration, species would not be able to adapt to changing environments. It appears that nature has developed both negative and positive controls for genetic diversity. In bacteria, for example, an inducible system (SOS) exists which generates genetic alterations in response to environmental stress (e.g. radiation, chemicals, starvation). Hence, the cost of generating diversity to adapt to changing conditions might be paid as sporadic gene alterations associated with disease.

1. INTRODUCTION

Perhaps the most telling lesson of the past forty years has been the recognition that very different forms of life are built around essentially similar mechanisms. All species are discovered to have more in common with each other than their differences would suggest.

(John Maddox in 'News and Views'
Nature, Lond. 1993 **363**, 13.)

The identification of two genes (and other unpublished candidates) (Fishcl *et al.* 1993; Leach *et al.* 1993; Bronner *et al.* 1994; Papadopoulos *et al.* 1994) linked to a predisposition to a hereditary form of colon cancer, hereditary non-polyposis colon cancer (HNPCC), was made possible due to the strong conservation among DNA repair functions between prokaryotes such as *E. coli* and eukaryotes such as the yeast *S. cerevisiae* (Reenan & Kolodner 1992*b*). The two genes discovered are human homologues to two components, *mutS* and *mutL*, from *E. coli*, of the so called mismatch-

repair system (MRS). Indeed, the crucial observations which led to the discovery of two genes involved in HNPCC were clearly reminiscent of the known phenotypes of such genes in other organisms (see below) with *E. coli* being the best studied. Linkage was detected using a 'microsatellite marker' on chromosome 2 revealing a previously unknown location for a colon cancer gene (Peltomaki *et al.* 1993). Such probes were designed to detect changes in microsatellite DNA characterized as short (1–6 base pair [b.p.]), repetitive DNA sequences occurring on average every 10^5 b.p. in genomic DNA. Surprisingly, the microsatellite linkage markers varied in size throughout the genome in most of the HNPCC tumours examined, indicating that nucleotides were both being added and deleted in microsatellite blocks (RER^+ phenotype for replication error) (Aaltonen *et al.* 1993; Thibodeau *et al.* 1993).

During DNA replication, DNA polymerases frequently misalign the newly synthesized template strand on short, tandemly repeated sequences creating small 'loop-outs' of unpaired bases that are normally

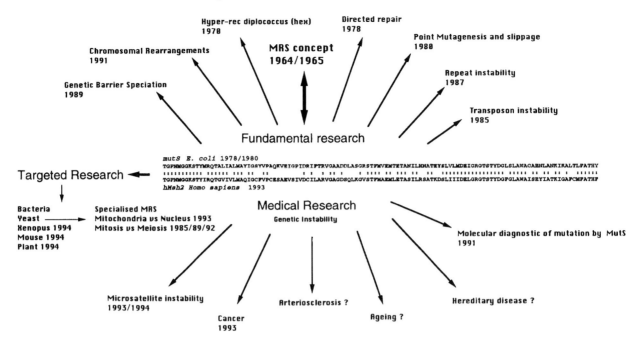

Figure 1. From bacterial mismatch repair system (MRS) to human genetic disease: a chronology. The centre of the figure presents the alignment of a well conserved region (including the ATP binding site) of the *E. coli mutS* gene with its human homologue *hMSH2*. The ':' indicate amino acid similarities. The years indicated provide the dates of the most important observations in the development of this field (see text for references). The association between MRS and arteriosclerosis is hypothetical but is suggested from studies on mutagenesis and clonality of arteriosclerosis plaques (Benditt & Benditt 1973). The possible link between the MRS, genetic disease and ageing is discussed in the text.

recognized and corrected by mismatch-repair enzymes (Dohet *et al.* 1986). Specific gene products encoded by the *mutS*, *mutL*, *mutH* genes are thought to operate on replication errors as a complex (Modrich 1991). Mutation in any of these three genes produces a strong mutator phenotype characterized by enhanced levels of base-substitution events, frameshift mutations at repetitive sequences, and recombination between homeologous (diverged) DNA sequences (Radman & Wagner 1986; Modrich 1991; Radman & Wagner 1993). As a result, it was thought that the genetic instability observed in human colon cancer cells probably reflected a defect in the maintenance of DNA integrity. This prediction was reinforced by the demonstration of a similar instability in $(CA)_n$ repeats, the most frequent form of microsatellite DNA in eukaryotes, in *E. coli mutL* and *mutS* mutants (Levison & Gutman 1987) and *S. cerevisiae msh2* (*mutS* homologue) *pms1* and *mlh1* (*mutL* homologues) mutants (Strand *et al.* 1993).

The striking sequence homology between components of the *E. coli* (MutS,L) and yeast (MSH2, MLH1, PMS1) mismatch-proteins was exploited and used to clone the first human homologue *hMSH2* and more recently, *hMLH1*, as well as homologues in *Xenopus* and mice (I. M. Varlet, M. Radman & N. D. Wind, unpublished results) (see figure 1). The Hopkins group speculated that approximately 40% of HNPCC non-hMSH2 tumours might be accounted for by another component of the mismatch-repair complex. To this end, a search for potential *mutL* homologues was initiated, using the expressed sequence tag method (EST) sequence data base which contains sequence information for approximately 10^5 cDNA fragments.

Three candidates were found: one with homology to the yeast *MLH1* counterpart and the other two with homology to the other yeast *mutL* homologue *PMS1*. Confirmation that the two genes *hMSH2* and *hMLH1* were indeed responsible for the majority of HNPCC cases was provided by substantial evidence. This included the mapping of these two genes to the regions of chromosomes 2 and 3 known to contain the HNPCC loci, the finding of mutations in these two genes in HNPCC-afflicted individuals (as heterozygotes in somatic cells and homozygotes in tumours) and the hypermutability of microsatellite-like $(CA)n$ repetitive sequences in tumour cell lines compared to somatic cell lines (Fishel *et al.* 1993; Ionov *et al.* 1993; Leach *et al.* 1993; Bronner *et al.* 1994; Papadopoulos *et al.* 1994), and from the failure of nuclear extracts to repair known heteroduplex DNA substrates for mismatch-repair enzymes (Parsons *et al.* 1993).

2. AN ARRAY OF DIFFERENT DISORDERS

HNPCC has been hallmarked as one of the most common genetic diseases of man, affecting as many as one in 200 individuals. In addition, as judged by microsatellite instability, afflicted individuals appear to manifest an increased susceptibility to other epithelial cancers such as endometrial cancer. However, microsatellite changes have also been detected at significantly high incidence in sporadic cases of colon, bladder (Gonzalez-Zulueta 1993), pancreas and gastric carcinomas (Han *et al.* 1993) and to a much lesser extent in breast and ovarian cancers (Wooster *et al.* 1994). These findings demonstrate that this type of genetic instability is not unique to HNPCC and suggests that sporadic tumours can acquire this phenotype during tumour initiation and/or progression.

In addition to a likely association of a mismatch-repair-deficient phenotype with the above mentioned cancers, a genetic instability that produces an expansion of 5′CXG 3′ trinucleotide repeat sequences has been observed in seven other hereditary neurological and neuromuscular diseases, including Huntington's disease and Fragile-X syndrome (Nelson & Warren 1993). Although at present the mechanism underlying the relatively large expansions observed for these syndromes is not known, it is possible that the instability associated with these syndromes results from a compromised DNA-editing function.

As the search for further human DNA repair homologues continues a number of cancer and hereditary disease-associated loci may emerge. For example, some mitochondrial disorders characterized by gene deletions, duplications and the accumulation of point mutations (reviewed by Schapira 1993) could be linked to mismatch-repair deficiencies. As described below, yeast *msh1* mutants display a 'petite' phenotype due to mtDNA mutations resulting in the loss of mitochondrial functions (Reenan & Kolodner 1992a). Because of the apparent specialization of eukaryotic mismatch-repair components (described below) in terms of compartmentalization (nuclear versus mitochondrial), life cycle (mitotic versus meiotic functions) and repair substrates recognized (replication versus recombination mismatches), malfunctions in components of the mismatch-repair machinery can be predicted to manifest an array of different disorders.

3. MULTIPLE PHENOTYPES OF MISMATCH REPAIR

Mismatch repair was first postulated thirty years ago to explain particular aspects of genetic recombination including non-mendelian segregation of genetic markers (e.g. gene conversion) and excess recombination between closely linked markers (Holliday 1964; Ephrussi-Taylor et al. 1965). The molecular evidence confirming that such marker effects result from two different mechanisms of mismatch repair was obtained in 1987 using a phage lambda assay for the repair of specific mismatches (Jones et al. 1987). The characterization of pneumococcal *hex* mutants which display a mutator phenotype and no marker effects (Lacks 1966; Lacks 1970; Tiraby and Fox, 1973) raised the question of how the repair of replication errors could be directed to the newly synthesized strand. In 1975, Meselson proposed that the transient hemi-methylated state of newly replicated DNA could provide the signal to differentiate nascent and template strands (for a historical review, see Radman & Wagner 1988). One year later this was demonstrated experimentally using hemi-methylated heteroduplex molecules (Radman et al. 1978, 1980). The isolation and characterization of E. coli *mutS*, *mutL*, and *mutH* mutants soon confirmed the first observation (Glickman & Radman 1980) and since then many laboratories have further characterized the specificity of the generalized MRS (Radman &

Wagner 1986; Claverys & Lacks 1986; Modrich 1991). *In vitro* repair assay has been developed (Lu et al. 1983) and the repair proteins have been purified facilitating *in vitro* reconstitution of mismatch-repair (Lahue et al. 1989).

The multiple phenotypes of *mutS* and *mutL* mutants in E. coli suggest that the MRS is the most versatile and multifaceted DNA-editing system known (see figure 2). The system involves mismatch (base–base or small insertion/deletion DNA loops) detection by MutS and MutL proteins and mismatch-stimulated unwinding by a helicase (helicase II, encoded by the *mutU* gene also known as *uvrD*). E. coli deficient in MutS, MutL, or MutU functions are genetically destabilized and show large increases in: (i) deletion events resulting from excision of transposable elements (Tex phenotype) (Lundblad & Kleckner 1985); (ii) spontaneous base substitution and frameshift mutagenesis (mutator phenotype) (Levison & Gutman 1987; Modrich 1991); (iii) large chromosomal rearrangements resulting from crossovers between diverged DNA repeats (chromosomal instability phenotype) (Petit et al. 1991; Radman & Wagner 1993b; Radman et al. 1993); (iv) recombination of genetic markers (hyper-rec phenotype) (Feinstein & Low 1986) and (v) recombination with related species such as *Salmonella* (disrupted genetic barrier phenotype) (Rayssiguier et al. 1989). The increases relative to wild-type bacteria range from tenfold to 10^3-fold, depending on the particular phenotype measured. All of these phenotypes result directly from the failure of the MRS or its components to operate on mismatched DNA. Deletions result from the replicative bypass of secondary structures (e.g. hairpins) in template strands which, when mismatch repair is functional, are presumably melted by the mismatch-stimulated helicase activity because such structures generally contain mispaired or unpaired bases. MRS controls the fidelity of DNA replication by repairing the newly synthesized strands and restores the parental sequence; strand direction occurs via adenine methylation of GATC sequences or strand discontinuities (for a review, see Modrich 1991). The chromosomal instability, hyper-rec and disrupted genetic barriers phenotypes all result from the failure of the disabled MRS to disrupt mismatched recombination-intermediates.

As previously mentioned, it appears that the bacterial MRS may also be well-conserved functionally in eukaryotes ranging from yeast to man and possibly plants as well (G. Cerovic & M. Radman, unpublished results) (see figure 1). The main difference is that mismatch repair genes in eukaryotes appear to be specialized, interacting with either nuclear or mitochondrial DNA. In yeast, *msh1* mutants (*mutS* homologue 1) accumulate mitochondrial DNA deletions and rearrangements and therefore display a 'petite' phenotype even when the wild type *MSH1* gene is subsequently reintroduced (Reenan & Kolodner 1992). *msh2* and *pms1* mutants show both mitotic mutator and meiotic hyper-rec phenotypes (Williamson et al. 1985; Kramer et al. 1989; Reenan & Kolodner 1992a,b). *msh3* mutants show a weak mutator phenotype but show an increase in recombination between

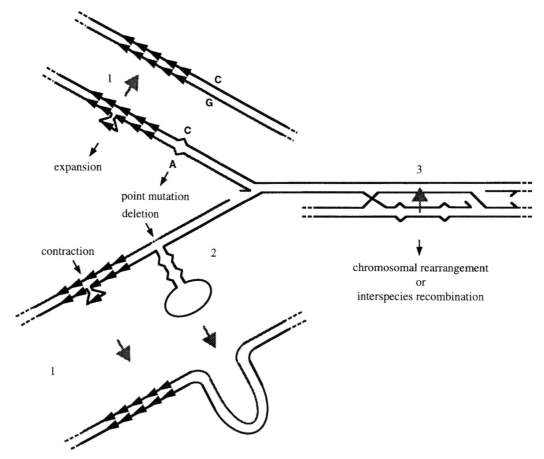

Figure 2. The maintenance of DNA integrity by the mismatch repair system (MRS).
Array of arrows indicate repeats of mono-, di-trinucleotides. Mismatched bases are indicated by opposing arrowheads.

   1. Editing of the newly synthesized strand. Avoidance of point mutations and small insertions and deletions by the excision of the nascent DNA strand containing mismatched or unpaired bases.

   2. Editing of the template strand. Avoidance of the formation of deletions by melting of deletogenic secondary structures containing mismatched base pairs.

   3. Editing of recombination intermediates. Prevention of the formation of recombination intermediates between diverged sequences, thus avoiding chromosomal rearrangements and interspecific recombination. The implication for speciation and the prevention of horizontal gene transfer are discussed in Radman & Wagner 1993*b*.

   The MutS protein detects mismatched and non-paired bases. The MutL protein binds to the complex to which helicase II (encoded by *mutU*) associates. The MutH protein of *E. coli* cleaves the newly synthesized strand at hemi-methylated GATC sites.

diverged repeated sequences (New *et al.* 1993). The *MSH4* gene is expressed only during meiosis and *msh4* mutant phenotypes are under investigation (S. Roeder, personal communication).

4. MODEL ORGANISMS AND GENETIC DISEASE

Because of the overall conservation of the MRS between prokaryotes and eukaryotes and the fact that phenotypes of mismatch repair mutants in model prokaryotic and lower eukaryotic organisms are known, a number of predictions can be made concerning the implications for human genetics. To begin with, one would predict that a mismatch-repair deficiency could be responsible for predisposition to a number of human genetic disorders as for the predicted and recently demonstrated mutator phenotype in human colon tumours. Furthermore, since the MRS is also involved in the editing of recombination intermediates, a link between

enhanced frequencies of chromosome rearrangements (as observed for such disorders as Fanconi's anemia or breast cancer) and a deficiency in mismatch repair could be predicted. Deletions between inverted repeat elements (such as Alu sequences or LINE elements) could be linked to a 'Tex-like' phenotype as described above. Ageing, in particular cases like progeria, could be linked to a mitochondrial mismatch repair deficiency, as characterized for yeast *msh1* 'petites'. The existence of a yeast gene (*MSH-4*) expressed only during meiosis and the hyper-rec effect of *msh2, pms1* and *mlh1* suggest a role for mismatch repair in fertility, as exemplified by bacteria in the maintenance of the genetic barrier between closely related species.

   The specificity of mismatch recognition by the MutS protein facilitates, on one hand, the diagnostic identification of mutation (based on the formation of heteroduplex DNA between normal and test DNA (Wagner *et al.* 1995)) and, on the other hand, provides an explanation for the instability of microsatellite sequences. The microsatellite sequences monitored during the mapping of the human genome are found to be more or less stable. In 'normal' cells, tetranucleotide repeats are apparently the most unstable (Weber & Wong 1993). Yet it is well known that polymerase slippage occurs more frequently at mono-, di-, and trinucleotides (as seen in HNPCC tumours) whereas the MutS protein has been shown to efficiently recognize small base loop-outs up to three bases in size. The degree of the 'accordion' effect observed at microsatellites in normal cells is therefore due both to polymerase slippage errors and the specificity of recognition of such errors by MutS. Therefore, repetitions of mono-, di- and trinucleotides are highly destabilized as seen in HNPCC tumours where the mismatch repair system is defective. Larger repeats, not well recognized by the MutS protein, are much less destabilized but for the same reason, appear as the most unstable microsatellites in cells with functional mismatch-repair.

5. EVOLUTIONARY IMPLICATIONS

In general, the MRS is an essential negative regulator of genetic alterations (see figures 2 and 3) linked to genetic disease (germinal mutation) or sporadic cases (somatic mutation). To avoid the toll of deleterious mutations, all organisms have evolved highly sophisticated mechanisms of mutation avoidance. However, without genetic diversity it would be impossible to adapt to a changing environment. Undesirable genetic alterations therefore can be seen as the price paid for the capacity to evolve. To minimize this cost to the

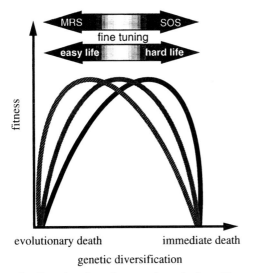

Figure 3. Genetic alterations and evolution. Too many mutations cause immediate death by error catastrophe. Too few mutations prevent adaptation to changing environments and lead to evolutionary death. The mutation rate which maximizes population fitness varies with adaptation to the environment, hence the necessity for fine tuning of the rate of genetic variability. Genetic diversification is fine tuned by an antagonistic control couple: mismatch repair and sos systems. The MRS appears to be constitutive and prevents all aspects of genetic diversification; whereas the sos system, which creates variability, is inducible and allows adaptation to adverse conditions. Genetic alterations, cancers and genetic diseases could appear as a price to pay for evolution.

organism, evolution has selected inducible systems for the creation of genetic diversity, i.e. positively regulated systems for the generation of genetic alterations (see figure 3). The induction of a mutator system, like the sos system in *E. coli* (Radman 1974; Walker 1984), increases on demand, the plethora of genetic alterations that the MRS normally suppresses (see figure 2). An inducible system is advantageous: in a favourable environment the mutation rate is maintained at a low level as compared to conditions of environmental stress (as a response to radiation, chemical agents, conditions of starvation etc.) when the sos-system is induced and variability enhanced. In this way, an inducible system, like the bacterial sos system, responding to environmental factors could be responsible for sporadic as well as hereditary forms of a number of human diseases. Bloom's syndrome, which constitutively synthesizes a number of proteins which are inducible in normal cells, could be an example of an unregulated sos-like response in humans which in turn could explain the associated enhanced genetic instability and elevated frequency of cancers characteristic of this syndrome (Mallick *et al.* 1982; Herrlich *et al.* 1984). Analogously to research on mismatch repair, pursuit of the mechanisms of inducible genetic alteration systems like the bacterial sos system should provide an understanding of the potential link between environment and genetic disease.

We have speculated that clones presenting a mutator phenotype in nature (found in approximately 1% of bacterial and human populations (Tröbner & Piechocki 1984; Peltomaki *et al.* 1993)) may represent population 'hotspots' for genetic defects and speciation events (Rayssiguier *et al.* 1989; Matic *et al.* 1994). Now we suggest that, in addition, conditions causing sos induction provide time 'hotspots' for the population of cells or organisms to produce sporadic genetic defects and stimulate speciation events. These considerations further weaken the notion of random genetic alterations. Untangling genetic control mechanisms involved in the timing of DNA sequence evolution will be instrumental to our understanding of the origins of species and of genetic diseases. The presence of mutator genes in the human population, even in a heterozygous state, raises a question of major concern: what is the impact of this subpopulation on the overall incidence of genetic diseases?

Thanks to the considerable conservation of systems responsible for the maintenance of DNA integrity from bacteria to man, bacterial genetics remains a source of new paradigms piloting research into the causes of genetic alterations in man. The finding that a defect in the human MRS provides a predisposition to colon cancer is the most recent example of such a 'targeted' research.

REFERENCES

Aaltonen, L.A., Peltomaki, P., Leach, F.S. *et al.* 1993 Clues to the pathogenesis of familial colorectal cancer. *Science, Wash.* **260**, 812–815.

Benditt, E.P. & Benditt, E.P. 1973 Evidence for a monoclonal origin of human atherosclerotic plaques. *Proc. natn. Acad. Sci. U.S.A.* **70**, 1753–1756.

Bronner, C.E., Baker, S.M., Morrison, P.T. *et al.* 1994 Mutation in the DNA mismatch repair gene homologue *hMLH1* is associated with hereditary non-polyposis cancer. *Nature, Lond.* **368**, 258–261.

Claverys, J.-P. & Lacks, S.A. 1986 Heteroduplex deoxyribonucleic acid base mismatch repair in bacteria. *Microbiol. Rev.* **50**, 133–165.

Dohet, C., Wagner, R. & Radman, M. 1986 Methyldirected repair of frameshift mutations in heteroduplex DNA. *Proc. natn. Acad. Sci. U.S.A.* **83**, 3395–3397.

Ephrussi-Taylor, H., Sicard, A. M. & Kamen, R. 1965 Genetic recombination in DNA-induced transformation of pnemococcus. *Genetics,* **51**, 455–475.

Feinstein, S.I. & Low, K.B. 1986 Hyper-recombining recipient strains in bacterial conjugation. *Genetics* **113**, 13–33.

Fishel, R., Lescoe, M.K., Rao, M.R.S. *et al.* 1993 The human mutator gene homolog *MSH2* and its association with hereditary nonpolyposis colon cancer. *Cell* **75**, 1027–1038.

Glickman, B.W. & Radman, M. 1980 *Escherichia coli* mutator mutants deficient in methylation-instructed DNA mismatch correction. *Proc. natn. Acad. Sci. U.S.A.* **77**, 1063–1067.

Gonzalez-Zulueta, M. 1993 Microsatellite instability in bladder cancer. *Cancer Res.* **53**, 5620–5623.

Han, H.-J., Yanagisawa, A., Kato, Y., Bark, J.-G. & Nakamura, Y. 1993 Genetic instability in pancreatic cancer and poorly differentiated type of gastric cancer. *Cancer Res.* **53**, 5087–5089.

Herrlich, P., Mallick, U., Ponta, H. & Rahmsdorf, H.J. 1984 Genetic changes in mammalian cells reminiscent of an sos response. *Hum Genet.* **67**, 360–368.

Holliday, R. 1964 A mechanism for gene conversion in fungi. *Genet. Res.* **5**, 282–304.

Ionov, Y., Peinada, M.A., Malkhosyan, S., Shibata, D. & Perucho, M. 1993 Ubiquitous somatic mutations in simple repeated sequences reveal a new mechanism for colonic carcinogenesis. *Nature, Lond.* **363**, 558–561.

Jones, M., Wagner, R. & Radman, M. 1987 Mismatch repair and recombination in *E. coli. Cell.* **50**, 621–626.

Kramer, W., Kramer, B., Williamson, M.S. & Fogel, S. 1989 Cloning and nucleotide sequence of DNA mismatch repair gene PMS1 from Saccharomyces cervisiae: Homology pf PMS1 to procaryotic MutL and HexB. *J. Bact.* **171**, 5339–5346.

Lacks, S. 1970 Mutants of *Diplococcus pneumoniae* that lack deoxyribonucleases and other activities possibly pertinent to genetic transformation. *J. Bact.* **101**, 373–383.

Lacks, S.A. 1966 Integration efficiency and genetic recombination in pneumococcal transformation. *Genetics* **53**, 207–235.

Lahue, R.S., Au, K.G., & Modrich, P. 1989 DNA mismatch correction in a defined system. *Science, Wash.* **245**, 160–164.

Leach, F.S., Nicolaides, N.C., Papadopoulos, N. *et al.* 1993 Mutations of a *mut*S homologue in hereditary nonpolyposis colorectal cancer. *Cell* **75**, 1215–1226.

Levison, G. & Gutman, G.A. 1987 High frequencies of short frameshifts in poly-CA/TG tandem repeats borne by bacteriophate M13 in *Escherichia coli* K-12. *Nucl. Acids Res.* **15**, 5323–5338.

Lu, A.-L., Clark, S. & Modrich, P. 1983 Methyl-directed repair of DNA base-pair mismatches *in vitro. Proc. natn. Acad. Sci. U.S.A.* **80**, 4639–43.

Lundblad, V. & Kleckner, N. 1985 Mismatch repair mutations of *Escherichia coli* K12 enhance transposon excision. *Genetics* **109**, 3–19.

Mallick, U., Rahmsdorf, H.J., Ponta, H., Wegner, R.-D. &

Herrlich, P. 1982 12-0-Tetradecanoylphorbal 13-acetate-inducible proteins are synthesized at an increased rate in Bloom syndrome fibroblasts. *Proc. natl. Acad. Sci. U.S.A.* **79**, 7886–7890.

Matic, I., Radman, M. & Rayssiguier, C. 1994 Structure of recombinants from conjugational crosses between *Escherichia coli* donor and mismatch-repair deficient *Salmonella typhimurium* recipients. *Genetics* **136**, 17–26.

Modrich, P. 1991 Mechanisms and biological effects of mismatch repair. *A. Rev. Genet.* **25**, 229–253.

Nelson, D.L. & Warren, T. 1993 Trinucleotide repeat instability: when and where? *Nature Genet.* **4**, 107–108.

New, L., Liu, K. & Crouse, G.F. 1993 The yeast gene *MSH3* defines a new class of eukaryotic MutS homologues. *Molec. gen. Genet.* **239**, 97–108.

Papadopoulos, N., Nicolaides, N.C., Wei, Y.-F. *et al.* 1994 Mutation of a *mutL* homolog in hereditary colon cancer. *Science, Wash.* **263**, 1625–1629.

Parsons, R., Li, G.-M, Longley, M.J. *et al.* 1993 Hypermutability and mismatch repair deficiency in RER + tumor cells. *Cell* **75**, 1227–1236.

Peltomaki, P., Aaltonen, L.A., Sistonen, P. *et al.* 1993 Genetic mapping of a locus predisposing to human colorectal cancer. *Science, Wash.* **260**, 810–812.

Petit, M.A., Dimpfl, J., Radman, M. & Echols, H. 1991 Control of chromosomal rearrangements in *E. coli* by the mismatch repair system. *Genetics* **129**, 327–332.

Radman, M. 1974 Phenomenology of an inducible mutagenic DNA repair pathway in *Escherichia coli*: sos repair hypothesis. In *Molecular and environmental aspects of mutagenesis* (ed. L. Prakash, F. Sherman, M. Miller, C. Lawrence & H. W. Tabor), pp. 128–142. Springfield, Illinois: Charles C. Thomas.

Radman, M., Villani, G., Boiteux, S., Kinsella, R., Glickman, B.W. & Spadari, S. 1978 Replication fidelity: mechanisms of mutation avoidance and mutation fixation. *Cold Spring Harb. Symp. quant. Biol.* **43**, 937–946.

Radman, M. & Wagner, R. 1986 Mismatch repair in *Escherichia coli. A. Rev. Genet.* **20**, 523–538.

Radman, M. & Wagner, R. 1988 High fidelity of DNA duplication. *Scient. Am.* **259**, 40–47.

Radman, M. & Wagner, R. 1993 *a* Missing mismatch repair. *Nature, Lond.* **366**, 722.

Radman, M. & Wagner, R. 1993 *b* Mismatch recognition in chromosomal interactions and speciation. *Chromosoma* **102**, 369–373.

Radman, M., Wagner, R. & Kricker, M.C. 1993 *b* Homologous DNA interactions in the evolution of gene and chromosome structure. *Genome Analysis* **7**, 139–52. Cold spring Harbor Laboratory Press.

Radman, M., Wagner, R.E., Glickman, B.W. & Meselson, M. 1980 DNA methylation, mismatch correction and genetic stability. In *Progress in environmental mutagenesis* (ed. M. Alacevic), pp. 121–130. Amsterdam: Elsevier.

Rayssiguier, C., Thaler, D.S. & Radman, M. 1989 The barrier to recombination between *Escherichia coli* and *Salmonella typhimurium* is disrupted in mismatch-repair mutants. *Nature, Lond.* **342**, 396–401.

Reenan, R.A.G. & Kolodner, R.D. 1992 *a* Characterization of insertion mutations in the *Saccharymyces cervisiae* MSH1 and MSH2 genes: Evidence for separate mitochondrial and nuclear functions. *Genetics* **132**, 975–985.

Reenan, R.A.G. & Kolodner, R.D. 1992 *b* Isolation and characterization of two *Saccharomyces cerevisiae* genes encoding homologs of the bacterial HexA and MutS mismatch repair proteins. *Genetics* **132**, 963–973.

Schapira, A.H.V. 1993 Mitochondrial disorders. *Curr. Opin. Genet. Dev.* **3**, 457–465.

Strand, M., Prolla, T.A., Liskay, R.M. & Petes, T.D. 1993

Destabilization of tracts of simple repetitive DNA in yeast by mutations affecting DNA mismatch repair. *Nature, Lond.* **365**, 274–276.

Thibodeau, S.N., Bren, G. & Schaid, D. 1993 Microsatellite instability in cancer of the proximal colon. *Science, Wash.* **260**, 816–819.

Tiraby, J.-G. & Fox, M.S. 1973 Marker discrimination in transformation and mutation of pneumococcus. *Proc. natn. Acad. Sci. U.S.A.* **70**, 3541–3545.

Tröbner, W. & Piechocki, R. 1984 Competition between isogenic *mutS* and *mut*+ populations of *Escherichia coli K12* in continuously growing cultures. *Molec. gen. Genet.* **198**, 175–176.

Wagner, R., Debbie, P. & Radman, M. 1995 Mutation

detection using immobilized mismatch binding protein (MutS). (Submitted.)

Walker, G.C. 1984 Mutagenesis and inducible responses to deoxynucleotide damage in *Escherichia coli. Microbiol. Rev.* **48**, 60–93.

Weber, J.L. & Wong, C. 1993 Mutation of human short tandem repeats. *Hum. Mol. Genet.* **2**, 1123–1128.

Williamson, M.S., Game, J.C. & Fogel, S. 1985 Meiotic gene conversion mutants in *Saccharomyces cerevisiae* I: Isolation and characterization of pms1-1 and psm1-2. *Genetics* **110**, 609–646.

Wooster, R., Cleton-Janson, A.-M., Collins, N. *et al.* 1994 Instability of short tandem repeats (microsatellites) in human cancers. *Nature Genet.* **6**, 152–156.

Index